anglistik & englisch
British Drama in the 1980s:

Hans-Jürgen Diller · Stephan Kohl · Joachim Kornelius · Erwin Otto
Gerd Stratmann (Hrsg.)

anglistik & englischunterricht

Band 41

British Drama in the 1980s:
New Perspectives

Verantwortliche Herausgeber für den thematischen Teil dieses Bandes:
Bernhard Reitz und Hubert Zapf

HEIDELBERG 1990
CARL WINTER · UNIVERSITÄTSVERLAG

CIP-Titelaufnahme der Deutschen Bibliothek

British drama in the 1980s: new perspectives / ver-
antw. Hrsg. für den thematischen Teil dieses Bd.:
Bernhard Reitz und Hubert Zapf. – Heidelberg:
Winter, 1990

(Anglistik & Englischunterricht; Bd. 41)

ISBN 3-533-04342-8

NE: Reitz, Bernhard [Hrsg.]; GT

Herausgeber:
Prof. Dr. Hans-Jürgen Diller · Prof. Dr. Stephan Kohl
Dr. Joachim Kornelius · Dr. Erwin Otto · Prof. Dr. Gerd Stratmann

Redaktionsassistent: Dr. Manfred Buschmeier

ISBN 3-533-04342-8
ISSN 0344-8266

Anschrift der Redaktion:
Dr. Joachim Kornelius, Dr. Manfred Buschmeier, Ruhr-Universität Bochum, Englisches Seminar
Universitätsstraße 150 · 4630 Bochum 1
Verlag: Carl Winter Universitätsverlag · gegr. 1822 GmbH · Heidelberg
Satz und Druck: Carl Winter Universitätsverlag · Abteilung Druckerei · Heidelberg
Alle Rechte vorbehalten. © 1990
Photomechanische Wiedergabe nur mit ausdrücklicher Genehmigung durch den Verlag
Printed in Germany · Imprimé en Allemagne

anglistik & englischunterricht erscheint in drei Bänden pro Jahrgang. Der Gesamtumfang beträgt ca. 540 Seiten
Preis des Einzelbandes DM 30,–.
Jahresabonnement DM 60,–. Studentenabonnement DM 50,–, zuzüglich Versandspesen.
In diesen Preisen sind 7% Mehrwertsteuer enthalten
Für unverlangte Einsendungen von Manuskripten wird nicht gehaftet
Mitarbeiter erhalten von ihren Beiträgen 30 Sonderdrucke und 2 Freiexemplare. Honorar wird nicht bezahlt
Der Verlag trägt die Kosten für die von der Druckerei nicht verschuldeten Korrekturen nur in beschränktem Maße
und behält sich vor, den Verfassern die Mehrkosten für Autorkorrekturen zu belasten

Inhalt

Vorwort

Die Entwicklung des britischen Dramas in den achtziger Jahren bestätigt, daß nichts beständiger ist als der Wandel. Aufbruchstimmung kennzeichnete die sechziger Jahre, in denen die neuen Dramatiker nicht weniger die Erwartungen beflügelten als die engagierten Regisseure der English Stage Company, der Royal Shakespeare Company und des National Theatre. Doch die siebziger Jahre, nicht unbeeinflußt von den wirtschaftlichen und politischen Konflikten Großbritanniens in diesem Jahrzehnt, wurden zu einer Dekade der wachsenden Polarisierung auch im Theater. Im Streit über Brentons *The Romans in Britain*, der für Edward Bond Anlaß war, das Theater Samuel Becketts und seiner angeblichen Nachfolger für tot zu erklären, erreichte die Konfrontation den Höhepunkt, standen sich politisch engagierte und sich dem "drama with a message" verweigernde Dramatiker scheinbar unversöhnlich gegenüber.

In den achtziger Jahren werden die unterschiedlichen Positionen nicht verwischt, doch hat sich die Konfrontation entschärft, obwohl – oder vielleicht gerade weil – sich im Jahrzehnt Mrs. Thatchers die ökonomische Situation der Dramatiker und der Theater erkennbar verschlechtert hat. Der Anspruch der politischen Dramatiker, auf der Bühne die Welt richtungweisend deuten zu können, wird zumindest verhaltener vorgetragen. Während auf ihrer Seite die Bereitschaft zu wachsen scheint, auch die ästhetische Dimension ihrer Stücke zu reflektieren, bezeugen die jüngsten Stücke Pinters und Stoppards, daß auch hier bislang scheinbar festgeschriebene dramentheoretische Positionen in Bewegung geraten sind.

An der Vielfalt des britischen Dramas der achtziger Jahre haben die Stücke von Dramatikerinnen einen maßgeblichen und wachsenden Anteil, der über ein dezidiert feministisches Engagement längst hinausgewachsen ist. Nicht ausgrenzen läßt sich auch das Schaffen jener englischsprachigen Dramatiker, die durch ihre Herkunft in Großbritanniens imperiale und koloniale Geschichte eingebunden sind und die hieraus resultierenden Konflikte thematisieren. Kennzeichnend für die Theaterlandschaft der achtziger Jahre ist schließlich auch die Erfolgsgeschichte des Musicals, das gegenüber dem Sprechtheater deutlich an Boden gewonnen hat und wie dieses den Spielraum zwischen anspruchsloser Unterhaltung und ästhetischem Engagement besetzt.

Die Beiträge des vorliegenden Bandes erläutern die Situation des britischen Dramas und Theaters der achtziger Jahre sowohl in übergreifenden Darstellungen wie in Einzeluntersuchungen. Mit Ausnahme des Beitrages von Günther

Klotz sind es Ausarbeitungen von Vorträgen zum Symposium "British Drama in the 1980s: New Perspectives", das mit großzügiger und dankenswerter Unterstützung des British Council und der Justus-Liebig-Universität Gießen im Oktober 1989 auf Schloß Rauischholzhausen stattfand.

Bernhard Reitz
Hubert Zapf

Louise Page, London

History of Contemporary British Drama

No playwright writes in a vacuum. Every play that we write is a product of the time we are writing in and is therefore a response to the circumstances which surround us. Thus my playwrighting career which spans almost exactly the years of the Thatcher government has inevitably been affected by that government and the effects of it's policies on society and the individual.

As a feminist I am acutely aware that the personal is the political. The plays I have written during the past years reflect this. The relationship of the individual to the society around her is obvious in my play *Golden Girls* which looks at the pressure on women in athletics. It is impossible for the women in *Golden Girls* to run honestly and cleanly, the whole sports system involving sponsorship precludes that, to get the sponsorship money you have to keep winning, the success ethic is all and all consuming. But the post-mortem of the play shows the women for what they are, victims of a system in which only success counts. The notion of a personal best has given way to a fanatical and unquestioning desire to come first. This quest is also true of Vivien and Hilary, they are the ultimate Thatcherite women using and manipulating other women to achieve their own power. When choosing names for my sponsor and doctor I deliberately choose names that in British society could be either male or female. But even as they exploit the runners Vivien and Hilary are being manipulated by forces outside themselves. For Hilary it is the world of multinationals and corporate finance, for Vivien it is the equally competitive world of medical academia. To gain power within their respective organisations they need to win. Winning is all.

And winning is particularly seductive for Dorcas who has suffered the huge racial and female prejudice which exists in British society. The play is not a political play in the terms of the big Agit-Prop plays of the early 70's which examined the society rather than the individual; like most of the plays of the past decade it is much more introspective. In the 1980's the overwhelming odds against each individual in our society has meant that plays about individuals as winners or losers in society became increasingly common, for example David Hare's *The Secret Rapture* and Alan Ayckbourn's *Man of the Moment*.

There is an uncanny parallel between the notion in *Golden Girls* that winning is good and the current assumption that plays which command large audiences – 'giving the audiences what they want' – are good. This 'bums on seats' and 'making the theatre cost effective' philosophy is held on to despite all the empirical evidence to the contrary, it would make the Victorian melodramatists our classic writers, we would have Boucicault on the back of our twenty pound notes rather than Shakespeare.

We all have the notion of the artist as an individual, the malcontent and the maverick who is not influenced by petty political concerns. While this may be true in other mediums it is certainly not true in the theatre. The process of getting a play staged is one of collaboration and consensus. This is true in both the subsidized and private sector of the British theatre. My advice to would-be playwrights is to study the medium and it would be a foolhardy would-be who looked just at the work produced without looking at the constraints imposed on it. A play does not exist as a theatrical text without performance and that performance necessarily takes place within the governing parameters of the society. So the Wakefield master could write about violence but he could only write about it within the context of the medieval mystery cycle. Shakespeare could write about power and government but governed by the Protestant Tudor world view. Fielding was forced out of the theatre altogether when Sir Robert Walpole, having been satirized in *The Historical Register*, introduced the 1737 Licensing Act.

Officially since the Licensing Act was abolished in 1968, no censorship has existed in the British theatre but in many ways this is far from the truth. If we wish to see our work performed there are many factors that we have to consider. Most of these factors are not to do with the content of the play (British audiences don't mind nudity but they don't like swearing, they love seeing royalty on stage but hate seeing politicians etc.), they are to do with money. It is cost that is the current censor of British playwrighting. The pen that signs the cheques is bluer than the Lord Chamberlain's was. Beckett was told that he couldn't have a picture of the Infant Jesus but a picture of the Infant Samuel would be allowed. Nowadays, I exaggerate (but not much) to make my point, you might write in a picture but the theatre might not be able to afford it. I had to choose between *Diplomatic Wives* being a four-hander and not being performed or a three-hander which was performed. A character called George was sacrificed nobly for the cause. I think I was right but I'm not sure. What I do know is that with three characters I was able to say much of what I wanted to but not all.

The critics certainly noticed the lack of characters, commenting that Libby's behaviour at the dinner party was reported rather than shown. It had to be. One cuts one's coat according to the cloth but that doesn't stop one, in cold times, wishing it reached to one's knees.

You only have to look at the cast list at the front of Edward Bond's *The Human Cannon* to see one very clear reason why it has never been professionally staged in Britain, there are too many characters. New plays, even from established playwrights, are a notorious risk. People like the tried and tested and *Macbeth*, though invested with much theatrical superstition because it's short and by Shakespeare and was brought out to bring the punters in when all else failed has been fairly risk-free for theatres and audiences over the years and "Shakespeare is dead so he doesn't have to be paid a royalty and what's more *Macbeth* just happens to be on the current 'A' level syllabus so we'll be able to sell a lot of tickets to school audiences but *Macbeth* has a lot of characters so let's try and think of ways of cutting the cast list down." And the six person *Macbeth* might be very interesting and the virtuosity of the actors astounding but it isn't actually *Macbeth*, it's a concept of the play but it's cheap. It could be cheaper. With serious thought you might even turn it into a monologue.

A young writer called W. Shakespeare submits a play called *Macbeth* to a repertory theatre in Warwickshire. It is read by various script readers (this is a rich repertory theatre) all of whom like it. An indication of how rich this theatre is is that they actually have a literary manager who has the task of responding to the rather good play from W. Shakespeare. Various questions are asked around the building to try and ascertain who W. Shakespeare is. Does the presence of three witches, a queen, a lady and a waiting woman mean that it's by a woman? Because a play by a woman would help balance the season of plays by six male, white and mostly dead writers. Any chance that the writer is from some other minority group because ditto. The literary manager replies to W. Shakespeare:

Warwickshire. 1990.

Dear Mr Shakespeare,

Thank you very much for letting us see your play which has been read by our theatre with great interest. Unfortunately we are unable to accommodate it within our budget. We would however be very interested in seeing a rewritten version and I hope the following points might assist you.

1 Do you really need three weird sisters? Couldn't the point be made just as well by one? As I write this I am reminded of your excellent scene where Macbeth imagines he sees a dagger. Wouldn't his imagining he sees the three sisters help maintain a continuity in the play?

2 The bloody captain seems to be an indulgence on your part. Whilst accepting your desire to represent the common man surely there are other characters who have seen just as much of the battle as he has. There is no indication of this in your cast list but I assume you were proposing that the actor playing the captain doubled as the porter and the doctor. I only mention this so you can have a look at these parts while you are about it. Do you really want the cameo role of the porter taking the focus off Macbeth?

3 Having established the character of Lady Macbeth you really don't seem to use her very much in the later half of the play. Actors don't like spending time in dressing rooms and although we never see them we never question the fact that Lady Macbeth had children. I think a couple of similar lines about Lady Macbeth from Macbeth would make her just as vivid a character. It would also solve your problem of what to do with the sleeping walking scene now you have cut the doctor.

4 Do we need both Malcolm and Donalbain? Surely one heir usurped is enough. You might even be able to get away with just presenting us with the thought of the usurped heir. But that's really to do with your confidence in yourself as a writer.

5 Lady Macduff's children? Have you considered the cost of the chaperones? Macduff is eloquent about them –

By this stage W. Shakespeare should have torn up the letter but is desperate to have his play staged and after all the success of *Shirley Valentine* has made the monologue a popular dramatic form.

It is extremely rare for a theatre to stage a play which it has not solicited from the playwright. Most new plays in Britain during the past fifteen years have come to fruition within the subsidized sector under the commissioning system. This system allows theatres to pay a playwright for writing a play for their theatre. The money provided to pay for the commission comes from either the Arts Council's or the Local Authorities' grant to the theatre. The great benefit of this system is that the playwright does not have to live on air whilst waiting for the royalties to arrive. There is also the thought that a theatre which has invested money in a play will try to do the play. This notion is at best hopeful, there is many a slip twixt commission and opening night, and at worst hurtful. Playwrights write plays to be performed. "We've paid you but we aren't going to do the play" doesn't touch on why the writer wrote the play in the first place.

The commissioning process works something like this: the director of a theatre approaches a playwright whose work interests him or her. A process of preliminary negotiation and discussing goes on. So for example when Jenny Topper at Hampstead Theatre decided she would like to commission me for her theatre she first rang my agent to check if I was likely to be available, i. e. not tied up in an epic television series or planning to spend the next few months of my life out of the country. Jenny and I then met for lunch where the discussion ranged between embroidery and politics. I put forward various ideas for plays and we discussed them. Over coffee we started talking about our relationships with our families. About the face one has to the world and the face one has to one's family. Jenny suddenly said, "That's the play I would like, if you think you can do it." It wasn't really the play I thought I wanted to do but I said I'd think about it.

Various circumstances then conspired to make me think about the way in which several well-known British media personalities make caricatures out of their families. The families are never seen and the mothers particularly never given a chance to reply to their alter egos. I rang Jenny and suggested I wrote a play about an artist of some description who for the content of their art is parasitic on their family. The play would look at the pride the family had in the creative output and the betrayal of their real selves. It was agreed that Hampstead would commission me.

Before anything was on paper either from the theatre's side or mine a discussion took place about the shape of the final play. I could not use a cast of more than eight and the number of sets required should be as small as possible. It couldn't actually be called censorship but the road down which the play could go was being decided. I fought one clause in my contract which was about the publicity for the play. I did not want any publicity about myself being sent out without having seen it first. The quest for publicity for plays is frantic, exposure means audiences but I did not want the audience to be titilated into coming to the theatre through inaccurate publicity about myself. I also felt if I was going to write about families being used as ideas by their artistic members I ought to protect mine as much as I could. I signed the contract and received my first half fee of just over one thousand pounds. The commissioning fee is split up into three portions, some on commission, some on delivery of the first draft and the rest on acceptance of the play. The acceptance money also allows the theatre to buy into a set of residual options such as the option to transfer the play to the West End, the West End option then triggers the New York option etc. In other words the payment of the acceptance money makes the play into a business commodity. Being paid in three parts also ensures that theatres don't waste too much money commissioning playwrights who never set pen to paper. So some commissions always fall by the wayside, things happen in the world and in writer's lives which mean that an idea which seemed attractive ceases to be so. And you have to have your heart in a play to write it well.

I wrote one and a half scenes, 25 pages of my Hampstead play before I realized that my focus on the subject had changed. I had become more interested in the betrayal element of the subject matter than anything else. And this had coincided with an interest in the current forms of historical manipulation and interpretation. It was an area of interest that had been triggered by writing my play *Hawks and Doves*, which had been a play which I wrote in response to Margaret Thatcher's call for a return to Victorian values by which she did not mean boys being sent up chimnies to sweep them nor husbands infecting their wives with venereal disease. One thing leads to a play and one play leads to another.

I had another lunch with Jenny and told her that I was disenchanted with what I was writing. What I wanted to do was a play about a father and a daughter, both archaeologists, and their relationship and the way that had altered during the years. The play examines the way in which they feel betrayed by each other. But in practical terms the political situation of the country has enforced those seeming betrayals.

The delivery date for the play, working title *Light Fantastic*, is now six months later than it originally was. The epic television serial I didn't have when the project was mooted suddenly materialized and I could not afford to turn it down. Theatre is my great, and since I saw *Noddy* at the age of three, my unrelenting passion but I have to subsidize my theatre work through my television work. The television series, *Rose Brinsley*, is hugely complicated and great fun to write but ultimately I am frustrated by the fact that television is a passive rather than an active medium. I love live audiences. I love first nights of my work because the audience is there. They are the people I write for and after four weeks of rehearsal I can go and sit amongst them. The audience are the final creators of the play but this does not necesarily mean that their numbers are the final arbiters of the play.

In a country where the mortgage rate is running at 15.4%, the buses stop running at 10.00 pm and many people are frightened to go in to city centres after dark the audience figures are financially censored. People can't choose to go to the theatre, it becomes a luxury. The government regard it as a luxury and take a 15% value added tax from the price of each seat sold. It has begun to charge value added tax on sponsorship in the grounds that theatres putting a companies logo on their programmes are providing a service to those companies.

What the government cannot do is tax the value that theatre can give to people's lives. Those moments of recognition that the theatre can provide. The sheer pleasure of coming together with other people to be part of an audience. Rousseau in his introduction to *Julie* said, "Big cities need plays and corrupt people need novels."

The bigger the cities get the more we need plays, the more we need to know it is still possible to be an individual and to stand up against the prevailing system.

Richard Humphrey, Gießen

The Stage in a State.
Public Financing of the Theatre in the First Thatcher Decade - an Historical Review

Behind every drama in the theatre there is another drama off-stage. As the Duke says in *As You Like It*, "This wide and universal theatre/Presents more woeful pageants than the scene/ Wherein we play it".[1] And so it has proved in the Britain of the Eighties. Behind the evident stage successes - *Amadeus* (1979), *The Mysteries* (1985), *Pravda* (1985), *The Cat on a Hot Tin Roof* (1988) - and the *succès de scandale* of *Romans in Britain* (1980) and *Short Sharp Shock* (1980), there have indeed been alarms and excursions behind the scenes.

One recalls the dismay at the appointment of Sir William Rees-Mogg as Chairman of the Arts Council in 1982, the uproar at the appointment of Luke Rittner to be his Secretary General in 1983, the applied histrionics of Sir Peter Hall protesting against government cuts in the arts in 1985, the tragi-comedy of the threats to the Royal Court and the real tragedy of the closing of the Cottesloe that same year, the ongoing drama of reduced grants to both building-based and touring theatre companies, the long-running farce of companies working on a shoe-string, the government string-pulling concerning the television drama *Tumbledown*, and - not least - the sinister spectacle of Clause 28.

Looking back over this decade of brouhaha off-stage, the latest Conservative Party document, *The Arts - The Next Move Forward*, begins with the following words: "Under the Conservatives the arts have been a success story in Britain."[2] More recently, the then Minister for the Arts, Richard Luce, has claimed, "I see a remarkable flowering of the arts in all regions and all art forms."[3] But he would say that, wouldn't he?

Looking back over the same decade of backstage hullabaloo, the Labour Party's latest policy review *Meet the Challenge, Make the Change* speaks of "the government's neglect of - and even hostility to - the arts".[4] It speaks of "crude curbs"[5] on creative freedom, and elsewhere in the tract *Breaking the Nation* the Party claims that the theatre in particular is being "clobbered".[6] But they would say that, wouldn't they?

As so often in British politics, it was the best of times and the worst of times, an age of light and an age of darkness. And the only way to discover what kind of age the Eighties really were is to read on – only in this case the reader must be prepared to do a different kind of reading, to turn his or her gaze from the theatre critics to the cultural critics, from the drama to the document, from the stage to statistics.

The following article attempts to pose and answer the following questions, to each of which a separate section is devoted. How have the arts been funded in past societies? How have they been funded in the British society of the Thatcher era? How does such funding differ from the funding in the British past? What are the difficulties in these differences – the difficulties intellectually and practically? What effects have the differences had? Further, given the effects, what are the reasons for the differences? Given the differences and the effects what should be done? And finally, what difference do the differences make or – to put it with blunt straightforwardness – does it all matter anyway?

I

Economists habitually describe the arts as an "economically abnormal" activity. The abnormality arises through the arts' involving a "spiritual" dimension, which is not easily calculated or priced. Perhaps because of this there is no unanimity among economists as to which (if any) of the seven or so historical forms of arts funding is most appropriate or most effective.

If one reviews these seven forms – private patronage, *panem et circenses*, state patronage in a command economy, a total command economy, total freedom of the market, state subsidy in a mixed economy, and mixed funding – one can, however, stake out the following minimal agreed territory. First, there is no direct correlation between government spending and the quality of artistic work or life. (Hitler, Stalin and Mussolini all spent more on the arts then than does Great Britain, Canada, Australia or the United States today.) And second, among these forms of funding those currently favoured are relatively young. To this second point there is an important corollary: the comparatively young form is still comparatively unresearched. Indeed, one feature of the Eighties has been the increased economic attention paid to state funding of the arts – attention which has led in Britain not only to the first chair in Arts Policy and Management[7] being established, but to none other than John Kenneth Galbraith delivering the Arts Council Lecture in 1983 on "Economics and the Arts".[8]

The relative youth and relative intractability of the area may help one to understand the uncertainties of arts funding in the Eighties. Here too, however, to understand is not necessarily to excuse.

II

Every student of the stage is a watcher of words. And among the words one could watch entering the English language in the first Thatcher decade have been the following: a "can-do" attitude, to "cash-limit" a project, a "chartist", the "commodification" of a good, to "de-access" an object, the "enterprise culture", to "go-get", the "loadsamoney" society, a "moneyman", a "mover and shaker", the "numerati" and so on.[9] It may be amusing to watch such words invade the English language: it is somewhat less amusing to see them invade also government thinking and policy on the funding of the arts.

The current Conservative view of the arts is encapsulated in the phrase "the arts and related industries".[10] Art, we are now told, has a "high value added".[11] Drama in particular is seen as a "growth industry"[12] with an "economic value"[13] – a recent policy review, indeed, claims that the arts are "as important as the motor industry".[14] Accordingly, theatres can have success in "planning and marketing themselves as businesses"[15], can attain "optimum production levels"[16] and can have an "excellent sales record".[17] As such, they can prove a "first rate investment"[18] with "welcome financial returns".[19]

If one asks why ·there is, in the words of Margaret Thatcher herself, "a great industry in other people's pleasures"[20], then the answer is both expected and surprising. It is on the one hand predictable that the arts should "create employment"[21], not least because they "attract tourists".[22] (There are indeed more than one million jobs in the arts in Britain today, and two-fifths of tourists to Britain are said to patronise the theatres.) And equally predictable is that the arts should play this role especially in the run-down inner-city areas. More startling, however, is the reason why they are to be accorded this role. Not only do you need "the whole of the arts to make the cities"[23], but "the arts create a climate of optimism – the 'can-do' attitude essential to developing the enterprise culture this government hopes to bring to deprived areas".[24] In short, the arts, once considered different because of their "spiritual" value, are now a multiple material factor in the balance sheet of the nation. They are – in the words of the Arts Council – "a small but successful part of Great Britain Inc.".[25]

Norman St. John Stevas, Mrs Thatcher's first Arts Minister, said to his credit that such terms had "no logical application to the Arts".[26] He, however, was one of the first of the "wets" to be released from his duties – and applied to the arts the terms have been.

The bare statistics[27] of arts funding in the first Thatcher decade are recorded in Tables A and B. Table A shows that spending on the arts as a whole rose from £192m in the financial year 1980–81 to £353m in 1986–87, while Table B reveals that Arts Council spending rose from £83m to £139m over the same period. Arts Council expenditure on drama – their annual reports reveal – moved from £14.9m in 1981–82, through £27.1m in 1986–87, to £27.5m in 1988–89.

Now, overall Arts Council spending in the late Eighties was nine times as high as in the early Seventies, and there are other figures too which might momentarily suggest that funding has substantially risen: in 1946, for example, the first Arts Council spent only £235,000 on drama, in 1956 the sum was only £820,000 and even in 1966–67 only £5.7m.

Equally beneficial might seem the fact that in the Eighties state funding of the arts was not to be their sole source of subsidy. On the contrary, there was to be a dual shift away from central funding towards, first, funding from Local Authorities and, second, funding through business sponsorship. Such sponsorship, declared Rittner, was a "civilised vehicle for business activity";[28] it was, an Arts Council report pronounced, "the motor for growth".[29] And over this period, as shown in Table C, income from this source too rose from under £1m in the mid-Seventies to some £25m towards the end of the Eighties.

Unfortunately, however, the bare statistics revealed so far barely tell the whole story. First, one must remember that in 1988–89, despite the "Glory of the Garden" and the "Theatre is for All" policies with their call for a wider spread of subsidy, almost half the funds – £13.2m – went to the national companies, the remainder being distributed among no fewer than 233 other recipients, the largest of which (Manchester) received £1m and the smallest, a paltry £464. Second, as Table B also reveals, spending on drama as a percentage of total spending on the arts actually declined over the period in question, from 20% in 1971–72 through 18% in 1981–82 to 14% in 1986–87. And above all, one must recall that expenditure in cash terms is not expenditure in real terms. In real terms, as the second half of Table A equally demonstrates, spending on the arts as a whole did increase in the Eighties, but only from £108m in 1980–81 to £138m in 1986–87, and even within this small increase there was a real fall between 1984–85 and 1985–86. If one adds to this the sombre fact that inflation in Britain was running at between 4 and 21.5% – and was never below 10% in the period from 1979 to 1982 – and that inflation in the arts is recognised to be substantially above the national average, then one can well understand why as early as July 1979 Peter Hall could claim that proposed cuts to the National Theatre budget "could actually wreck everything that has been built up in the last twenty-five years"[30] and why by Autumn 1989 even Rittner himself could speak in the Arts Council Report of "strains being felt throughout the arts world" and of a "rising tide of client organisations facing financial difficulties".[31] However can-do the attitudes they aroused in others, the arts, by the end of the first Thatcher decade, were feeling markedly less can-do themselves.

III

In Britain, state funding of the arts is not a long-standing tradition. This is partly because Britain, the land of liberty rather than equality, has a dislike of countries with a centralized cultural policy, and partly because in Britain, the "snail shod with lightning"[32], state provision is habitually retarded.

A brief chronology of state funding would include the following:

1845–50   The first public money for the arts: the Museum Act 1845, the Public Libraries Act 1850

1918   The first manifesto mention of the arts: the Labour Manifesto calls for the promotion of "music, literature and fine art, which under capitalism have been so neglected and upon which [...] any real development of civilization fundamentally depends"

1924   The first Labour Government proposes a 1d rate for arts and entertainments but is opposed by the commercial theatre

1938   The Entertainments National Service Association (ENSA) is founded

1939   The Council for the Encouragement of Music and the Arts (CEMA) – the second chairman of which is John Maynard Keynes – is founded with the aim "to carry music, drama and the arts to places which would otherwise be cut off from all contact"

1945   CEMA becomes the Arts Council of Great Britain

1948   The Local Government Act introduces a 6d rate for the arts

1960   TUC support for the arts leads to "Centre 42" founded by Wesker at the Round House

1965   The first Minister of the Arts: Jennie Lee

Among all these developments, which was the key one for British theatre? Undoubtedly that with the most potential was the 6d rate of 1948. It, however, remained unrealized – the average local rate for the arts is still only 1d – and among the local "arts" the theatre anyway ranks only fourteenth behind band concerts, indoor art exhibitions, children's entertainment, ballroom dances, lectures, swimming galas, football and even professional wrestling, beauty concerts and the like.[33] Instead, the development of central importance for the theatre has become the Arts Council. Its significance for the arts as a whole should not be overstated: there, it is only the fourth biggest sponsor behind the Local Authorities, central government and the BBC. The first-named, however, devotes much of its funding to libraries, the second-named to museums and the British Library and the third-named to art and artists. For the British theatre, the Arts Council has indeed emerged as the largest sponsor, as *the* institution one must study if one wants to analyse the relation between stage and state.

The emphasis must be on the word "relation". For the Arts Council is not – at least in theory – the state. Its much-trumpeted policy is to have no policy, to be "at arm's length" from government. It is, in the words of Raymond Williams, "an important and relatively original attempt to create a kind of intermediate body which distributes public money without being under the direct control of a governmental organization".[34] In reality, however, this principle is modified by the very power structure of the Council and by appointments to it. As Table D depicts, the power of the Prime Minister over appointments in the arts is such that the arm's length is a mere wrist's length – and in the Eighties was no longer than a finger-tip.

The essential difference between theatre funding in the Eighties and such funding previously was hence threefold. A different concept of the theatre as business led to a different structure and quantity of funding – concept, structure and quantity being both promoted and promulgated by a different group of appointees to the Arts Council.

IV

On both an intellectual and a practical level, these differences are fraught with difficulties. Intellectually, there is the contradiction which Galbraith located at the heart of the monetarist philosophy: private affluence but public squalor – with, in this case, the former being called on to assuage the latter. Further, there is the contradiction frequently cited as lying at the heart of Thatcherism: an avowedly libertarian philosophy bent on "setting the people free" in fact introduces a series of new controls. And third, there is a shallowness in much of the New Right's understanding – or misunderstanding – of art and its effects. It is rarely, for example, true that art has a "high value added": of actors in Britain, fewer than a quarter, and of writers fewer than one in ten manage to live well from their professions.[35] Nor is it always the case that the arts foster a "can-do" approach to living: one may feel more can-do after attending a Madonna concert; one is somewhat less likely to feel so after a performance of *Oedipus Rex*.

The major intellectual weakness, however, lies in the concept of the theatre as an "industry" of a modern type. For the theatre can indeed be seen as an industry – but as a labour-intensive industry which flourished before the twentieth century on cheap labour. At the outbreak of the First World War, 206 British towns had a playhouse; Manchester had eight; Liverpool had twelve. In a well-known process, however, these theatres had to cede to the cinemas, which in turn were ousted by the television. The successive electronic arts could achieve vast increases in productivity from which the pre-electronic theatre was by nature barred. (Indeed, when the theatre does use the new technologies, the evidence is that it employs not fewer staff but more.[36]) Some 80% of theatre costs are off-stage[37], and on-stage not all theatre can be as economical in cast as *Not I*, not all as economical in costume as *Oh, Calcutta*. This largely ineluctable economic process, best formulated by the American economist William Baumol and now known as the "Baumol principle"[38], is the overlooked bottom line in the Conservative audit of this "growth industry".

The intractability of this final intellectual problem makes all the more acute the sheer practical problems encountered by those who try to put into actual effect the New Right's thinking on sponsorship. For sponsorship is largely for the already established. As the chief executive of Royal Insurance – now a sponsor of the RSC – has put it: "it was in our overall interests that such sponsorship should be undertaken with a highly respected organisation of national, and indeed international, stature".[39] And the corollary is that sponsorship is rarely for the controversial. The Theatre Royal in Stratford East employed for two years a professional fund-raiser to drum up sponsors – but without one single success: the recurrent stumbling-block was one sketch in their repertoire which featured a strip-teasing Mrs Thatcher. Moreover, even when sponsorship is forthcoming, it can have the most material of motives: the American Digital Equipment Co. funds dance groups since they bring together potential customers for its type of computer; Beck's Beer funds the mime group Théâtre de Complicité since it performs in Beck's target zone – the pub.[40] And yet, even such manifest motives can be considered preferable to the less manifest. For some companies, it has been claimed, sponsorship is part of a "softening-up process, forming the vanguard of a larger economic strategy".[41] Thus one of the more sinister Maecenas figures to emerge in the Eighties was the Sikorsky company, previously less known for its involvement in the arts than for its production of military helicopters and Cruise Missiles. And even if a theatre company does overcome its scruples and does go in search of such funding, it may well be unable to overcome one further obstacle to theatre sponsorship in the Thatcher years: in an age of private affluence and public squalor, the slowly increasing amount of private funding is being sought after by a rapidly rising number of would-be beneficiaries. By the end of the Eighties, major firms were registering a 20% increase in sponsorship requests per year. The inevitable result is that less and less is given to more and more, with an increasing number of begging-bowls left less than full or quite empty. One of the least lovely entrants to the English language in the Eighties has been the tell-tale phrase, "compassion fatigue".

Of all the practical problems besetting theatre sponsorship, however, one towers above all the above-mentioned: it is the uncomfortable because unconscionable but nevertheless unavoidable truth of the matter that – despite a decade of government effort – sponsorship of drama has signally failed. It is true that sponsorship of the arts as a whole rose from £4.6m in 1979–80 to £25m in 1987. In the specific case of drama, however, the figures offer naught for one's comfort. In 1989, theatre income came 10% from Local Authorities, 36% from Arts Council subsidy and 51% from box office revenue, but only 3% from private or commercial sponsors. Even within the arts, the theatre fares badly in competition with the visual arts, which receive 6% of total income, dance, which derives 8%, and music, which garners 11% from sponsorship.[42] Indeed, of all the arts, only literature fares worse. If sponsorship is indeed to be the "motor for growth" in British drama, then that growth, one must conclude, will be stunted.

V

Despite these difficulties both intellectual and practical, the successive Thatcher administrations have adhered to their policy and have superintended its implementation in three main areas: in appointments to the Arts Council, in a restructuring of the Council, and in the consequent re-allocation of funds.

The central appointment was that of Sir William Rees-Mogg – now Lord Rees-Mogg – who was made Chairman of the Arts Council for seven years from 1982. Educated at Charterhouse and Balliol, and a former editor of *The Times*, Rees-Mogg was a co-disciple of Hayek and a supporter of the Thatcherite cause, a man well suited to becoming "the most eloquent mouth-piece for the new 'arts as industry' movement."[43] In addition, however, he adhered to the traditional Conservative philosophy of art having a spiritual role. "At its most important," he wrote in a devotional book *An Humbler Heaven*, "art is a way of apprehending God."[44] In a more recent article entitled "Disturbingly Quiet On the Western Front", he admits that he does "not understand" much modernist art but nevertheless insists that the first half of the present century brought "a simultaneous cultural, spiritual and political breakdown" – a "horrifying" decline. Among the "50 Mastersingers of Europe" whom he chooses to single out, only seven are from this century and none (not even Beckett) from our post-war period.[45] Whatever the rights and wrongs of such attitudes, they clearly augur less than well for modern drama.

Alongside Rees-Mogg in the central years stood a man of quite different pedigree. With no university education (and indeed no "O"-Levels), Luke Rittner, appointed Secretary General for five years in 1983 and re-appointed for a further five in 1988, was indeed – as one Council member remarked – "not quite our type".[46] He was, however, in one sense very much the government's type: for after training as an actor and stage manager and having been Stage Manager and later Administrative Director of the Bath Festival, Rittner became in 1976 the first Director of the Association for Business Sponsorship of the Arts. Now, one should not overstate the case: of Rittner it has been said that he "could not be more pro-arts" and that he is "one of those over whom the arts have exercised a hypnotic fascination"; and of Rees-Mogg, that he "believes in state subsidy for the arts and, indeed, that it should represent a higher proportion of government spending than it does at present".[47] Nevertheless, together with Anthony Blackstock, Director of Finance from 1984–89, the two were indeed prepared – in the latter's notorious phrase – to "talk to this government in a language it understands".[48]

Changes in Arts Council structure and policy were not slow to follow. New departments – for Planning and for Marketing and Resources – were founded. Booklets were produced with titles such as "Partnership – Making Arts Money Work Harder". A glossy magazine, *The Arts In Britain*, was launched. All these works and – as shown earlier – the annual Arts Council Reports themselves became suffused with the weasel-worded "language it understands", the verbal pieties of the new orthodoxy. And not least, the staff of the Council was severely cut back, from over 300 in 1983 to 175 in 1989.

Cuts in arts funding had been both mooted and practised soon after the Conservatives' accession to power in 1979, but it was under Rees-Mogg and Rittner that they assumed more methodical form. In 1982, cuts of £10m were imposed and in 1983 a cut of 1% across the board. Then in November 1983, following a major conference of the Arts Council in Ilkley, Rittner sent to all Council clients his "Ilkley Letter". Having asked how recipients would react, first, to a 25% increase and, second, to a 25% cut in funding, Rittner continued:

> The arts, like seeds, need to grow if they are to blossom. Some of the seeds we have nurtured over the years are now bursting to grow but are held back by lack of space and nourishment. This strategy will help the Council to thin out the seed-bed to give more room for them to develop, and for new seeds to be planted.[49]

The writing was on the wall: a horticultural virtue was to be made of a financial necessity. In practice, however, British drama in the Eighties was viewed less as seed than as weed.

It would be invidious to decide who suffered more – the national companies, the regional or the fringe. That the latter was affected – and the more affected the more left-wing it was – is as well-known as it was predictable. The situation in 1985 is documented in Table D, the entry for John McGrath's 7:84 Theatre Company being the most striking. As that table makes clear, however, cuts also fell elsewhere, notably on the building-based theatres in the regions, often on those established in the Sixties and Seventies – be they at Worthing or Chester, Guildford or Bromley. Perhaps most striking, however, because most surprising, and most surprising because most prominent, were the curbs equally imposed on the national companies, successful flag-ships though they were.

The fate of the National Theatre in the Eighties is documented in the final column of the chronology. Having been itself strike-bound in the "Winter of Discontent", it remained in the forefront of developments. It too faced cuts in real terms. It too had to seek sponsors, even for major productions. It too fell back on the musical as money-spinner. It too undertook more foreign touring to boost its finances. It too had to close part of its complex, reopening it only with GLC money. And not least, it too offered fewer new productions – far fewer in fact since the potential of the Cottesloe, opened in 1978, was never to be realized in the Eighties. In 1978 there had been 27 new productions: in the Eighties there were never more than 18. Just how far the National has come since the heady days of the Sixties and Seventies is evinced in the following words from its new Director, Richard Eyre:

> Our priorities now have to do with good housekeeping: the old artistic licence to fail has been to some extent revoked by a new Thatcher reality [...]. The National now has to run on mixed funding, and that means more sponsorship but it doesn't necessarily mean bland subscription seasons of familiar classics; we don't have a charter for controversy, but we can't be anodyne either.[50]

And as the National Theatre so the Royal Shakespeare Company. Although the Priestley Report of 1983 stated that the RSC was "underfunded", and although it was thereafter given an additional grant of £1m, it too has suffered from the fact that its grant was not index-linked. It too, therefore, has had to have recourse to the soft option of the musical. And as RSC so many another ensemble. "What is happening to the RSC", David Edgar has written, "is a microcosm of what has happened or might happen to a swathe of cultural institutions."[51]

One final example, however, must suffice. In 1989, the English Shakespeare Company, led by Michael Bogdanov and Michael Pennington, conceived a complete seven-play, modern-dress *Wars of the Roses*. Despite a modicum of initial Arts Council funding, however, they found it difficult to gain any other sponsorship at all. They distributed the 257 parts among 25 actors. They put up their own houses as security against loans. They spent more time on the phone than on rehearsing. And they finally took on far more foreign touring than envisaged. When the show took to the road, they had had time for only three full rehearsals but had still found only the Allied Irish Bank to sponsor them, and that to the tune of a mere £150,000. It is hard not to concur with Bogdanov's remark after the experience that "reliance on commercial funding is a dead end"[52] – unless, that is, one adheres to Auden's dictum that a creative artist needs as much neurosis as he or she can get.

24

The Conservative Party, of course, had quite other dicta in mind. The initial reason why they adhered throughout the Eighties to so evidently flawed a policy for the funding of drama, is that the policy embodied not one but two of their central shibboleths: monetarism *and* Victorian values. It should not be forgotten that, in Margaret Thatcher's vision, "The Victorian Age, which saw the burgeoning of free enterprise, also saw the greatest expansion of voluntary philanthropic activity."[53] And from these shibboleths the Lady and her Party were avowedly "not for turning". Indeed, so central did the unswerving, unflinching stance become to the ideology of Thatcherism that it too must be added to the web of causation behind this policy. To those who have elevated resolution into dogma, mere lack of success is no dissuasion.

It would be a simplification, however, to see the causes of this Conservative policy solely in terms of the causation behind their other policies. For from the early years of Thatcherism onwards, quite different causes were becoming apparent. Key figures and organizations on the Conservative Right – Norman Tebbit, Teddy Taylor, Kingsley Amis and the Confederation of Conservative Students – were attacking the phenomenon of subsidized left-wing theatre as such. And the Arts Council too was increasingly perceived as "broadly soft left".[54] The attacks were partly a reaction to a changing situation: in 1967, Britain had had one left-wing theatre troupe, of independent financial means; by 1978 it had at least 18 in receipt of state funding. But the attacks were also an expression of a largely unchanging Conservative philosophy as to what art is. In 1979, this philosophy and its application to drama found petulent expression in "An Arts Policy?", a pamphlet written by Kingsley Amis, published by the Centre for Policy Studies and containing not only a disparagement of "plays without plots" but also the following consequence for the funding of drama: "I cannot say I fancy paying the bills of some supposedly promising young person while he writes his political (equals left wing) or experimental (equals nonsensical) play, these being apparently the only two categories tolerated."[55]

Now, no other Conservative document has been so outspoken. On the contrary, *The Arts – the Next Move Forward* lists it as one of the government's tasks to "provide the seedcorn cash to support more experimental work and get new projects off the ground".[56] Nevertheless, that same pamphlet makes quite clear where Conservative priorities are more likely to lie. The Conservative Party, it claims, has "demonstrated a tradition of generous support for the arts" because the Party is "the guardian of the best of our tradition for the benefit of posterity"; because art is the product of individual genius and the Party has "always upheld the rights of the individual"; because art is "an expression of spiritual values"; and because "it is the essence of Conservatism to encourage creativity and quality, excellence and pride in achievement."[57] Just what is absent from this philosophy is perhaps best clarified by comparison with the parallel passage in the latest Labour policy document, *Meet the Challenge, Make the Change*:

> The arts are also an element of growing significance in the quality of our lives. That significance does not only lie in their basic function of providing entertainment and enjoyment, but reflecting and shaping the values of our society. Their role in voicing dissent, in challenging prevailing orthodoxies with unpopular or uncomfortable views is essential.[58]

One need not espouse either of the competing parties to see which of their philosophies was the more likely to foster British drama in the Eighties.

VII

In the light of the above, many reforms of the funding of drama in Britain suggest themselves and many have indeed been suggested in recent years. Among the more tenable are the ideas that the Arts Council should be run more by artists and less by mandarins; that its composition and decision-making be democratized; and that its new-found regionalism be reinforced.

The burden of the present article, however, is that a different emphasis is required. None of these reforms (nor any others) could be of much avail for the theatre unless accompanied by an additional act of understanding – a recognition of the particular locus of the theatre as a labour-intensive, and hence ineluctably costly art form evolved irretrievably early in the development of Western art.

VIII

It may seem, in the context of the present volume, otiose or heretical to conclude this article by asking whether it all matters anyway. It is surely, however, for the sake of perspective, important to point out that in three ways it doesn't really – or doesn't so much.

First, this first Thatcher decade saw many other "woeful pageants", in many of which the woe was far deeper. The arts, in J. P. Stern's splendid phrase, are just "the most necessary of the unnecessary pursuits of mankind"[59] and the Eighties saw many of the necessary pursuits cut as well. Second, the creative artist – like the university don – is one of the best able to act in self-defence. Just as the boffin can always bamboozle the bureaucrat, so the playwright can always outwit the politician. (Indeed, there will always be those writers and performers who, like

Gustav von Aschenbach, actually flourish in adversity.) And finally, as David Edgar has pointed out, here too there is solace in the thought that it could have been worse. After all, the Arts Council was not abolished, the Royal Court did not close its doors, and some of the political groups still "totter on".[60]

And yet, and yet. Of course, if there are fewer productions at the National Theatre, if there are fewer theatre companies to choose from, if the political spectrum is narrowed, if actors are at the end of their tethers and directors tend to avoid risk-taking, if the major work makes way for the musical and the home season is supplanted by the season abroad, then emphatically it does matter – at least to those people to whom such things do matter.

If culture entails variety (and T. S. Eliot told us that it did[61]), if culture entails criticism (and Raymond Williams told us that it did[62]), if culture hates hatred (and Matthew Arnold told us that it did[63]), if culture entails excellence (and the Conservatives themselves repeatedly tell us that it does[64]), then the Thatcher governments have failed the culture of British drama in the Eighties on each score. British drama in the past decade needed monetarism like a sea-gull needs an oil-slick. And as with other slicks what is now needed is thorough corrective action, in the spheres both of short-term financing and of long-term historical understanding.

Notes

1 Shakespeare, W.: *As You Like It*, II,7.
2 Banks, R., et al.: *The Arts – The Next Move Forward. A Plurality of Riches: A Plurality of Funding.* London, 1987, p. 7.
3 Luce, R.: "Foreword". – In *The Arts in Britain.* London, 1988, p. 3.
4 The Labour Party: *Meet the Challenge, Make the Change: A New Agenda for Britain. Final Report of Labour's Policy Review for the 1990s.* London, 1989, p. 74.
5 Ibid.
6 Manwaring, T., Sigler, N. (Eds.): *Breaking the Nation. A Guide to Thatcher's Britain.* London, 1985, p. 189.
7 The chair is held by John Pick at the City University, London.
8 Galbraith, J. K.: *Economics and the Arts.* London, 1983.
9 Ayto, J. (Ed.): *The Longman Register of New Words.* London, 1989.
10 Palumbo, P.: *Arts Council Conference Booking Form.* London, 1989, p. 1.
11 J. Myerscough, quoted in Pick: "Arts Under the Hammer". *Times Higher Education Supplement*, 20. 1. 1989, 13 and 18.
12 Brown, I.: "Drama". – In *Arts Council 44th Annual Report and Accounts.* London, 1989, p. 12.
13 Pick: "Arts Under the Hammer", p. 18.

14 Davison, J.: "Urban Renaissance". - In *Arts Council 43rd Annual Report and Accounts.* London, 1988, p. 28.

15 Brown: "Drama", p. 12.

16 Pick: "Arts Under the Hammer", p. 18.

17 Mulgan, G., Worpole, K.: *Saturday Night or Sunday Morning? From Arts to Industry - New Forms of Cultural Policy.* London, 1986, p. 24.

18 Pick: "Arts Under the Hammer", p. 18.

19 Banks et al.: *The Arts - The Next Move Forward*, p. 7.

20 Daly M., George, A. (Eds.): *Margaret Thatcher in Her Own Words.* London, 1987, p. 59.

21 Banks et al.: *The Arts - The Next Move Forward*, p. 7.

22 Pick: "Arts Under the Hammer", p. 18.

23 Davison: "Urban Renaissance", p. 29.

24 Pick: "Arts Under the Hammer", p. 18.

25 *Arts Council 40th Annual Report and Accounts*, quoted in J. Pick: *The Arts in a State. A Study of Government Arts Policies from Ancient Greece to the Present.* London, 1988, p. 89.

26 Appleyard, B.: *The Culture Club. Crisis in the Arts.* London, 1984, p. 56.

27 Table A: Griffin, T. (Ed.): *Social Trends 17.* London, 1987, p. 171; Tables B and C: Griffin, T. (Ed.): *Social Trends 18.* London, 1988, pp. 165-6; Table D: Manwaring/Sigler (Eds.): *Breaking the Nation*, p. 189; Table E: Mulgan/Worpole: *Saturday Night or Sunday Morning?* p. 130.

28 Mulgan/Worpole: *Saturday Night or Sunday Morning?*, p. 24.

29 Banks et al.: *The Arts - The Next Move Forward*, p. 9.

30 Goodwin, J. (Ed.): *Peter Hall's Diaries. The Story of a Dramatic Battle.* London, 1983, p. 454.

31 Rittner, L.: "Secretary General's Report". - In *Arts Council 44th Annual Report and Accounts.*

32 Tessimond, A. S. J.: "England". - In ders.: *Collected Poems.* London, 1938, p. 39.

33 Mulgan/Worpole: *Saturday Night or Sunday Morning?*, p. 27.

34 Williams, R.: *Resources of Hope.* London, 1989, p. 42.

35 Pick: "Arts Under the Hammer", p. 18.

36 Pick: *The Arts in a State*, p. 64.

37 Goodwin (Ed.): *Peter Hall's Diaries*, p. 168.

38 Mulgan/Worpole: *Saturday Night or Sunday Morning?*, p. 23.

39 Rushton, R.: "Business and the Arts". - In *Arts Council 44th Annual Report and Accounts*, p. 36.

40 Thorncroft, A.: "Business and the Arts". - In *Arts Council 43rd Annual Report and Accounts*, pp. 30-31.

41 W. Januszczak, quoted in Mulgan/Worpole: *Saturday Night or Sunday Morning?*, p. 25.

42 *Arts Council 44th Report*, pp. 6-7.

43 Pick: "Arts Under the Hammer", p. 18.

44 Rees-Mogg, W.: *An Humbler Heaven.* London, 1977, p. 2.

45 Rees-Mogg, W.: "Disturbingly Quiet on the Western Front". *The Independent*, 2. 10. 1989.

46 Appleyard: *The Culture Club*, p. 89.

47 Ibid., p. 88-89.

48 Mulgan/Worpole: *Saturday Night or Sunday Morning?*, p. 24.
49 Appleyard: *The Culture Club*, p. 63.
50 Morley, S.: "New Faces, New Directions". –In *The Arts in Britain*, p. 42.
51 Edgar, D.: *The Second Time as Farce. Reflections on the Drama of Mean Times.* London, 1988, p. 20.
52 Durrant, D.: "Who Pays the Piper?". – In *The Arts in Britain*, p. 34.
53 Thatcher, M.: *The Revival of Britain. Speeches on Home and European Affairs 1975– 1988.* London, 1989, p. 57.
54 Appleyard: *The Culture Club*, p. 63.
55 Amis, K.: *An Arts Policy?* London, 1979; Amis, K.: "Speaking up for Excellence". – In Cormack, P. (Ed.): *Right Turn.* London, 1978, p. 56.
56 Banks et al.: *The Arts – The Next Move Forward*, p. 8.
57 Ibid.
58 The Labour Party: *Meet the Challenge*, p. 74.
59 Stern, J.P.: *On Realism.* London, Boston, 1973, p. 184.
60 Edgar: *The Second Time as Farce*, p. 19.
61 Eliot, T. S.: *Notes Towards the Definition of Culture.* London, 1962, Ch. 3.
62 Williams: *Resources of Hope*, p. 16.
63 Arnold, M.: *Culture and Anarchy.* Cambridge, 1969, p. 69.
64 Banks et al.: *The Arts – The Next Move Forward*, p. 7.
65 Goodwin, T.: *Britain's Royal National Theatre. The First 25 Years.* London, 1988.

	Politics and the Arts	The Arts Council
1979	Margaret Thatcher elected for first term	
1980	National Heritage Memorial Fund (NHMF) established	
1981		Drama budget: 18%
1982	Public Lending Right (PLR) Select Committee Report: *Public and Private Funding of the Arts*	Sir William Rees-Mogg becomes Chairman Cuts of £10m introduced
1983	Thatcher elected for second term Priestley Report on ROH and RSC	J. K. Galbraith: *Economics and the Arts* Luke Rittner becomes Secretary-General Rittner's "Ilkley Letter"; 1% cut on all clients
1984	Business Support Incentive Scheme (BSIS) Cable TV licences granted to 11 companies	"The Glory of the Garden" policy launched Anthony Blackstock re-joins as Finance Director
1985	Films Act abolishes quota system VAT on books and newspapers mooted National galleries' purchasing funds cut 13%	Severe cuts on 7:84, M6, Temba, CAST etc. Drama budget: 17%
1986	OAL announces new pilot arts marketing scheme Budget gives new tax reliefs for charities Adam Smith Inst.: *Ex Libris*	Cork Enquiry: *Theatre is for All* Drama budget: 14%
1987	Thatcher elected for third term Education Year in London theatres Museum of Moving Image opens (Getty-funded)	Drama budget: £27.1m
1988	The Liverpool Tate opens Abolition of the GLC and the Mets	Luke Rittner re-appointed for further 5 years Drama budget: £26.5m
1989		Peter Palumbo becomes Chairman Lew Hodges becomes Finance Director Drama Budget: £28.75m

The National Theatre[65]

Theatre-Going	The National Theatre[65]
1979 Box office income: 37% (grant-aided companies)	Unofficial strike over pay closes all three NT theatres in March 70 strikers dismissed: £¼ m loss *Amadeus* most successful NT production to date 15 plays open (1978: 27)
1980	Uproar at premiere of *Romans in Britain* Mary Whitehouse brings prosecution *Hiawatha* becomes first NT tour for children 18 plays open
1981 Theatre attendance: 37 m	*The Oresteia* is filmed for new Channel 4 17 plays open
1982	AC grant cut in real terms Success of *Guys and Dolls* helps Anon. sponsor funds £2 m Bargain Nights for 14 months NT Education Dept. sends out first production to 20 towns Mary Whitehouse drops prosecution 15 plays open
1983 Box office income: 41% (grant-aided companies)	New musical, *Jean Seberg* flops *Peter Hall's Diaries* published 14 plays open
1984 Theatre attendance: 39 m £1 m added to RSC grant, but no index-linking	AC grant falls short of inflation First NT deficit for 6 years NT Studio founded on private funds Regular Studio nights in Cottesloe 15 plays open

Theatre-Going	The National Theatre[65] (Fortsetzung)
1985	Cuts force Cottesloe to close Peter Hall makes savage attack on Government policy Great success of *Pravda* Cottesloe re-opens on GLC grant 15 plays (and 2 bills) open
1986 Alcohol 26x more popular than theatre	*The Threepenny Opera* is first NT production to be sponsored More foreign touring than ever 17 plays open
1987 Theatre attendance higher than that at football 5% reduction in grant to building-based companies	International Theatre Festival privately sponsored 16 plays open
1988 Box office income: 50% (grant-aided companies)	Peter Hall's last productions Richard Eyre succeeds as Director Lady Soames becomes Chairperson 14 (?) plays open
1989 Box office income: 51% (grant-aided companies)	

Public expenditure on the arts, museums, and libraries

Great Britain

£s million

		Cash				Real terms [1] (base year 1984-85)			
		1980-81	1984-85	1985-86	1986-87	1980-81	1984-85	1985-86	1986-87
Central government									
The arts [2]	— current	84	117	121	152	108	117	115	138
	— capital	2	2	1	1	3	2	1	1
Museums and galleries	— current	60	94	96	115	77	94	92	105
	— capital	6	11	16	15	8	11	15	14
Libraries [3]	— current	46	52	56	57	59	52	53	52
	— capital	− 6	7	9	13	− 8	7	9	12
Total central government expenditure		192	283	299	353	247	283	285	322
Local authorities									
Museums and galleries	— current	44	66	71	68	57	66	68	62
	— capital	15	17	16	6	19	17	15	5
Libraries	— current	282	388	412	398	363	388	392	363
	— capital	21	28	28	14	27	28	27	13
Total local authority expenditure		362	499	527	486	466	499	502	443
Total public expenditure on the arts, museums, and libraries		554	782	826	839	713	782	787	765

1 Real terms figures are the cash outturns or plans adjusted to
  1984-85 price levels by excluding the effect of general inflation as
  measured by the GDP deflator.
2 Includes a grant-in-aid to the National Heritage Memorial Fund.
3 Includes PSA administration and building costs.

Source: HM Treasury

33

Arts Council expenditure

United Kingdom

Percentages and £s thousand

	National Companies [1]	Regional Arts Associations	Art	Drama	Music	Dance	Literature	Other [2]	Total (= 100%) (£s thousand)
1971-72	29	5	5	20	20	4	2	15	12,096
1976-77	26	8	6	20	21	4	2	13	38,100
1981-82	27	11	6	18	19	4	2	12	83,028
1982-83	28	12	5	18	20	4	2	11	94,099
1983-84	29	12	5	18	20	4	2	10	100,068
1984-85	29	12	5	18	19	4	2	11	104,746
1985-86	29	15	5	17	18	4	2	10	109,966
1986-87 [3]	23	21	4	14	17	5	1	15	139,288

1 Includes the English National Opera in London and on tour, the National Theatre (in three auditoria), the Royal Opera and the Royal Ballet Companies in London and on tour, and the Royal Shakespeare Company in Stratford-on-Avon and in London

2 Includes arts centres and community projects, training in the arts, housing the arts, and general operating costs

3 The total for 1986-87 includes £25m to cover the consequences of the abolition of the GLC and the Metropolitan Counties. £8.8m of this was paid to the South Bank Board and has been included in the 'Other' category. Most of the remainder was paid to Regional Arts Associations.

Source: Annual Reports, Arts Council of Great Britain, Arts Council of Northern Ireland

Table B

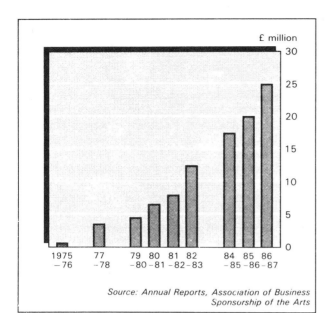

Table C

Business sponsorship of the arts

Great Britain

Source: Annual Reports, Association of Business Sponsorship of the Arts

Table D

Drama cuts

	Grant reduction (£)
Building-based companies	
Basingstoke: Horseshoe Theatre Company	72,000
Chester: Gateway Theatre Trust	87,500
Guildford: Yvonne Arnaud Theatre Management	108,000
London: Churchill Theatre Trust (Bromley)	90,500
Croydon Alternatives Theatre Company	73,500
Hornchurch Theatre Trust	148,000
King's Head Theatre Trust	55,000
Wakefield Tricycle Theatre Company	87,000
Harrogate (White Rose) Theatre Trust	132,500
Worthing and District Connaught Theatre Trust	76,000
Touring companies	
CAST Presentations	47,000
M6 Theatre Company	44,500
Mikron Theatre Company	28,500
7:84 Theatre Company (England)	92,500
Temba Theatre Company	72,000

35

Table E

How decisions are made

NOW:

Prime Minister appoints:

1. Ministers for: 2. Members of:

*Office of Arts and
Libraries*
responsible for:
Arts Council, museums
and galleries, British
Library, BFI, etc.

*Department of
Environment*
responsible for local
authorities, zoos, historic
buildings, heritage, inner
city projects

*Department of Trade and
Industry*
responsible for film,
publishing, tourism,
copyright law

Home Office
responsible for broadcast-
ing, cable and DBS,
theatre and cinema
licensing, censorship

Arts Council:
responsible for funding
"living arts"

BBC Governors:
responsible for overseeing
BBC

IBA:
responsible for award of
ITV, ILR franchises and
overseeing activities

Cable Authority:
responsible for awarding
cable licences

Local authorities: responsible for arts funding, public libraries,
parks, museums and galleries, etc.

Hubert Zapf, Paderborn

Plays of the Cultural Imagination.
On British Drama of the Nineteen-Eighties

If one looks at the past decade, one first of all notices a remarkable continuity of play-writing in Britain. A considerable number of playwrights from the first generation of the New English Drama are still prominent figures in the 1980s. Arnold Wesker, whose seminal play *Roots* returned to the London stage in 1989[1], has continued to produce new plays. Edward Bond since the 1960s seems to have personified an institution of political drama of his own. Harold Pinter with his peculiar blend of hyperrealism, Tom Stoppard with his intellectual metaplays, or Peter Shaffer with his combination of epic and psychological drama remain dominating presences. Even John Osborne has risen from his grave of temporary oblivion, and his *Look Back in Anger* has currently been revived in a production by Judi Dench in London.[2]

Joe Orton, too, who perfected the farce as a medium of social criticism, has come, two decades after his death, to posthumous fame, which goes together with the enormous successes of other playwrights associated with farce, notably Michael Frayn and Alan Ayckbourn, both of whom, however, have been writing since the 60s or early 70s. Furthermore, those authors who had shaped the political drama of a decade ago have meanwhile become established figures and have also, as with Caryl Churchill's *Top Girls* (1982) or with Howard Brenton and David Hare's *Pravda* (1985), attracted large audiences. Something similar applies to the more consciously 'literary' plays of Christopher Hampton or to the refined philosophical comedies of Simon Gray, whose styles had also already been shaped in the 1970s.

If all of this seems to suggest that English drama has largely followed into the 1980s the models established in earlier decades, a closer look reveals that already within the individual careers of the authors mentioned above there occurred substantial thematic and stylistic changes which make it increasingly difficult to maintain earlier categories and classifications. Thus Harold Pinter, for example, after he had been safely filed away as the English exponent of Absurd Theatre, and seemed for some time to be buried alive in his fame, has emerged in the 1980s as a political playwright after all. Tom Stoppard, too, who had been put into a similar category, has more and more clearly included sociopolitical issues in his theatrical experimentalism. In a different way, John Arden has unsettled critical certainties by consciously placing himself, as a once highly acclaimed avantgarde writer of British drama, *outside* the theatrical establishment, having developed, in his creative symbiosis with Margaretta D'Arcy, into a kind of radical fringe figure. Arnold Wesker has moved in a somewhat opposite direction in that his earlier preoccupation with working-class themes and with kitchen-sink naturalism has given way to a more general interest in questions of cultural identity and communication and to a more experimental kind of writing which, as in the monologues of *Annie Wobbler* (1983), almost reminds one of a Beckett or Pinter.

Similarly, leading exponents of that second generation of angry young men and women who had gained their reputation with provocative plays that challenged the political and theatrical institutions have largely given up their association with agitprop and have come to embrace a more differentiated and artistic kind of theatre which consciously includes elements of play and entertainment, as is illustrated in the more recent works of David Hare, David Edgar, or Howard Brenton. Even such a topical play as Tariq Ali and Howard Brenton's *Iranian Nights* (1989), which was produced at the Royal Court Theatre as a response to the Salman Rushdie affair[3], largely refrains from direct references and instead uses the literary frame of *One Thousand and One Nights* for a complex dramatization of Islamic culture and of its various historical manifestations and distortions. The intended criticism is not diminished by this attempt at an intercultural understanding but is rendered even more persuasive by the use of poetic, ironic, and even comic elements, because the open form of the play and the pluralism inscribed into its aesthetic experience represent in themselves counterpoles not merely to this, but to all kinds of political or ideological totalitarianism.

On the other hand, playwrights formerly associated with boulevard and with an apolitical theatricalism like Frayn or Ayckbourn have not only gained more recognition among critics but have produced markedly different plays in the sense of a greater seriousness of purpose and of an increased interest in questions of contemporary culture and society. The comic surface of their farces often conceals an almost apocalyptic vision of cultural chaos and dissolution, as in the case of Ayckbourn's *Woman in Mind* (1986), which utilizes apocalyptic imagery to illustrate the schizophrenic disintegration of a middle-aged woman under the strain of her conventional role as wife and mother, and under the false promise of the idealized images of life propagated by the mass media. The play is composed from the subjective view of the protagonist, so that the audience experience as if from inside her character her frustrations with her daily life and her fantasies of an ideal counter-family which gains hallucinatory presence in the play, but which in the end turns into a terror of empty cultural signifiers and extinguishes her as an independent personality.

What these shifts in attitudes and styles suggest is that significant changes have indeed occurred which justify the assumption that after the First Wave of the

1950s and 60s, and the Second Wave of the 1970s, the 1980s can be said to demarcate a *third phase* in the evolution of Modern English Drama. What seems most characteristic about these plays is a tendency to combine and fuse themes and styles that had often been opposed to each other in the preceding periods.

Above all, the emergent type of play can be described as the product of a mutual assimilation and in many cases even of a fusion between the two major directions of British drama that had developed in relative separation before, namely between *political drama* on the one hand and what Rodney Simard has called *postmodern drama* on the other, which he sees represented by figures like Pinter, Stoppard, or Shaffer, and characterized by a high degree of semiological self-awareness, by the pluralization of the dramatic world on all levels, and by an all-pervading consciousness of *play* which fully exploits the possibilities of the stage and of interacting with the audience.[4] The political drama which had so forcefully asserted itself in the 1970s, in the words of Christopher Bigsby, "within a decade [...] had been infiltrated by a degree of doubt which turned ideological assurance into ontological insecurity."[5] As a consequence, the theatre itself is foregrounded as a medium, as a structure of signs on which the communication of the plays' intended meanings depends. Political drama explodes the primacy of the referent and, in its combination with techniques of experimental meta-drama, develops new, polystylistic forms of play-writing.

This is particularly well illustrated by Howard Barker, who in his wildly imaginative and yet intellectually sophisticated plays reminds one of Heiner Müller, and who is undoubtedly one of the most interesting, if not uncontroversial, younger playwrights. His *The Power of the Dog* (1985), for instance, shows in the example of Stalinism that any attempt at an adequate representation of postwar European history on the basis of social realism must inevitably fail, because the diversity and the semiotic mediation of the material requires the inclusion of more and more perspectives. Under the strain of these multiplying frames, the play abandons all semblance of surface realism and becomes a bizarre and in some ways tragic farce about the labyrinthine infinity of what is commonly called 'reality'.

Different yet comparable ways of synthesising political and postmodern drama, drama as a cultural statement and drama as a self-conscious sign structure, also characterize the works of other playwrights who have recently come to the fore such as, for example, Caryl Churchill, Louise Page, Peter Nichols, or Nigel Williams. And in this lies, it seems to me, a specifically productive tension and a major source of innovation in contemporary British drama, which also manifests itself in the works of such established playwrights as Edward Bond, who has recently published what he calls *Two Post Modern Plays*.[6]

Moving now from the aesthetic evolution of recent British drama to some characteristic themes and attitudes, it seems clear that, on one level, there is an unmistakable response in many plays to the new sociocultural climate, and a critical reflection of the political changes in an era of *Thatcherism*. What appears as one of the most irritating problems here is the ambiguities in which this new, success-conscious era entangles the idea of political and personal emancipation which continues to be a strong normative concept in the consciousness of individuals. On the one hand, this is a decade of a radical neoconservatism, which in many ways represents the very opposite of the political hopes of the earlier generation of dramatists. But on the other hand, it is also a decade of the rise of a number of *women playwrights* and their recognition as a major force of dramatic innovation, in which feminist themes in a broad sense began to exercise a considerable influence also on the works of their male colleagues.[7] In many recent plays, there are female protagonists, and the lives and characters of women are examined in their various aspects ranging between the personal and the social sphere.

At the same time, the partial realization of earlier emancipatory ideas is caught in a highly ambivalent and indeed almost schizophrenic relationship with the commercial and political power-structures in whose context it is defined. Examples of this are Caryl Churchill's plays, notably *Top Girls*, which portrays a 'Thatcherized' career woman, or her extraordinary experimental play *Serious Money* (1987) about the international world of finance and stockmarket speculation, which, quite ironically, was a big success with the Yuppies of London. Women act on a virtually equal basis with men here. But in the process they also become part of the dehumanizing system which is exposed in *Serious Money*, and they are shown to fall, in the same way as the men, under the corrupting influence of the merciless power games going on behind the scenes. On one of its many levels, this is a detective play in which a woman – another 'top girl' in the stock-trading business – acts as her own private detective. She tries to find the murderer of her brother, who had been dealing in illegal financial transactions. But her search results not in the unmasking of a murderer but in her own participation in the kind of dubious high-profit deals in which her brother had been involved. There is of course a strong parodistic and farcical element in this, which is underlined by Churchill's use of rhyme and of musical forms like the round in the dialogue of the stockbrokers. The rhymed newspeak of the international money market becomes an ironic comment on the contemporary cultural imagination, and on the impossibility of poetic drama in the postmodern business world into which it is projected. In the use of techniques such as plural settings, simultaneous dialogues, and the dissolution of a clear sense of reality into polyphonic clusters of fragmented information, *Serious Money* exemplifies the assimilation of postmodern elements in the type of political drama emerging in the 1980s.

Another example which exposes the ambiguities of the new success-ethic is Louise Page's *Golden Girls* (1984). A racially mixed women's 4x100m relay squad is trained, with the scientific advice of a psychiatrist and the sponsorship of a big firm, for the gold medal at the Olympic Games, which they actually succeed in winning, but which is denied them later because of doping. The members of the squad, who are turned into national idols by the mass media, have internalized their roles as figures of the public imagination – of the contemporary 'realms of gold', as it were – and have dedicated themselves to their goal with an ambition which consumes all of their private lives. But this is also true for the two representatives of science and commerce in the play, who, by the way, are also women, and for whom the project becomes a test case for their own careers.

There is also a recognizable shift in recent plays in social theme and setting from the working class to the office, to the world of finance, of media and high tech. In *Serious Money*, central scenes are set in offices filled with computers and multiple telephones. In Stephen Poliakoff's *Coming in to Land* (1986), the stage is a HiFi shop full of video screens which reproduce the multiplied image of the central female character. David Edgar in *Maydays* (1983) speaks of a new society of spectacle, where the "theatre of struggle has [...] shifted from the factory to the supermarket."[8] *Maydays* is a critical review of the failure of attempted social revolutions in the manner of an intertextual play with earlier models of committed drama in Britain (referring, among others, to Osborne's *Look Back in Anger*, Wesker's *Roots*, Griffiths's *The Party*, Mercer's *After Haggarty*, and Brenton's *Weapons of Happiness*), but is also a tentative affirmation of new, undogmatic political perspectives.

What also becomes apparent in *Maydays* is a more strongly felt presence of what could be called the *international* or *intercultural theme*, which exposes the worldwide implications of the apparently 'national' issues of Thatcherism. The relationship of East and West is also explored in Poliakoff's *Coming in to Land* or in Edward Bond's *Summer* (1982). Europe and America are shown in typical cultural attitudes in Christopher Hampton's *Tales from Hollywood* (1983), while the relationship of England and America is dramatised in Caryl Churchill's most recent play *Icecream* (1989), in which the mutual clichés and stereotypes, rather than the characters, become the agents of the play. Problems of Britain's colonial past and of its postcolonial relationship to the Third World are a central concern in Peter Nichols's *Poppy* (1982), a play about the opium war with China in the 19th century, which helped to establish the English habit of tea-drinking. The play makes ironic use of the English Pantomime as the dominant form of popular theatre in Victorian England, with its sensational and melodramatic effects, and "with excruciating rhyme, / So typical of English Pantomime".[9] It thereby dismantles that theatrical convention and reveals it as an aesthetic ideology through which the realities of English culture and history are mediated.

If we can therefore speak of an expansion and multiplication of the external world of the plays, there is also a simultaneous tendency towards an exploration of the private life of individuals. An example of this is *sexuality*. As June Schlueter puts it: "[...] the political spine that gave structure to the theatre of a decade ago has splintered into sinews of dramatic subjects, not the least of which is sex."[10] Again, this means that the idea of sexual liberation, which in an earlier phase had been closely linked with the idea of political liberation itself, is continued and further developed. Different forms of sexual partnership are explored in a kind of experimental attitude of the protagonists towards their own lives. Thereby, new patterns of intimacy and character relationships are introduced into the plays, breaking up conventional monogamous partner relations into various kinds of homo- or heterosexual partnership.

This includes the traditional, gender-based role distribution between men and women, which is frequently undermined by its variation or reversal, and by the use of the androgynous theme. Such a gender role reversal occurs, for example, in Louise Page's *Real Estate* (1984). In this play, which characteristically presents everyday activities as deeply entwined with archetypal structures of the subconscious, the two female protagonists – mother and daughter – are active, rationally-minded real estate agents, whereas the husband and father is on early retirement, does the housework and the cooking, and is attributed traditionally female character traits like emotion, domesticity, or an instinctive relationship to nature. Caryl Churchill and David Lan's *A Mouthful of Birds* (1986) is an attempt at a contemporary Dionysian theatre based on Euripides's *The Bacchae*, in which women are cast in traditionally male roles and are ascribed ambition, aggression, and a potential for physical violence. The conventional opposition of gender clichés is transcended in the interplay of elemental passions and spiritual obsessions, which culminate in an explicit scene of gender transformation and in the actual appearance of the mythological figure of a hermaphrodite upon the stage.

But the idea of a many-sided, fully realised sexuality is again shown to be subverted by the sociocultural context. Rather than advancing political liberation, the new sexual permissiveness is seen to reinforce the depoliticization of consciousness. "But sexy greedy *is* the late eighties", says one character in *Serious Money*, a view, however, which is ironically qualified in the ensuing dialogue in that, because of Aids and of the hectic struggle for professional success, real sex has been replaced by less dangerous substitutes: "The more you don't do it, the more it's fun to read about."[11] The personal indifference of sexual behaviour threatens to lead to an instrumentalization of the partners and their intimacy in the sense of a permanent power struggle. This form of 'sexual politics', which recurs in many plays, is the central theme of Christopher Hampton's adaptation of Laclos's novel *Les Liaisons Dangereuses* (1985), which in the form of a parody of the comedy of manners dramatizes the refined virtuosity and yet the emotional paralyzation of a sexuality which has become a mere functional element in a self-sufficient social power game.

The modification of earlier concepts of emancipation, however, has its reasons not only in sociopolitical changes but in a shift in attitude which can be described as a new existentialism, not so much in the sense of the philosophical existentialism of the mid-century, but in the sense of an anthropological or even *biological existentialism* which is clearly distinct from the more sociologically-minded plays of the 1970s. The discovery of the *body* as a source of potential meaning simultaneously increased the awareness of the dependency of human life on the contingencies and the finite nature of bodily existence in time and space. It thus sharpened the sense for those dimensions of the life process which resist rational explanation and manipulation, whether it be in the form of unpredictable and irreversible consequences of actions, or of the pre-rational and therefore not wholly explainable element in interpersonal experience.

Physical processes of organic life are presented on the stage with unprecedented concreteness and intensity within a more comprehensive and holistic view of human existence. In Louise Page's *Real Estate*, the time span of the action is defined by the months of pregnancy of the daughter of the family, and the unborn child becomes a catalyst for an entirely new arrangement of the relationships between the adults. The hectically accelerated pace of the real estate business in which mother and daughter are involved is counterbalanced by the slow pace of the natural life process, which Page presents in a subtle use of mythopoetic motifs, thereby opposing the indeterminacies and biopsychological complexities of that process to the bureaucratic one-dimensionality of the business world. In David Rudkin's *The Triumph of Death* (1981), a birth is shown on the stage, in Pam Gems's *Loving Women* (1986), the wish for children becomes an all-consuming impulse for the female protagonist who is also a political activist, whereas in David Hare's *Wrecked Eggs* (1986) the frequency of abortions signifies the failure of meaningful perspectives in human relationships.

At the same time, mental or bodily disability and old age have become more prominent themes. In Arnold Wesker's *Whatever Happened to Betty Lemon?* (1986), an isolated old woman who is dependent on her wheelchair and communicates with her absent daughter only via the answering machine of her telephone, still manages to maintain her self-respect with heroic irony. In Peter Shaffer's *Lettice and Lovage* (1987), too, an elderly woman is the protagonist, who fights against what she sees as a catastrophic loss of cultural imagination as is exemplified in the mere functionalism of modern city architecture.

But above all, *dying* and *death* as borderline experiences which transgress the prevailing ideology of utilitarianism and of the economic and technological availability of human life are put on the stage with far more insistence than previously. In Edward Bond's *Summer* (1982), the play's focus is on the dying of an old woman, which is integrated into the more general framework of European history since World War II. But death loses some of its individual bitterness through the awareness of a process of history which, in the breaking up of cultural and class divisions, contains at least the potential of meaningful social change. In Catherine Hayes's *Skirmishes* (1982), a play for three women, there is a more pessimistic note in that the dying of a mother becomes an insignificant and, in its decisive stage, virtually unnoticed background event for the conflict of her two daughters. Their life-long animosity erupts in a fiercely egocentric battle for positions, which reveals an abyss of human isolation and indifference, and which is contrasted by Hayes with the unobtrusive brutality and the enervating slowness of the mother's dying, who is degraded to a kind of living human waste whose disposal is already arranged before her actual death.

A similar situation with male protagonists underlies Nigel Williams's *My Brother's Keeper?* (1985), where a father is in hospital beyond hope of recovery and his two sons, a playwright and a businessman, engage in aggressive verbal battles at his death-bed. The experience of death becomes a test case for the validity of the characters' values and views of life, and for the "wonderful radical paradise"[12] the playwright had devised for himself. Most of all, it becomes a challenge for his play-writing itself, which becomes indistinguishably intermingled with the dramatic events, confronting Nigel Williams's fictitious *alter ego* with the failure of his play-in-progress. The blurred focus of the play, and the loss of a clearly identifiable dramatic purpose are explicitly formulated in *My Brother's Keeper?* in a way which pinpoints the more general transformation of political drama in Britain: "The play's a swinging attack on something or other. I forget what. The National Health Service probably. Or maybe I've gone really deeper this time. It's an attack on illness. I hit illness pretty hard. I expect the critics will have a hard time coming to terms with that. I'm doing my errand you know. [...] I'm not coming to the point, am I? [...]"[13]

If we can see in this play another manifestation of the semiological and existential turn in contemporary British drama, this does not mean a weakening or a loss of its critical impulse but rather its anthropological extension and concretisation. For the themes and concerns mentioned above are precisely those which are neglected in the contemporary image of an autonomous, self-reliant, successful and well-functioning human being which is the cultural stereotype of the time. Nor does the new 'existential' interest posit an unquestionably given basis of reality. On the contrary, it replaces conventional ways of thinking in terms of progress, causality and binary logic by a thinking in terms of pluralism and of the simultaneous interplay of various levels of meaning and frames of interpretation. It thereby intensifies the reflexive attitude that pervades the plays on all levels, and that raises into consciousness with even sharper acuteness the constitutive role and the epistemic limitations of the linguistic, cultural and theatrical signifiers that they employ. By presenting no longer one world but a multiple world of competing interpretations, the plays become dramas of the cultural imagination, in which 'reality' is replaced by images of reality that are brought to interact in a way which includes the theatre itself as an integral part of that cultural imagination.

The concurrence or fusion of different, sometimes contradictory tendencies that we saw as characteristic of much of recent British drama can also be observed in the relationship between the dramatic and the theatrical side of the plays. On the one hand, the scepticism about the referential and representational functions of dramatic language leads to a strong emphasis on the *nonverbal element*, on the signs and the body-language of the theatre, and on the concrete here-and-now of the performance itself as a communicative act which is increasingly composed into the plays themselves. The pre- or translinguistic signifiers of theatrical communication like acoustic or optical signs, dance, song, gesture and ritual, are used in the sense of maximising and, as it were, of authenticating the dramatic experience. In this tendency, one can see a semiological parallel to the new existentialism in the themes of the plays, a search for a new vitality and concreteness of the theatre vis-à-vis the clichés and implicit ideologies of conventional forms of aesthetic communication with which any 'realistic' theatre of representation is inevitably entwined.

On the other hand, however, there is, often within the same plays, an opposite tendency towards what can be called a *reliterarisation* of drama, towards a breaking up of cultural clichés from within the potentials of language and dialogue themselves. There is in this a new affirmation of the aesthetic, the imaginative and indeed the poetic dimensions of dramas and of their characters as literary works of art. This is shown in the frequent use of literary sources from the past; in the dramatic exploration of the role of the artist in society; and in an at least partial, if often highly self-ironical, revival of forms of verse and poetic drama.[14]

What I see as a common motive behind these complementary tendencies is that they continue and further differentiate that fundamental *opposition to an abstract society* which has characterised Modern English Drama since the 1950s. By an abstract society I mean that particular change in the relationship between the individual and contemporary society which has irreversibly transformed our experience of reality by superseding the primary world of our senses by a secondary world of abstraction. This is illustrated in such phenomena as the explosion and specialisation of scientific knowledge; the computer revolution; the bureaucratisation of conflicts and decisions; or the virtual omnipresence of the electronic media and of their multiplication of simulated realities. The individuals are confronted with a cultural world of incommensurable proportions, and enmeshed in a labyrinthine network of highly indirect and existentially indifferent relationships. This appears, in many plays, as a kind of 'unreal superreality' which, as it were, 'colonializes' the primary world of the senses and of communicative action, and thus the world on which drama depends for its material. Abstract society poses a specific resistance to its dramatization because it is impersonal and therefore essentially *undramatic*.[15]

The tension which results from this conflict can be felt behind many contemporary plays. Indeed, most of those mentioned in this paper could be taken as examples, notably Shaffer's *Lettice and Lovage*, Poliakoff's *Coming in to Land*, Wesker's *Betty Lemon*, or Churchill's *Serious Money*, where one character expresses his own derealization in the world of abstract money transactions by affirming that, in comparison with it, "matters of life and death come a poor second".[16] Howard Brenton's *The Genius* (1983), too, is a case in point, where the progress of modern physics leads to discoveries which endanger the survival of humankind, so that a scientist and his young female student, who is a mathematical genius, desperately try to find ways of preventing their political misuse. In Sarah Daniels's *Byrthrite* (1987), something similar is shown in the field of genetic technology, in which the reproduction of the human race is gradually removed from the female body and becomes part of an artificial world of genetic manipulation; and against this threat, Daniels's play actualises a mythopoetic female self-consciousness which is based on 'ecological' principles in a broad sense. Alan Ayckbourn's *Henceforward* (1988), produced in 1989 in Berlin by Peter Zadek[17], dramatizes the crisis of a composer surrounded by a computerized environment and threatened in his creativity by the replacement of real communication and real characters by their technological counterparts. And in Harold Pinter's *Mountain Language* (1988), to name a final, and as I think particularly impressive, example, the agent of the play is an anonymous state, which rules with computer-based, arbitrary decrees. The state enforces its centralized power by an act of linguistic imperialism, which outlaws and in effect eliminates the concrete language of the mountain people, who in the play represent human communication and cultural difference, and whose identity and forms of life are destroyed by an all-pervading language of dominance and bureaucratic abstractions.

But beyond these explicit examples, the problems of an abstract society can be said to form an almost universally present background to which the plays, in their various ways, respond. In their aesthetic pluralism, in their biological existentialism, as well as in their emphasis on the concrete semiotic process of the theatre and on the living communication with the audience, they can be seen as reactions to and indeed as defence strategies against that intensely felt cultural *loss of reality* which is not merely the result of a postmodern scepticism but a symptom of the derealization of experience in an abstract society.

Notes

1 London, Cottesloe Theatre, January 1989.
2 London, Lyric Theatre, August 1989, directed by Judi Dench.
3 London, Royal Court Theatre, April 1989, directed by Penny Cherns.
4 Simard, R.: *Postmodern Drama. Contemporary Playwrights in America and Britain.* Lanham/Md., London, 1984. The 'aesthetic of play' which Dieter A. Berger sees at work in contemporary British drama has affinities to Simard's concept of postmodern drama: cf. D. A. Berger: „Ästhetik des Spiels im zeitgenössischen britischen Drama". *Forum Modernes Theater* 3, 1988, 17–30.
5 Bigsby, C. W. E.: "The Politics of Anxiety: Contemporary Socialist Theatre in England". – In Brown, J. R. (Ed.): *Modern British Dramatists. New Perspectives.* Englewood Cliffs/N. J., 1984, pp. 161–176, here: p. 164.
6 Bond, E.: *Two Post Modern Plays (Jackets* and *In the Company of Men).* London: Methuen, 1989.
7 For introductions to contemporary feminist theatre see H. Keyssar: *Feminist Theatre. An Introduction to Plays of Contemporary British and American Women.* Basingstoke, London, 1984; M. Wandor: *Look Back in Gender. Sexuality and the Family in Post-War British Drama.* London, 1987.
8 Edgar, D.: *Maydays.* London: Methuen, 1983, p. 63.
9 Nichols, P.: *Poppy.* London: Methuen, 1982, p. 110.
10 Schlueter, J.: "Adultery Is Next to Godlessness: Dramatic Juxtaposition in Peter Nichols's *Passion Play*". – In Brown (Ed.): *Modern British Dramatists*, pp. 153–160, here: p. 153.
11 Churchill, C.: *Serious Money. A City Comedy.* London: Methuen, 1987, p. 92.
12 Williams, N.: *My Brother's Keeper?* London, Boston: Faber, 1985, p. 56.
13 Ibid., p. 16.
14 The claims for a new artistic, imaginative, and indeed tragic theatre have been put forward probably most explicitly and provocatively by Howard Barker in his "49 Asides for a Tragic Theatre" (*Englisch Amerikanische Studien* 8, 1986, 474–475), where he expresses his credo as a dramatist in the context of the 1980s with such heretical formulations as: "The opposition in art has nothing but the quality of its imagination./ The only possible resistance to a culture of banality is quality. [. . .] Tragedy was impossible as long as hope was confused with comfort. Suddenly tragedy is possible again./ [. . .] The tragedies of the 60s were not tragedies but failures of the social services." (474)

15 For a more extensive exposition of this theory see H. Zapf: *Das Drama in der abstrakten Gesellschaft. Zur Theorie und Struktur des modernen englischen Dramas.* Tübingen, 1988.
16 *Serious Money*, p. 75.
17 Berlin, Theater am Kurfürstendamm, April 1989.

Plays Referred to:

Ali, Tariq, Brenton, Howard: *Iranian Nights*. London: Nick Hern, 1989.
Ayckbourn, Alan: *Woman in Mind. December Bee*. London, Boston: Faber, 1986.
–: *Henceforward*. London, Boston: Faber, 1988.
Barker, Howard: *The Power of the Dog*. London, New York: Calder and Riverrun, 1985.
Bond, Edward: *Summer*. London: Methuen, 1982.
–: *Two Post Modern Plays*. London: Methuen, 1989.
Brenton, Howard: *The Genius*. London: Methuen, 1983.
–: Hare, David: *Pravda. A Fleet Street Comedy*. London: Methuen, 1985.
Churchill, Caryl: *Top Girls*. London: Methuen, 1982.
–: *Serious Money. A City Comedy*. London: Methuen, 1987.
–: *Icecream*. London: Nick Hern, 1989.
–, Lan, David: *A Mouthful of Birds*. London: Methuen, 1986.
Daniels, Sarah: *Byrthrite*. London: Methuen, 1987.
Edgar, David: *Maydays*. London: Methuen, 1983.
Gems, Pam: *Three Plays*. Harmondsworth: Penguin, 1985.
Hampton, Christopher: *Tales from Hollywood*. London, Boston: Faber, 1983.
–: *Les Liaisons Dangereuses*. London, Boston: Faber, 1985.
Hare, David: *The Bay at Nice* and *Wrecked Eggs*. London, Boston: Faber, 1986.
Hayes, Catherine: *Skirmishes*. London: Faber, 1982.
Nichols, Peter: *Poppy*. London: Methuen, 1982.
Osborne, John: *Look Back in Anger*. London: Evans, 1979 (1956).
Page, Louise: *Golden Girls*. London: Methuen, 1985.
–: *Real Estate*. London: Methuen, 1985.
Pinter, Harold: *Mountain Language*. London: Methuen, 1988.
Poliakoff, Stephen: *Coming in to Land*. London: Methuen, 1986.
Rudkin, David: *The Triumph of Death*. London: Methuen, 1981.
Shaffer, Peter: *Lettice and Lovage*. London: André Deutsch, 1987.
Wesker, Arnold: *Roots*. London: Evans, 1961.
–: *One Woman Plays*. Harmondsworth, 1989.
–: *Whatever Happened to Betty Lemon?. Englisch Amerikanische Studien* 8, 1986, 493–504.
Williams, Nigel: *My Brother's Keeper?* London, Boston: Faber, 1985.

Günther Klotz, Berlin

Zwischen Erfolgszwang und Engagement: Tendenzen im englischen Drama der achtziger Jahre

Die Lage im englischen Theater hat sich in den letzten zehn Jahren gründlich verändert[1] (die Konservativen regieren seit 1979) und mit ihr der Sprachgebrauch. Die Begriffe *industry, enterprise, products, investments, market needs, marketeers, consumer, productive efficiency, monitoring committees* gehören nun zur Denkweise und zum Instrumentarium des Arts Council, der die staatlichen Subventionen verteilt (die aufgezählten Begriffe sind seinem Bericht von 1987 entnommen).[2] Die Praxis und die Theorie des radikalen Monetarismus haben die Künste ergriffen. An die Stelle des Wortes „Zuschauerreaktion" ist „Zufriedenstellung des Kunden" getreten. Elemente des Musicals und der *soap opera* breiten sich aus, die sinnlose Zurschaustellung von Überfluß, von Ausstattungen und technischen Raffinessen nimmt zu, in einer wachsenden Anzahl von Inszenierungen scheint sich wie im Fernsehen der geistige Anspruch fast gesetzmäßig zu verringern. Endlich, so heißt es im herrschenden Sprachgebrauch, müßten sich die Künste dem „Neuen Realismus" stellen. Dieser *new realism* ist freilich kein ästhetischer Begriff, sondern er beschreibt die Tatsache, daß sich die Theater dem Prinzip der "cost effectiveness", den Bedingungen des Finanzgeschäfts unterordnen müssen.

Gewährte der Arts Council früher den, wie es hieß, "centres of excellence" Zuschüsse, wendete er also Kriterien künstlerischer Qualität an – wie fragwürdig diese auch zuweilen waren –, so unterstützt er heute jene Theater und Ensembles, welche die meisten auf Werbung basierenden Sponsorenbeträge auftreiben; das gelingt natürlich denen am besten, die einen Grad von Popularität besitzen. Finanziers und Firmen geben auch lieber den großen nationalen Einrichtungen Geld, weil diese eine internationale Publicity erlangen. Große, aufwendige Inszenierungen werden auch oft ins Ausland übernommen; d. h., es geht nicht etwa das Ensemble samt Technik z. B. von London nach Wien, sondern nur der Regisseur und der Ausstatter, manchmal auch nur das Logbuch einer Inszenierung mit den Videokassetten. Allmählich nähert sich das Theater dem Einheitsfutter internationaler Restaurantketten. Führende Regisseure lockt das ganz große Spektakel, sie treten zur Oper über. Shakespeare und das Erbe werden mit Hilfe großer Namen vermarktet: Derek Jacobi als Richard III., Dustin Hoffmann als Shylock. Stars als Publikumsmagnet, der Rest der Inszenierung ist nicht so wichtig. Wenn die Künstler, die, so hört man, von Natur aus in Finanzdingen inkompetent seien, weil sie sich mit so imaginären Sachen wie dem zweifelnden Selbst, der Moral und illusorischen Idealen beschäftigen, erst einmal begriffen, wie das Geschäft läuft, werde auch die Kunst aufblühen, eben als eine Industrie. Dieser Zwang zum Geschäftserfolg, zur Anpassung an den Markt, an die nationalen und internationalen Kapitalbewegungen ist ein Zwang zur Konformität. Herausforderungen, Stücke, die Scheinprobleme demaskieren und wirkliche Probleme ausbreiten, werden an die Wand gedrückt, marginalisiert oder ganz ausgeschlossen.

Fanden in dem Jahrzehnt nach 1968 das englische und das schottische Nationaltheater auf kleinen Bühnen, an Orten fern der großen Theater, auf dem Lande, in Kneipen, Schulen, Gemeindesälen und alternativen Studios statt, gespielt von fahrenden Theatertruppen vor einem Publikum, dem das bürgerliche Salonstück nichts gab oder das überhaupt noch nie eine Theateraufführung gesehen hatte, so ist dieser Quell einer vielgestaltigen, teilweise experimentellen oder engagierten Weiterentwicklung des Theaters in Großbritannien nun in Gefahr zu versiegen. Theatergruppen wie Footsbarn oder Pip Simmons sind erloschen oder weggezogen, viele mußten aufgeben, die Spielstätten der Fahrenden stehen nun häufiger leer oder Diskotheken ziehen ein. Diese Gruppen können gar nicht den Anforderungen eines werbeintensiven Finanzmanagements entsprechen, weil sie zu klein sind. Auch hat sich das Schema ihrer Subventionskonkurrenz gewandelt. Früher konkurrierten sie nach künstlerischen Kriterien mit anderen Theatertruppen um die staatlichen Gelder. Heute konkurrieren sie um Sponsorengelder mit anderen Projekten der Unterhaltungsindustrie, mit Vergnügungsparks, Festivals und Unternehmungen, die mehr „Verbraucher" finden, mehr Touristen anlocken und für Geldgeber und Kommunen profitabler sind. Nur wenige Theatergruppen können sich da halten. Früher zum alternativen Theater zählende Theatermacher wie Ken Campbell oder Gavin Richards haben sich dem Erfolg um jeden Preis verschrieben, die Gruppen Cheek by Jowl und Wildcat finden alle Unterstützung, wobei Wildcat (Glasgow), eine professionell hochqualifizierte Band, die gelegentlich mit Schauspielern höchst politische Programme inszeniert, mehr Geld einspielt als jedes andere Theater in Schottland.

Die ästhetischen und funktionalen Konsequenzen dieser gesellschaftlichen Entwicklung in der Kultur und in den kulturellen Institutionen sind unabsehbar. Überall spürt man das Trauma einer Niederlage, weil das politische Theater der Nach-68er-Jahre die Rechtswende von 1979 nicht habe verhindern können. Also ist, so scheinen viele Beteiligte zu denken, das politische Theater passé, zumal für sie unklar ist, ob es eine Arbeiterklasse und eine Klassengesellschaft überhaupt noch gibt (verkündete doch Mrs. Thatcher, es gebe keine Gesellschaft, nur Individuen). Übrigens, was heute rückblickend „politisches" Theater genannt wird, war durchaus nicht durchgehend politisch, doch immerhin gesellschaftskritisch.

Wie kann man sich, grob vereinfachend, in der heutigen Theaterlandschaft Großbritanniens orientieren? Tun wir das in fünf Kapiteln, so haben wir zunächst (1. Kapitel) das Mainstream-Theater bürgerlicher Natur. Es findet im Londoner Westend und in den großen Theatern statt. Zu seinen Autoren gehören Alan Ayckbourn, Ray Cooney, Michael Frayn, Nigel Gray, Tom Stoppard, Harold Pinter. Es herrschen *domestic comedies* vor, Farcen, psychologische und sexuelle Spiele, auch absurde Situationen, Entfremdungen und Identitätsschwierigkeiten, doch alle, auch im Endspielschmerz, aufgehoben in bürgerlichen Weltverständnissen. Von diesem Mainstream-Theater gehen keine anderen gesellschaftlichen Impulse aus als die, daß Entertainment ruhig "out of touch with reality" sein dürfe und daß die wohlhabenden zwei Drittel der Gesellschaft trotz kleiner individueller Probleme sich im großen und ganzen doch zufrieden und gelassen zurücklehnen können – auch wenn Ayckbourn zwischendurch einmal wieder düstere Prognosen stellt wie in *Henceforward* und wenn Pinter in *Mountain Language* (beide 1988) mit dem Land, in dem die Folter gebilligt und jede Kommunikation überwacht wird, vielleicht doch das künftige England meint.

Wichtiger und strittiger ist die Frage danach, welche Wege die Dramatiker des alternativen Theaters der siebziger Jahre gegangen sind (2. Kapitel). Einer nach dem anderen wanderten sie, von besagtem Trauma gezeichnet, in die großen Häuser ab, ins Mainstream-Theater, ins Fernsehen. Ich bin nicht der Ansicht, daß Howard Brenton, David Hare, David Edgar, Trevor Griffiths, Pam Gems und andere als Dramatiker in den siebziger Jahren gescheitert sind. Vielleicht überschätzten sie die Wirkungsmöglichkeiten des Theaters. Doch ihre Dramaturgien des Schocks und der politischen Debatte haben das Theater außerordentlich bereichert. Mit ihren Stücken beteiligten sie sich an den großen öffentlichen Diskussionen, sie gewannen neue Zuschauer und sie bewiesen, daß ein problemorientiertes, die offiziellen Verlautbarungen, Sprüche, Bilder und Zeichen entmystifizierendes Theater vergnüglich und lebensfähig sein kann. Ihr Beitrag zur Entwicklung des englischen Dramas und Theaters bleibt unverloren.

Nach ihrem Einzug in die etablierten Einrichtungen, wo sie nach Griffiths eine "strategic penetration" versuchen wollten, haben sie allerdings dem Widerspruch ihrer Situation Tribut zollen müssen und um des Erfolges willen ihre einstigen Intentionen so weit reduziert, daß ihre Worte und Werke nun ziemlich hohl klingen. Ihre Desillusionierung, die Früchte der zwangsweise eingegangenen Kompromisse und ihre enttäuschenden Kassenschlager sind inzwischen zum Hauptgegenstand der Kritik und Forschung zum englischen Theater der Gegenwart geworden.[3] Hervorstechende Merkmale ihres Schaffens in den Achtzigern sind ihre Unausgeglichenheit und Unsicherheit, vielleicht sogar Unentschiedenheit in den Gegenständen, Themen und Mitteln der Stücke. Nehmen wir Beispiele.

David Hare, Mitbegründer von Portable Theatre (1968), später auch der Joint Stock Theatre Company verbunden, avancierte zu einem der Schauspieldirektoren des National Theatre. 1989 lief dort mit großem Erfolg *The Secret Rapture* (1988), von *Drama* und *Plays and Players* zum besten Stück des Jahres erkoren. Hare veranschaulicht die korrodierende Wirkung des Thatcherschen Ethos in privaten Partnerbeziehungen. Die Schwestern Isobel, Graphikerin, und Miriam, Staatssekretärin für Umweltschutz und Thatcher-Typ, begegnen sich am Totenbett des Vaters und haben Fragen der Erbschaft und des Verbleibs von Katherine zu klären, der jungen, vulgären, trinkenden Stiefmutter. Mit ihren Finanzaktionen ruinieren die kalte Miriam und ihr halbtrotteliger Mann Isobels kleine Firma und auch deren Liebe zu Irwin, ihrem Mitarbeiter, der Miriams Kuhhandel aus Gewinnsucht mitmacht. Die altmodisch aufrichtige, liberale Isobel steht am Ende mit leeren Händen da, weil sie der neuen britischen Welt nicht gewachsen ist, in der Täuschung, Geldgier, über Leichen gehendes Kalkül und Karrieresucht gutgeheißen werden. Treffsicher erzielt Hare Lacher, wenn die eiserne Miriam ihr schieres Unverständnis für Gefühle und Menschlichkeit preisgibt. Doch der melodramatische Schluß schiebt dann den Kontrast der beiden Schwestern auf ausgetretene psychologische Pfade, als beruhe alles auf Neurosen, die mit etwas gutem Willen zu überwinden seien. So verschwindet der Sarkasmus der Komödie im Märchen. Da ist kaum etwas geblieben von dem ernsten Engagement, mit dem Hare in *Fanshen* und *Teeth 'n Smiles* (beide 1975) Fragen jener Jahre aufgriff und in *Brassneck* (1973), gemeinsam verfaßt mit Howard Brenton, die Verflechtung korrupter Politiker, Unternehmer und Krimineller aufdeckte.

Auch in den Achtzigern schrieben Brenton und Hare ein Stück zusammen, *Pravda* (1985), ein Renner im großen Haus des National Theatre. Im Mittelpunkt steht ein faszinierender Schurke des britischen Pressewesens, ein Ausländer wie Rupert Murdoch, der mit clubfeinen Gangstermethoden die alte Fairness-Liberalität außer Kraft setzt und sich die ehrwürdigen Blätter der Fleet Street kahlschlagartig unter den Nagel reißt. Die Fabel ist als Folge persönlicher Auseinandersetzungen angelegt, in liberalistischer Moralität. Der gesellschaftliche Nexus und die wirkliche Macht des öffentlichen Diskurses kommen nicht vor. Der interessante Böse, die alte *Vice*-Figur, spricht die besten Wahrheiten, die pragmatischen: Wenn alle Welt lüge, warum nicht auch die Presse. Dieser Show unterliegt die Gewißheit, daß Individualismus, Privateigentum und die Macht der Reichen unverändert gelten, keine Sorge. Damit sind die Autoren im alternativlosen Theater angekommen.

Howard Brenton, der mit der Bradford Theatre Group und auch mit Portable Theatre gearbeitet hatte, offenbarte 1983 in *The Genius* seine Ratlosigkeit, was zu tun sei. Sein Held, ein Atomwissenschaftler, zieht sich zurück, um der politischen Manipulation zu entgehen; wer aber könnte das System der

Manipulation abschaffen? 1988 wurde seine Dystopia von 1974, *The Churchill Play*, von der Royal Shakespeare Company im Barbican neuinszeniert, überarbeitet vom Autor. Es ist eine Warnung vor der Abschaffung der Menschenrechte in Großbritannien (für die es schon Beispiele gab: geheimdienstliche Unterwanderung der Medien, Eingriffe in die Interviewpraxis und in die Fernsehberichterstattung vom Parlament, ein neuer Zensurindex). Das ist politische Aufklärung. Gemeinsam mit Tariq Ali verfaßte er 1989 *Iranian Nights*, eine intertextuell gekleidete Entrüstung über islamische Bücherverbrennung in Bradford, über die Todesdrohung an einen Schriftsteller und die religiöse Überheblichkeit, die die Identität islamischer Einwanderer in England bekräftigen soll. Der Gedanke des Theaters als öffentliche Anstalt, nicht nur als Unterhaltungsindustrie, ist also noch lebendig.

Das Engagement D a v i d E d g a r s war und ist unbestritten, was die Sammlung seiner wichtigsten Aufsätze *The Second Time as Farce* (1988) belegt. Aber sein bislang wichtigstes Stück der achtziger Jahre, *Maydays* (1983), bedeutet nach Meinung einstiger Mitstreiter eine Abkehr von den Anliegen des alternativen Theaters, wenn nicht einen Verrat. Edgar hatte mit der Theatergruppe The General Will agitpropartige Stücke herausgebracht und später, z. B. mit *Destiny* (1975), ein großes kritisches Panorama der britischen Gesellschaft entworfen. Dieses Stück warnte vor einer faschistoiden Entwicklung und kritisierte die Haltung der Labour-Regierung. In *Maydays* nun setzt Edgar die Linke mit der Rechten gleich. Die beiden Hauptgestalten des europäisch angelegten Geschichtsrahmens kommen aus dem Osten und aus dem Westen. Sie kappen ihre Wurzeln und laufen über, von links nach rechts. Im Sekundären und Psychologischen sind es genau gezeichnete Charaktere, doch selbst *Time Out* und *Plays and Players* vermerkten, daß die Geschichte der Linken verzerrt und wesentliche Vorgänge weggelassen wurden. Links und rechts sind im Stück nicht mehr verschieden, die ideologische Ausstattung des einzelnen ist austauschbar. Dissens erscheint als eine Lebensform, "contained", die Grundlagen einer Frontstellung gegen das Establishment werden diskreditiert, das Individuum kehrt bei sich selbst ein. 1987 hingegen plädierte er in *That Summer*, einem Stück vor dem Hintergrund des Bergarbeiterstreiks, wieder für die Solidarität in der Klassenauseinandersetzung.

C a r y l C h u r c h i l l setzte feministische Akzente im englischen Theater, ohne sektiererischen Dogmatismus, in den Achtzigern u. a. mit *Top Girls* (1982). In Geschichts- und Gegenwartsstücken geht es ihr um übergreifende gesellschaftliche Fragen. Im Mai 1989 lief am Royal Court das kurze Stück *Icecream*, ein Spiel mit den Klischeevorstellungen, die sich Engländer von Amerikanern und Amerikaner von Engländern machen. Es ist eine bittere Farce um die falsche Suche nach geschichtlichen Wurzeln und um selbstgefällige Geschichtslosigkeit, die dem Verbrechen nahesteht. Churchills voraufgegangene Satire auf den

Monetarismus, *Serious Money* (1987), auf das Geldmachen als politisch beglaubigte Tugend, zog genau die Kritisierten an, die Banker, Broker und Yuppies, die sich auf die Schenkel klopften, weil die Autorin die Machenschaften, die Sprache, den Witz und die Gesinnung so genau ausstellte. Was vermag Satire, wenn die Regierung, die Finanziers und die Neureichen in Parlament, Fernsehen und Presse ohnehin kein Blatt vor den Mund nehmen und selbst offen über die Unrentabilität von Menschlichkeit sprechen?

Das ist die Frage, die sich diesen Theaterleuten stellt. Sie sehen ihr gesellschafts-kritisches Potential zwischen Erfolgszwang und Engagement aufgehen in einer sich amüsant selbst ironisierenden und bestens unterhaltenden Selbstgefälligkeit. Seit dem Einzug in die etablierten Theater haben sie es mit einem Publikum zu tun, das zum großen Teil aus den Nutznießern der konservativen Umverteilung besteht. Außer den pauschalreisenden Touristen kann sich niemand anderes als besagte zwei Drittel die Eintrittskarten leisten.

Neben den ehemals alternativen Dramatikern zeichnen sich andere Trends ab. Zu erwähnen ist zunächst der Ein-Mann-Trend H o w a r d B a r k e r (3. Kapitel). Aus der intensiven Überzeugung, daß sowohl das kommerzielle Theater als auch das linke sich auf Hegemonie gerichteten Ideologien unterwirft und also disziplinierend, Harmonie suggerierend wirkt, sagt er den herkömmlichen Dramaturgien ab und bietet ein *theatre of catastrophe* an. Er will ein Theater machen, das gegen die Kunst der Banalität und Beschönigung und gegen die selbstzufriedene Berufung auf eine Kultur der Arbeiterklasse auftritt, die es seiner Meinung nach nicht gibt.[4] Für Bühne, Funk und Fernsehen schrieb er mehr als dreißig Stücke, und 1985 verschaffte ihm eine erfolgreiche Saison im Barbican mit drei Inszenierungen der Royal Shakespeare Company einen Durchbruch. 1988 wurden drei Werke anderer Bauart von ihm gespielt. *The Possibilities* besteht aus zehn "short plays", angesiedelt in Krieg und Verwüstung; *The Last Supper* zeigt, angelehnt an das Neue Testament, Szenen vom Ende eines Gurus, von der Entstehung eines Mythos, der der Gewalt dienstbar gemacht werden kann; und *The Bite of the Night* blickt zurück auf das zwölfmal zerstörte Troja, auf Ruinen, welche auch die Ruinen einer englischen Universität sind.

In einem der Kurzstücke von *The Possibilities* tritt die Familie eines türkischen Webers auf. Während die Stadt von Christen bombardiert wird, weben sie weiter, um den Lebensunterhalt zu verdienen. Als ein gewebtes Stück vom Blut eines Soldaten getränkt wird, entdecken sie eine wunderschöne Farbe. Sie finden aber keine Zeit, die neue Ware auf den Markt zu bringen, weil sie selbst umkommen. In einer der in *The Last Supper* eingestreuten Fabeln will ein blinder Geiger eine Nonne ausrauben und vergewaltigen. Soldaten kommen, und alle verbünden sich, die Bauern auszuplündern. Auch die Szenen der Anhänger des Gurus oder Führers sind von solcher Struktur. Sie brechen die Handlung auf, Charaktere mit individuellem Profil und Motivationen gibt es nicht mehr, die Kategorien gut und böse sind irrelevant geworden. Das Abendmahl wird zum Mord, jeder der zwölf Anhänger sticht einmal zu, bevor sie den Leichnam zerteilen und aufessen; statt Kommunion die Zersetzung des "body" und des "body politic".

In *The Bite of the Night* sehen wir den englischen Literaturwissenschaftler Dr. Savage, der zwei Bücher über Homer schrieb. Er wird in den Trojanischen Krieg und die nachfolgenden Zerstörungen verwickelt, ist Gefangener, dann Ratgeber des griechischen Königs Fladder, der aber auch eingekerkert wird. Savage wird Liebhaber von Fladders Frau Helena. Er heiratet die Trojanerin Creusa, wird an eine Tonne gekettet, soll eine Verfassung aufsetzen. Man droht Homer, ihn zu waschen. Zwei Moslems mit einem europäischen Diener stecken Fähnchen in den Wüstensand, Schliemann tritt in imperialistischer Gebärde auf. Helena, Hure und Idol, erklärter Kriegsgrund und vermeintliche Garantin göttlichen Glücks, erleidet das Altern und wird stufenweise gestutzt: Man hackt ihr die Arme, dann die Beine ab, doch sie wird als Objekt des Hasses gebraucht. Den letzten Untergang vollzieht das Volk selbst. Es verbrennt sich, nachdem es die Grausamkeit der Mordlüsternen, der Machtbesessenen, der Befehlsempfänger, der Unschuldigen und der Babies erfuhr.

Diese Vorgänge werden nicht als Fabel erzählt, die irgendwie auszulegen wäre. Es sind Bilder aus der Geschichte Trojas, einer Geschichte, vor der sich Homer drückte und die sein großes Epos im herrschenden Diskurs ausschloß. Howard Barker fragt wohl damit, welche wirklichen Erfahrungen heute ausgeschlossen werden und was die Medien in ihrer Informationsfülle verbergen. In *The Last Supper* spricht er vom Charme vor den Kameras, der unser aller Tod sein wird.[5]

Statt Handlung gibt es also Tableaus und Bilder, Minimalszenen von Gewalt und eine Sprache, welche die Tabus des letzten Schmerzes abstreift. Es wird eine Welt jenseits der Geschichtlichkeit auf dem Grat zwischen Sein und Selbstzerstörung gezeigt. Die Bilder aber fügen sich nicht ein in ein Erklärungssystem. Sie bedeuten nichts jenseits der Bilder, sie selbst sind die Sache. Barker verwirft das konventionelle bürgerliche Drama des privaten Konflikts in relativ stabiler Gesellschaft, auch die Tragödie, die über der Leiche des Helden die öffentliche Moral bekräftigt, auch die agitatorischen Stücke der Identifizierung mit einer alternativen Ordnung, ja er verwirft im Grunde die gesamte klassische Dramenästhetik des allegorischen Kunstverständnisses, die von der Renaissance bis zum Modernismus gültig war und weiterlebt, die Ästhetik nämlich, die das Theater als Zeichen der Welt nimmt und das Bühnengeschehen den Universalien einpaßt, sei es dem christlichen Weltbild, dem bürgerlich-liberalen, der humanistischen Ethik; einem materialistischen Geschichtsmodell, einem anthropologischen oder Schicksalsfatalismus, dem Prinzip der Absurdität allen Handels und

Seins oder einem anderen geschlossenen Denkschema. Der Zuschauer erfährt im Erlebnis des Bildertheaters, daß ihm die bisher zur Verfügung gestellten Ideologien in dieser globalen Bedrohung nicht helfen; er sollte die Verantwortung selbst übernehmen. Im *Guardian* schrieb Barker vor der Premiere von *The Bite of the Night*:

> But in a theatre of catastrophe there is no restauration of certitudes, and in a sense more compelling and less manipulated than in the epic theatre, it is the audience who are freed into authority.[6]

Auch wenn Barkers Theater elitär jegliche Solidarisierungsimpulse verweigert, ist es höchst aktuell und theatralisch. Von der Struktur her besitzt es Ähnlichkeiten mit Robert Wilsons ästhetisierendem Bildertheater und mit den politisch und philosophisch radikalen Texten und Inszenierungen Heiner Müllers. Die Kritik in Großbritannien tut sich schwer damit, weil sie mit Dramen ohne Fabel, ohne Charaktere und ohne Inhalt und Sinn im konventionellen Sinn wenig anzufangen weiß. Barkers Strategien der Sinnkonstitution in seinem Theater der letzten Warnung sind postmodernistisch, nicht kausal oder argumentativ, sondern metadramatisch, intertextuell, assoziativ, audiovisuell, die heutigen Gewohnheiten der Medienrezeption einkalkulierend.[7]

Wo ist nun eigentlich das gesellschaftskritische Theater, das zu überleben vermag, ohne daß es mit den öffentlichen Widersprüchen und dem Abbau der Demokratie besänftigend ausgesöhnt? Es ist schwer zu finden, denn es zeigt sich zersplittert, fragmentarisiert. Früher brauchte man nur die jeweils neuesten Publikationen von Methuen, Calder und wenigen anderen Verlagen herzunehmen, um sich ins Bild zu setzen. Doch auch in den Verlagen wirken die finanziellen Ausschließungsmechanismen. Was ist z. B. aus Methuen geworden? Zunächst wurde der Verlag von einem anderen Verlag übernommen, von Associated Book Publishers, danach aber von dem Konzern International Thompson. Der wiederum bot seine "book division" bald auf dem Markt an, wo sie von der meistbietenden Octopus Group gekauft wurde. Der renommierte Leiter der Dramenabteilung Nick Hern verließ daraufhin den Verlag und gründete einen eigenen.

In dieser Fragmentierung splittern auch die Themen der Stücke und das Publikum auf (4. Kapitel). So gibt es Stücke mit feministischem Anliegen und vor allem solche, die sich der Probleme der Minderheiten annehmen, der ethnischen Gruppen, der Einwanderer, der Arbeitslosen, der Behinderten, der Homosexuellen und Lesbierinnen, der entlassenen Strafgefangenen, Drogensüchtigen und der regionaler Besonderheiten. Punktuell und manchmal mit übergreifenden Implikationen wecken sie die Bewußtheit für soziale Fragen, doch es fehlt ein allgemeinerer Fokus. Aus diesem reichen Potential möchte ich, stellvertretend für andere, drei Namen nennen.

Sarah Daniels begann 1981 zu schreiben; es liegen acht oder mehr Stücke vor. In ihrem harten feministischen Engagement wollte sie gelegentlich nicht einmal männliche Regisseure akzeptieren. *Masterpieces* (1983) klagt die Diffamierung der Frauen in der Pornographie an. Nach der Uraufführung an der Royal Exchange in Manchester wurde es vom Royal Court in London übernommen, wo sie 1984 "writer in residence" wurde. In *Byrthrite* (1986) untersucht sie, welche Konsequenzen heute noch von jenem denkwürdigen Eingriff aus dem 17. Jahrhundert wirksam sind, der die Kontrolle der menschlichen Reproduktion und der Geburt von den Frauen auf die Männer übertrug, auf Ärzte mit einer Zange. Die Frauenfrage verbindet sie mit der der Ausbeutung in *The Gut Girls* (1988). Die Geschichte beruht auf Tatsachen; im viktorianischen England wurden die aus Südamerika importierten Rinder in den Schlachthöfen von Deptford von Männern getötet und von Frauen ausgenommen. In dem grimmigen und komischen Stück verstehen die Frauen es, mit dem Messer umzugehen und sich zu behaupten, auch wenn sie wegen ihres handgreiflichen Kontakts zu nacktem Fleisch kaum für besser als Huren erachtet werden. Lady Albany, Schwiegertochter Viktorias, will sie aus christlicher Nächstenliebe auf den rechten Weg führen. Sie eröffnet für die Arbeiterinnen einen frommen Club, wo man ihnen Gottesfurcht und Haushaltspflichten beibringt. Als die Schlachthäuser von Deptford schließen, müssen sich die Frauen als Bedienstete in den Häusern der Reichen verdingen und verlieren so ihre relative Selbstbestimmung.

Mit *Beside Herself*, geschrieben für The Women's Playhouse Trust (gegr. 1981), 1990 im Royal Court aufgeführt, verschiebt Sarah Daniels (hierin ähnlich Ayckbourn) die gesellschaftskritische Sicht um einige Nuancen auf eine psychologische und moralische: soziale Probleme in einem Londoner Bezirk; ein Heim oder Haus für wiedereinzugliedernde Nervenkranke unter der Aufsicht von Ärzten, Sozialarbeitern und ehrenamtlichen Wohlfahrtsausschüsslern. Der Ausschuß versucht, die bürgerlichen Alltagsmiseren zu verbergen oder auf dem Wege des *business as usual* zu erledigen. Unter dieser Oberfläche enthüllen sich Formen des Versagens und Leidens, in einem Falle die Vernachlässigung einer Tochter, die leicht radikalisiert aus der Fremde wiederkehrt, im Falle der Heldin der in ihrer Kindheit liegende sexuelle Mißbrauch durch den Vater, den sie lange verdrängt. Das Gewissen dieser respektierten Frau, das sie immer "beside herself" auf der Bühne begleitet, der Gedanke an das ihr zugefügte Verbrechen, durchbricht schließlich das Schweigen gegenüber dem Vater in einer Revolte gegen die von ihm repräsentierte soziale Herrschaft der Männer. Dramaturgisch akzentuiert bleiben freilich der Mittelklassenalltag zwischen Terminen, die Wohlfahrtsarbeit und die privaten Nöte des Überlebens mit moralisch heiler Seele.

Noel Greig war Mitbegründer der Brighton Combination (1968) und arbeitete ab 1973 mit The General Will in Bradford zusammen, ab 1977 mit Gay

Sweatshop. Seit 1975 schreibt er Stücke über Arbeiter und über Homosexuelle. In *The Dear Love of Comrades* (1979) berührt er beides im Porträt eines einfachen Mannes vor dem Hintergrund der politischen Ereignisse zwischen 1890 und 1900. Im Mai 1989 lief in der Drill Hall in London *Plague of Innocence*, das in die Serie der Dystopias gehört, die vor einer rechten Diktatur in Großbritannien warnen. Das Stück projiziert den Abbau der Demokratie in einer Zukunft, in der Homosexuelle und Aids-Kranke als Risikofaktoren ausgesondert werden. Mit den verordneten medizinischen Tests, deren Ergebnisse nicht mitgeteilt werden, kann die Regierung zugleich alle Unliebsamen und Nonkonformen, die Minderheitler und Fragensteller erfassen und in eine abgeschirmte Gegend, d. h. in ein Lager abschieben. Sie bedient sich dabei terroristischer "gun gangs". Propaganda und totale Kontrolle schüren Vorurteile, beuten Ängste aus und halten das Volk im Fesselgriff. Die Schauspieler erzählen und spielen gleichzeitig. Die Suche nach einem Bruder und die nach einer Mutter bilden die Handlung. Am Ende flackert die Hoffnung auf Widerstand auf.

1990 kam eine Inszenierung der irischen Field Day Theatre Company nach London (Hampstead Theatre Club), die eine neue Facette des linken Theaters darstellt. Der Oxforder Literaturprofessor und marxistische Kulturtheoretiker T e r r y E a g l e t o n schrieb (nach seinem ersten Roman *Saints and Scholars*, 1987) sein erstes Stück, *Saint Oscar* (1989). Wie sehr den Autor auch Oscar Wildes Rolle als "socialist proto-deconstructionist"[8] gefesselt haben mag, der die Sprache als selbstreferentiell und die Wahrheit als textuelle Fiktion begriff, er spricht Wilde offenbar vor allem deshalb heilig, weil dieser subtil und frech und gewiß auch unverfroren selbstgefällig die Scheinheiligkeit des Viktorianismus entschleierte. Das Stück inszeniert weniger Wildes sexuelle Perversität als seine sozialen und künstlerischen Abweichungen von der Norm, die durchaus politische Qualität besaßen. Die Bezüge zur Gegenwart sind handgreiflich: So wie der pro-britische Staatsanwalt Edward Carson Wilde verfolgte und letztlich aus der Gesellschaft ausschloß, verfährt das britische Establishment heute in Irland, "with brutality of a different kind".[9] Dieses Spiel der Ideen, der Masken und der surrealistischen Bilder beschwört die beunruhigende, spöttische Präsenz eines nonkonformistischen Potentials, das sich gerade auf die Fähigkeit stützt, Texte zu entlarven und Texte zu kreieren, offizielle Vorstellungen zu unterminieren, das Gewöhnliche zu bezweifeln und die Energie des Ungewöhnlichen zu nutzen.

Bei Daniels, Greig und anderen gibt es also doch politisches Theater. Seine Existenz kann sich in diesen Fällen auf die inzwischen gewachsene und bewußt gewordene feministische bzw. homosexuelle Gesellschaft in der Gesellschaft stützen. Doch es gibt auch umfassendere Anstrengungen (5. Kapitel). Hierzu sind die *community plays* zu rechnen. Sie verbinden die Aufarbeitung von Geschichte mit dem Gemeinschaftserlebnis und der Aktivierung der Volkskultur. Die Dramatikerin Ann Jellicoe hat sie in Dorset praktiziert und weiterentwickelt, und John McGrath benutzte in einer Reihe seiner Stücke die schottische volkstümliche Unterhaltungsform des *ceilidh*, lange bevor die Bachtin-Rezeption in England das zeremonielle Volksfest und die subversive Kraft des Karnevalesken wieder stärker ins Bewußtsein rückte. David Edgar steuerte zu Jellicoes Projekt 1988 *Entertaining Strangers* bei, an dem 180 Bewohner von Dorchester mitwirkten. Es ist ein geschichtliches Lehrstück über den viktorianischen Puritanismus und den kapitalistischen Gründergeist, die sich nicht immer deckten, eine Aktion mit folkloristischen und karnevalesken Elementen.

John McGrath, Gründer und Leiter der 7:84 Theatre Company (1971–1988) und einer der wenigen, die sich nicht vom Mainstream absorbieren ließen, brachte 1989 im alten Transportmuseum Glasgows gemeinsam mit Wildcat *Border Warfare* heraus, ein Stück über die Geschichte der Beziehungen zwischen England und Schottland. Im Programmheft schreibt er:

> [...] Union came as a polite form of conquest [...]. But now a new, more insidious set of forces is at work [...] the sly penetration of our society and our lives by the lizard-eyed, auto-cued, super efficient salesman of Thatcherism. The moment is fast approaching when these and other forces of the 1980s – privatisation, sanctified greed, the reduction of human life to service a multi-national money making machine – will, if unchecked, make Scotland no more than a loss-making subsidiary of England Ltd.[10]

McGrath verwendete Lieder, historische Aufzüge, Possenreißer, Schwertkämpfe, ein Fußballspiel, eine parlamentarische Abstimmung mit den Zuschauern. Zwischen beweglichen Bühnenflächen mußte sich das Publikum je nach dem Gang der Geschichte selbst bewegen. Das geschah im März, wenige Wochen bevor Mrs. Thatcher in Schottland angesichts der Europawahl für die Einheit mit England warb. Es ist ein facettenreiches, aktivierendes und relevantes Theater, den Traditionen des Volkes verpflichtet, ernst und lustig, überraschend und besinnlich, unterhaltsam sich einmischend in das Denken und Leben der Menschen.

Dieses Stück, kürzlich im Channel Four Television zu sehen, hat im Jahr 1990, das Glasgow zur Kulturhauptstadt Europas machte, an gleicher Stelle (nun Tramway Theatre genannt) seine Fortsetzung gefunden. *John Brown's Body*, ebenfalls unter der Regie des Autors von Wildcat gespielt, zeigt im gleichen Stil des lebenden Geschichtsbuchs oder der "epic promenade" das Leben einfacher Menschen vom Beginn der Industrialisierung im 18. Jahrhundert bis in unsere achtziger Jahre, dem Jahrzehnt der Yuppies: Aufstände der Weber, Robert Owens praktizierte Utopie, der Chartismus und die Arbeitskämpfe am Clyde in unserem Jahrhundert, mit der Schließung der Werft John Brown. Auch wenn am Schluß ein Lied fragt, "Is the dream over?", bleibt die Realität einer langen

Tradition von Solidarität und eines Ringens um Demokratie und ein menschenwürdiges Leben.

Vielleicht gibt es in der vielgestaltigen englischen Theaterlandschaft und unter dem Publikum mehr Stimmen für eine Art kulturellen Gegenspiels gegen das kommerzielle Entertainment und für eine neue künstlerische Belebung, als im Augenblick zu erkennen sind.

Anmerkungen

1 Gehalten als Gastvortrag am Englischen Seminar der Ruhr-Universität Bochum am 28. 6. 1989. – Die hier vorgelegte Übersicht muß aufgrund des beschränkten Raumes notwendigerweise sehr raffen und enthält insofern natürlich Lücken.

2 Vgl. J. Pick: "The 'Arts Industry'". *The Journal of Arts Policy and Management* 3, 1988, i, 2–3. – Vgl. auch C. Barker: "Character and Discourse in Contemporary British Productions of Shakespeare". *Shakespeare-Jahrbuch* [Weimar] 126, 1990, 149–159.

3 Unter dem Thema „Englisches Drama seit 1980" brachte die Zeitschrift *Englisch Amerikanische Studien* 1986 in H. 3/4 einschlägige Beiträge von K. P. Müller, G. Klotz, J. Bull, S. Bassnett, A. Sinfield, T. Dunn, St. Lowe, M. Wandor, H. Keyssar, J. Arden, H. Barker und St. Gooch, nebst einer Bibliographie. Weiter sei verwiesen auf: D. Edgar: *The Second Time as Farce. Reflections on the Drama of Mean Times.* London, 1988. – J. McGrath: *A Good Night Out. Popular Theatre: Audience, Class and Form.* With a Foreword by Raymond Williams. London, 1981. – C. Chambers, M. Prior: *Playwrights' Progress. Patterns of Postwar British Drama.* Oxford, 1987. – J. Bull: *New British Political Dramatists. Howard Brenton, David Hare, Trevor Griffiths and David Edgar.* London, Basingstoke, 1984. – V. Gottlieb: "Thatcher's Theatre – or, After 'Equus'". *New Theatre Quarterly* H. 14, 1988, 99–104. – I. Maassen: „Twenty Years After. Eindrücke von der Londoner Theaterszene 1988". *Hard Times* H. 35, 1988, 41–44.

4 Vgl. dazu: "Energy – and the Small Discovery of Dignity. Howard Barker interviewed by Malcolm Hay and Simon Trussler". *Theatre Quarterly* H. 40, 1981, 9. – T. Dunn: "Interview with Howard Barker". *Gambit* 11, 1984, 41, 33–44 (diese Howard-Barker-Sondernummer enthält auch Beiträge von E. Mottràm, T. Dunn, I. McDiarmid und R. Shade). – "Oppression, Resistance, and the Writer's Testament. Howard Barker Interviewed by Finlay Donesky". *New Theatre Quarterly* H. 8, 1986, 338.

5 "[...] instead we praise the actors, the geniuses posing for the cameras, how effortless they are and charming, this never-ageing charm will be the death of us, only catastrophe can keep us clean [...]." (H. Barker: *The Last Supper. A New Testament.* London: John Calder, 1988, p. 23)

6 Barker, H.: "The Triumph in Defeat". *Guardian*, 22. 8. 1988, 34.

7 Zu Barker vgl. auch G. Klotz: „Elitäres Theater kontra Massenkultur: Die unpopuläre Dramaturgie Howard Barkers". *Zeitschrift für Anglistik und Amerikanistik* 37, 1989, 124–135, und D. I. Rabey: *Howard Barker: Politics and Desire. An Expository Study of His Drama and Poetry, 1969–87.* London, Basingstoke, 1989.

8 Eagleton, T.: *Saint Oscar.* Derry: Field Day, 1989; "Foreword", S. VIII.

9 Ebd., S. XI.

10 McGrath, J.: "About the Play". – In Wildcat & Freeway present: *Border Warfare by John McGrath.* Programm, o. O., o. J. [1989], o. S. [S. 12].

11 Stevenson, R.: "Compelled by History. John McGrath: Border Warfare". *Times Literary Supplement*, 10.–16. 3. 1989, 250.

RUDOLF MELDAU

Sinnverwandte Wörter der englischen Sprache

Unter Mitwirkung von Ralph B. Whitling
1981. 642 Seiten. Kartoniert DM 200,-. Leinen DM 230,-
(Anglistische Forschungen, Band 154)

Eine moderne englische Synonymik benötigt der Anglist ebenso dringend wie eine Anzahl guter Wörterbücher, denn jede Sprache – und ganz besonders die englische – verfügt über einen reichen Schatz an sinnverwandten Wörtern, deren richtige Anwendung selbst Fortgeschrittenen oft Schwierigkeiten bereitet. Ihre Kenntnis und Unterscheidung ist jedoch auf dem Wege zur Beherrschung der englischen Sprache unerläßlich.

Ein wesentliches Merkmal des vorliegenden Buches ist völlig neuartig: die Begriffsbestimmung nach den englischen und amerikanischen Standardwörterbüchern. Sie ist für den Benutzer die notwendige Autorität, auf die nicht verzichtet werden kann. – Das Buch ist im wesentlichen einsprachig: Übersetzungen der englischen Beispielsätze stehen in Klammern und sind nur in schwierigen Fällen aufgenommen worden. Da die Aussprache eine besondere Schwierigkeit der englischen Sprache darstellt, wurde bei Tausenden von englischen Wörtern die Aussprachebezeichnung beigefügt. Gleichzeitig ist das Buch durch seine ausführlichen Verzeichnisse der wichtigsten deutschen und englischen Wörter und Wendungen ein wertvolles Satzlexikon des gegenwärtigen Sprachgebrauchs. Die eigentliche literarische Sprache ist nur in Ausnahmefällen angeführt worden. Es ist jedoch manches zu finden, was im Wörterbuch vergeblich gesucht wird, soweit es zur alltäglichen Sprache des gebildeten Engländers und Amerikaners gehört.

CARL WINTER · UNIVERSITÄTSVERLAG · HEIDELBERG

Beate Neumeier, Würzburg

Past Lives in Present Drama:
Feminist Theatre and Intertextuality

0. Intertextual Gender-Construction

> [...] I, a little child, would crouch
> For hours upon the floor, with knees drawn up,
> And gaze across them, half in terror, half
> In adoration, at the picture there, –
> That swan-like supernatural white life,
> Just sailing upward from the red stiff silk
> Which seemed to have no part in it, nor power
> To keep it from quite breaking out of bounds.
> [...]
> [...] And as I grew
> In years, I mixed, confused, unconsciously,
> Whatever I last read or heard or dreamed,
> Abhorrent, admirable, beautiful,
> Pathetical, or ghastly, or grotesque,
> With still that face ... which did not therefore change,
> But kept the mystic level of all forms
> And fears and admirations; was by turns
> Ghost, fiend, and angel, fairy, witch, and sprite,
> A dauntless Muse who eyes a dreadful Fate,
> A loving Psyche who loses sight of Love,
> A still Medusa with mild milky brows
> All curdled and all clothed upon with snakes
> Whose slime falls fast as sweat will; or anon
> Our Lady of the Passion, stabbed with swords
> Where the Babe sucked; or Lamia in her first
> Moonlighted pallor, ere she shrunk and blinked
> And shuddering wriggled down to the unclean;
> [...][1]

With these words the fictional autobiographer Aurora Leigh in Elizabeth Barrett Browning's verse novel recollects the times in her childhood which she spent staring at her dead mother's picture. The heroine thus addresses the problem of recovering the absent mother from the past and of making her visible in the child's present life. The description of the process by which this is achieved shows the process of gender-construction at work and reveals this gender-construction as an intertextual process encompassing a variety of literary/cultural models from "dauntless Muse", "loving Psyche", to Medusa, and Lamia. Aurora's ambivalent feelings towards her mother, evident from these conflicting roles in the child's fantasy, can be interpreted as a result of the uneasy internalization of the culturally constructed images of women. Nevertheless, Aurora's reflections seem to reach – in her own words – towards a "breaking out of [the] bounds" of gender-construction by the conflation of these pre-existing gender images into a "mystic level of all forms". Thus, instead of being caught in the constraints – or rather the myth – of a definable unified identity, the mother is made present precisely through her absence.

Aurora's attempt to recover the absent mother from the past parallels one of the prevalent concerns of feminist critics, namely the need of "the archeological and rehabilitative act of discovering and recovering 'lost' women writers".[2] In this context her ambivalent feelings towards the mother can be seen as part of an 'anxiety of influence', as admiration for a female tradition, but at the same time as fear of being trapped into a still male-defined women's literature. By implication this points towards the necessity of "a reconstituted record of predecession and prefiguration, debts acknowledged and unacknowledged, anxieties and enthusiasms."[3] These aspects draw attention to the disparate and changing attitudes apparent among feminist writers and feminist critics towards the past, ranging from a celebratory acclaim of past literary heroines to a critical questioning of their role as token women within patriarchal society. This shift in emphasis is closely linked to the growing problematisation of the concept of identity by feminist critics and writers. While the enthusiastic re-appraisal of a particular female heritage implies the belief in the existence of a unified female identity even within a patriarchal culture, the sceptic re-evaluation of the past tends to reveal the absence of such a unifying principle, which – if at all – is to be envisioned in the gaps of a universal intertextual process of gender-construction. Accordingly, this new perspective seems to be accompanied by the changing use of the concept of intertextuality, as "less a name for a work's relation to particular prior texts than a designation of its participation in the discursive space of a culture".[4] The stated shift in emphasis can also be viewed in the context of a widely acknowledged distinction between three generations within the European feminist movement, aptly formulated by Julia Kristeva: The first being marked by an attempt at the insertion of women into history, the second by "the radical refusal of the subjective limitations imposed by this history's time on an experiment carried out in the name of the irreducible difference", the third by an interest in analysing "the potentialities of victim/executioner which characterize each identity, each subject, each sex [. . .] to demystify the identity of the symbolic bond itself […] in order to bring out […] the relativity of his/ her symbolic as well as biological existence".[5] But, as Kristeva rightly emphasizes, "the word 'generation' implies less a chronology than a signifiying space. […] So it can be argued that as of now a third attitude is possible, thus a third generation, which does not exclude – quite to the contrary – the parallel existence of all three in the same historical time, or even that they be interwoven one with the other."[6]

My analysis of these issues proceeds from such a third attitude with regard to contemporary feminist drama in England. It will focus on four plays, Michelene Wandor's *Aurora Leigh*, Liz Lochhead's *Blood and Ice*, Pam Gems' *Queen Christina*, and Caryl Churchill's *Top Girls*. The term feminist theatre as substratum for all of them is used in a very broad sense, as applied by Helene Keyssar, referring to plays "self-consciously concerned about the presence – or absence – of women as women on stage."[7] Furthermore, all four plays give a presence to the lives of outstanding women of the past, thereby referring directly or implicitly to notions of biography and autobiography, and thus to questions of intertextuality and identity.

Michelene Wandor dramatizes Elizabeth Barrett Browning's verse novel and fictional autobiography *Aurora Leigh*, in an effort to re-claim a heroine from the past for the present. Liz Lochhead re-constructs the links between Mary Shelley's life and her novel *Frankenstein* (thereby creating a fictional autobiography of the writer) in her play *Blood and Ice*, in a demonstration of the therapeutic process of re-constructing one's own identity by re-reading the fictionalized self. Pam Gems re-creates the life of *Queen Christina* of Sweden by re-visioning the romantic myth of the Hollywood Garbo-movie in an attempt to re-veal the coercive power of cultural gender-construction. Caryl Churchill, finally, radically de-constructs not only the lives but the very notion of *Top Girls* of the past – and the present. In each play the life story, and thus biography and autobiography, are used as exemplary forms of textualisation, the constitutive elements of which – namely identity and narrativity – can be reinforced or disrupted through the possibilities of the stage: the former most obviously in Wandor's deliberate neglect of the use of theatrical means, the latter most radically in Churchill's multiple casting and a-chronological presentation of events.

1. Re-presentation as Re-citing: Michelene Wandor's Aurora Leigh (1979; 1981)[8]

In *Aurora Leigh*, dramatist, poet, and critic Michelene Wandor turns in reverence to "the grand mother of all modern women poets in England and America"[9], Elizabeth Barrett Browning, and her depiction of nineteenth-century woman's struggle for autonomy and recognition as a writer. Thus Wandor joins the ranks of feminist critics who have hailed *Aurora Leigh* as "boldly self-assertive"[10], and calls it "clearly a feminist work"[11], while others have criticised it as being "aligned with feminine ideology"[12], or even more directly as "a woman's voice [speaking] patriarchal discourse".[13]

In Michelene Wandor's stage version Aurora remains the narrator, in control of her own story, the plot outline of which is closely followed, the whole play being almost exclusively a compilation of quotations from the pre-text in iambic verse.[14] All the more significant are the omissions and shifts in focus in Wandor's re-citation of the story. Like Barrett Browning, Wandor starts out with a short description of Aurora's childhood in Italy before the orphan is transferred to England after her father's death, and left in the care of her spinsterly aunt Leigh who unsuccessfully tries to impose Victorian ideals of femininity onto the young heroine. No mention, however, is made in Wandor's play of the father's forming educational influence, the similarity between father and daughter ("I am like, They tell me, my dear father"; *AL*, p. 7), and the father's admonition on his deathbed: "Love, my child, love, love!" (*AL*, p. 8) Thus, whereas Barrett Browning's Aurora is left with the *double* parental legacy of an interest in art, and an admonition to love, Wandor's Aurora has to develop her identity as a poet and woman more exclusively (out of herself and) in defense against the imposed values of Aunt Leigh. As in Barrett Browning's novel, two opposing female images, Lady Waldemar and Marian, are set off against Aurora, teaching her a lesson in female rivalry and sisterhood respectively. But whereas living with the tender-hearted Marian and her child has an important impact on Aurora's outlook on life in Barrett Browning's verse novel, this 'biological' aspect of womanhood is played down in Wandor's drama.

Particularly striking is Wandor's change of the story's ending. As in Barrett Browning's verse novel Aurora initially refuses to marry her cousin Romney – the political reformer, but conservative male – and accepts him only after a gradual and painful learning process, whose ramifications are, however, entirely different in both texts. Barrett Browning's Romney has not only lost Leigh Hall in a fire enkindled by farmers enraged at his turning Leigh Hall into an almshouse and thus – in their eyes – into a hideout for city scum, but he has also lost his sight in this fire and therefore becomes dependent on female help. At the same time Aurora has experienced the consequences of an artist's self-aggrandizement, namely loneliness and isolation, and has learnt to appreciate the virtues of human sympathy and altruistic service to others. This represents the well-known nineteenth-century compromise between female self-assertion and submission.[15] Barrett Browning's new Aurora admits:

Art is much but Love is more!
[...] Art symbolises heaven, but Love is God

and makes heaven. I, Aurora, fell from mine:
I would not be a woman like the rest,
A simple woman who believes in love...
I must analyse, confront and question;
I am changed since then, changed wholly, – for indeed
If now you stoop so low to take my love
and use it roughly without stint or spare, [...]
The joy would set me like a star, in heaven.
[...] Yet in one respect,
Just one, beloved, I am in no wise changed:
I love you. [...]
[...] [You] mistook the world:
But I mistook my own heart, – and that slip
Was fatal. Romney, will you have me here?
So wrong, so proud, so weak, so unconsoled,
So mere a woman! (*AL*, pp. 357f.)

Michelene Wandor's Romney on the other hand is not blinded in the fire that destroys his home; neither is her Aurora changed. The playwright explains her omission of the motif of blindness on feminist grounds:

> [In Barrett Browning's novel] Romney loses everything, and comes to find Aurora to declare himself totally wrong and her totally right. His blindness is profoundly symbolic – his darkness against Aurora's light. But as a feminist I found it impossible to accept such capitulation as representing any real solution. [...] I could not see how it could be credible if male domination was simply replaced with female domination.[16]

Aurora's speech quoted from Barrett Browning's novel, however, shows how far her heroine is from claiming female domination. Wandor's omission of Romney's blindness, therefore, rather than being used to prevent the impression of female domination, is necessary to justify Aurora's renewed emphasis on self-assertion at the end of the play, as Wandor's version of the same speech reveals:

Oh I

Would not be plain woman like the rest.
I must analyse, confront and question.
In this last I have not changed and could not.
But in one respect I see I am changed.
Marian saw, and Lady Waldemar saw
What I was too proud and dishonest to
See: that I loved you then and love you now.
(*AL*, p. 132)

Wandor's Romney doesn't have to be blinded to make Aurora's change acceptable, because Wandor's Aurora does not change her position in the first place. While Romney has to change to be acceptable for her, Aurora remains largely unchanged throughout the play. In order to re-cite Aurora's nineteenth-century story for a twentieth-century audience as a story of female autonomy and self-assertion, Wandor has to remove the "self-abnegating servitude with which Barrett Browning's *Aurora Leigh* concludes."[17] However, this also implies the removal of the "rage for social transformation concealed behind th[is] veil of self-abnegating servitude"[18], reflected in the very structure of Barrett Browning's *Aurora Leigh*.

Elizabeth Barrett Browning's fusion of genres – *Bildungsroman, Künstlerroman,* spiritual epic, social satire, and poetical treatise – has been rightly claimed as a "particularly striking example of what Bakhtin terms the 'novelized' epic", the style of which is 'dialogized', "reflecting a 'multi-languaged consciousness' that disrupts epic stylization with parody and self-parody".[19] Consequently, when Wandor "disentangles the story from the elaborations"[20], she 'monologizes' Barrett Browning's dialogization of the epic form. Similarly Wandor's transformation of Aurora's interior monologue into dramatic dialogue is not used to diminish, but rather to enforce her authoritative voice by objectifying her inner conflicting views as outward manifestations of reality. Thus, whereas the disruptive form of Barrett Browning's verse novel contradicts the conciliatory ending on a notion of feminine ideology, the conventional, straightforward form of Wandor's play with its emphasis on identity and narrativity reinforces its bourgeois feminist ideology (as Wandor herself terms it), proclaiming individual female self-assertion within the existing patriarchal structure.[21] However, although Wandor's use of language as "the primary gesture of her drama" has been criticized[22], the preservation of the pre-text's verse form can also be seen as implicitly reminding the audience of the historicity of the proclaimed viewpoint within the development of a feminist consciousness.

2. Re-presentation as Re-construction: Liz Lochhead's Blood and Ice (1984)[23]

Poet and playwright Liz Lochhead's *Blood and Ice* centers on a dramatization of Mary Shelley who re-constructs the links between her life and her novel *Frankenstein* by re-considering past events and by re-reading her own fiction, possibly before re-writing it for the second edition. Art is thereby interpreted as the result of an autobiographical impulse, a desire for revealed self-expression. Consequently Lochhead's play, taking place within the consciousness of Mary Shelley, reflects the act of autobiographical exploration as the therapeutical process of a re-construction of the self through the dialogue between life and art.

Framing the story is Mary Shelley at the age of thirty, who sits in her home's "ghostly nursery" (*BI*, p. 83), full of nightmarish toys, absorbed in re-reading her story *Frankenstein* and in meditating on the past. This time of her life also serves as a reference point for flashbacks to the summer at lake Geneva when the idea of *Frankenstein* was conceived, and further back to childhood experiences with her half-sister Claire. Lochhead establishes Mary's image through her interaction with Shelley, Byron, Claire, and Elise, the maid and children's nurse. The uninterrupted flow of the first of the two acts of the play in one scene presents Mary's unquestioned identity as a construct of her parents' and Shelley's ideas on the one hand, and remnants of conventional feminine ideology on the other: Mary, who as a child was wont to quote from her parents' works by heart, continues to speak in the manner of Godwin's discourse on *Political Justice* and Wollstonecraft's discourse on *The Vindication of the Rights of Women*. And, as the Byron of the play notices, she now has added to that the phraseology of Shelley's discourse on liberty, repressing her own "senses and the imagination" in favour of the abstract teaching of "intellect and moral nature" of her literary authority figures (*BI*, p. 101). Byron consequently warns Mary that the suppression of the heart by the head will produce monsters. Mary's adherence to conventional ideas about feminine behaviour, noted above, becomes evident, for example, in her attitude towards Shelley's 'indecency' (*BI*, pp. 84f.), or her 'moral' advice for Claire (*BI*, pp. 86f.).

The episodic sequence of eight scenes in the second act mirrors the gradual dismantling of this constructed identity through life and art. Life's intrusion manifests itself mainly as jealousy, guilt and grief, linked to the ultimate realities of birth and death: as jealousy towards Claire, as guilt and grief over the deaths of her own children and her miscarriage, and as grief over the death of Claire's child and over the deaths of Byron and – above all – Shelley. The importance of art in the process of self-discovery is pointed out by Byron who functions – just as in the first act – as an initiator of change, this time by advising Mary: "Read your story." (*BL*, p. 111) He thus hints at the hidden relation between Mary's life and her "silly work of fantasy", as she denounces her own novel (*BL*, pp. 109f.). Towards the end of the play Mary confronts Shelley with a changed view of life and self, stressing the need for a re-definition of the relation between freedom and responsibility, theory and reality, art and life, male and female.[24] This re-cognition is linked to Mary's ongoing re-evaluation of her own fiction in relation to her life in the very last lines of the play:

> I thought: I am Frankenstein, the creator who loves creation and hates its results. Then I thought: no, I am the monster, poor misunderstood creature feared and hated by all mankind. And then I thought: it is worse, worse than that, I am the female monster, gross, gashed, ten times more hideous than my male counterpart, denied life, tied to the monster bed for ever. [...] But

now I see who I am, in my book. I am Captain Walton, explorer. Survivor. My own cool narrator. The one who once dreamed of that land of wonder, where, way beyond the pole, sailing over a calm sea, further than the flickering Northern Lights – Men and Women Might Live In Freedom. The one who turned back. The one who, when the ice came, stuck fast, unable to go back or forward. [...] And I hear Frankenstein, calling from my own book. [...] 'The ice cannot stop you if your hot hearts say it shall not!' [...] Oh, Shelley. (*BI*, pp. 115–116)

This ending of the play refers back to the hidden feminist significance of the historical Mary Shelley's *Frankenstein* as an expression of the desire for a new gender relationship. As has often been observed, Mary Shelley shaped her own ambivalent attitude towards the nineteenth-century woman artist's dilemma between artistic self-assertion and feminine self-effacement in the form of three interlocked autobiographical narratives by the created monster, by the creator Frankenstein and by the spectator Captain Walton.[25] By setting off the egotistical, anti-social creative impulse of Frankenstein against Walton's ultimately altruistic abandonment of these desires, Mary Shelley could give form to this impulse without having to take responsibility for it. This split of self is what Mary has to become aware of in the course of Lochhead's play: The (psycho)-analytical reading of her own imaginative writing is presented as the therapeutical process of a re-construction of the self, which, however, does not necessarily lead to a new unified self. Even if Mary believes in the concept of a unified identity till the end, as her successive attempts at establishing an identity with just one of her fictional characters in the quotation above reveal, the audience is made aware of the multiplicity of selves within Mary, who *is* all of the characters of her novel at once. The last lines of the play can thus be interpreted not only as an acknowledgment of Mary's siding with the self-effacing Walton, but at the same time as an unrelenting expression of Frankenstein's self-assertive desire, which is linked to the utopian vision of an 'undiscovered country' for men and women, a country free of cultural gender-construction. In comparison to Michelene Wandor's play, Liz Lochhead's drama thus marks a shift in emphasis: Michelene Wandor reinforces the concepts of identity and narrativity in her straightforward re-citation of fictional autobiography with the declared aim of presenting an outward picture of a self-assertive bourgeois feminist heroine of the past. Liz Lochhead reveals the concept of identity as (at least partly) culturally constructed in her re-construction of the relation between life and art as an intertextual process in her heroine's mind.

3. Re-creation as Re-vision: Pam Gems' Queen Christina (1977)[26]

Many of Pam Gems' plays focus on historical or mythical women[27] – Queen Christina, Rosa Luxemburg, Piaf, Guinevere, Camille – whose lives (rather than being merely represented) are re-created in a process of de-mythologizing public images.[28] *Queen Christina* presents a particularly interesting example, insofar as the play draws upon two pre-texts, the historical figure and the film version of the life of the seventeenth-century Queen of Sweden, re-vealing especially the latter as a textual strategy of gender-construction. This is achieved by first conflating and then separating the historical and the cinematic images of Christina in the audience's consciousness. In her afterword to the play Gems explains:

> I'd seen the Garbo movie ... I had the idea, like, I suspect, many people, that Christina had been a shining, pale, intellectual beauty,[29]

who, as Mary Remnant specifies in her introduction to the play,

> abdicates in order to marry her lover, who is immediately killed in a duel, leaving her tragically alone and kingdomless to make her way in the world.[30]

Gems' two-act life chronicle opens with the episode of a miscarriage, one of numerous failures of Christina's mother to deliver an heir, and the subsequent decision to educate the female offspring Christina for the throne, which means educating her as a man. Thus the very first scene establishes a rigidly divided world in which the female is linked to private life and breeding, the male to public power and duty. At the same time, however, the cultural (as opposed to the biological) construction of gender is implicitly acknowledged by the very fact that Christina is supposed to be able to transcend the female gender stereotype through education. With the Garbo film in mind, the audience easily accepts this notion without realizing its ultimate consequences, which, however, will become evident in the second scene which centers on a prearranged betrothal between Christina and a German prince, who is shocked to find out that she is a manly, "slightly crippled", "battered figure in hunting clothes" (*QC*, p. 18) with a lesbian relationship to her beautiful lady-in-waiting Ebba.

Throughout the remainder of the first act, which functions as a kind of parody of the 'female' life-cycle between birthgiving, betrothal and wedding, Christina is presented as a 'man' trapped in an 'imperfect' woman's body, deploring the "ludicrous pattern[s]" (*QC*, p. 19) of her own monthly cycle, abhorring the sight of pregnancy in Ebba, and deriding the hysterical emotionality displayed by her mother. At the same time, however, there is a growing awareness of desires which remain unfulfilled, foremost an unrequited love for a man who prefers the beauty of Ebba. In a confrontation with the chancellor of the state just before Christina's abdication, this split of personality is finally thematized. Whereas for the chancellor Christina's "unique position demands both the manly qualities of a king, and the fecundity of a woman" (*QC*, p. 29), Christina realizes the incompatibility of these demands. By making a man of her, "a man, despising women" (*QC*, p. 29), the men of the court have cut her off from the role as wife and childbearer. Contrary to the Hollywood myth Gems' Christina abdicates to avoid marriage and childbirth and to seek spiritual freedom.

The second act of the play starts where the Hollywood movie ends, tracing Christina's life after her departure from Sweden and – by implication – from a fixed, though unhappy gender-construction. Yet, the resultant feelings of uncertainty and the fear of an impending loss of identity lead to acts of violence perpetrated in her retreat into the 'male' world, e. g. Christina's attempts at securing the throne of Naples through warfare and her murder of a lover turned political traitor, as the ultimate act of male assertion of power. This deed, however, marks the turning-point in Christina's development and initiates her descent into madness and her 'rebirth' as a woman. The latter development, however, is at least to a certain extent – rather than being mystified – ironized as yet another aspect of gender-construction. Thus it is no mere coincidence that Christina's education as a woman after her breakdown starts by her being fed, scolded and slapped as a sort of substitute doll by the child of Christina's maid. In a further step, Christina is presented in feminine attire trying to please the visiting Cardinal, who, she imagines, has come as a suitor. When she complains that one room "is now my whole world. To go as far as [the] door fills me with terror" (QC, p. 43), this is a reference to her slow recovery as well as an ironic comment on the 'female sphere' in general. Christina's liberation from this extreme confinement is linked to her saving the life of her maid's daughter in an act of instinct rather than deliberation, which leads to a conscious re-evaluation of womanhood and motherhood. Finally Christina is able to voice an incipient new self-understanding:

> I have *been* as a man. I have commanded. I have signed death warrants, consigned regiments to the sword. All done in my name. I have even committed murder. What more do you want?
> […]
> […] By God, half the world are women … they've learned subversion, to keep their teeth in their mouths and the rope off their backs, why not try that?
> […] I was bred as a man, despising the weakness of women. I begin to question the favour. […]
> […] They know how to share rather than take … by God, they share their very bodies with their own young, with us! […]
> […] I begin to perceive that I am a woman. What that is, heaven knows … the philosophy is yet to be written, there is a world to be explored. (QC, pp. 44f.)

The play, however, does not end on a note of utopian hope, but rather on an ironic insistence on the power of gender-construction, contrasting Christina's sudden hysterical sexual advances towards the Cardinal with the Cardinal's and her maid's pitiful comments on Christina's lack of beauty, echoing statements from almost all the characters throughout the play.[31] Thus the play leaves the characters with a partial awareness, but presents them as still caught in the web of the old text. This is reflected in Gems' particular use of the old form of the biography of the exceptional woman[32], the narrative sequence of which is adhered to, but the identity concept of which is disrupted. Pam Gems' play creates a re-vision not only of the specific myth of Christina, but of the general process of gender-construction as part of a larger cultural textualisation.[33]

4. Re-creation as De-construction: Caryl Churchill's Top Girls (1982)[34]

Caryl Churchill's play *Top Girls* has been called a "warning of the price to be paid by women if we either ignore or glamourize our own histories."[35] In this sense she sets out to radically deconstruct the conventional notions of individual identity and progressive history. The play opens with the main character Marlene's promotion to managing director of the employment agency 'Top Girls', which the heroine celebrates together with other top girls from the past in a (fantasy) restaurant scene. Scenes two and three of the first act present Marlene in her new position, and the dreary country life of her sister Joyce and daughter Angie, who rightly suspects her admired aunt Marlene to be her real mother. The final act presents Angie's visit to Marlene's office and ends on a troubled reunion between Marlene and her sister which, however, took place one year earlier in Joyce's kitchen. Thus (as has been noticed by a number of critics) the movement of the play turns backwards, from a refined place of opulent consumption to a simple place of basic production, thereby disrupting the audience's sense of chronological progression.[36] The play's last word, Angie's remark "frightening" (*TG*, p. 87), refers not only to a nightmare Angie has had, but also to women's future beyond the limits of the play. Significantly this bleak picture is reinforced by the chronologically last line of the play, a comment by Marlene about the prospects of her daughter Angie: "She's not going to make it". (*TG*, p. 66) That she seems to have to *make it within* a patriarchal structure, is, however, what is really frightening according to the play's logic.

In marked contrast to the plays discussed so far, which are all one-woman shows, Churchill reveals the marginality of the achievement of being a 'top girl' by presenting the first scene as a "dramatized Women's Studies class"[37] as Marlene's introduction of the women to each other shows:

> This is Joan who was Pope in the ninth century, and Isabella Bird, the Victorian traveller, and Lady Nijo from Japan, Emperor's concubine and Buddhist nun, thirteenth century [...] and Gret who was painted by Brueghel. Griselda's in Boccaccio and Petrarch and Chaucer because of her extraordinary marriage. (*TG*, p. 20)

By first presenting and then discarding this illustrious assembly after the first scene, Churchill can at the same time point out the continuity of female struggles and the historicity of individual achievements. The overlapping dialogue of the women at the dinner table is not a mere reproduction of the cliché of feminine chatter, but a conscious strategy on the part of the author to show them as being "locked in separate discourses".[38] The life stories which emerge from these discourses further prove the women's identities to be just as culturally constructed as their historical costumes. Marlene's (and maybe the audience's?) hoped-for "concept of female homogeneity"[39] applies – if at all – to a unison in distress (Marlene: "O God, why are we all so miserable?" *TG*, p. 18), not to common views or characteristics, as the conversations about a variety of subjects (love, family, religion, morals) make unmistakably clear. Ironically the women spot the injustices within other historical contexts, but are blind to those of their own time, as Joseph Marohl's detailed discussion of this issue shows.[40] Gender-construction is thus clearly presented as part of cultural textualisation.

This impression is further emphasized by Churchill's multiple casting, the 'doubling' or 'tripling' of roles played by the same actress, which is not used as a means to suggest an underlying continuous identity but on the contrary to stress the cultural encoding of femaleness.[41] Moreover the fact of an all-female cast avoids the superficial identification with a male/female opposition, the cultural construction of which the play wants to unravel.

The play's foremost target of criticism is undoubtedly the bourgeois feminist notion of the top girl personified in Marlene, and her embracing middle class egotistical individualism and Thatcherism (Marlene: "She's a tough lady, Maggie" *TG*, p. 84). Her sister Joyce's advocacy of altruism and socialism, however, is rendered impotent by passive suffering and subdued bitterness, and therefore (in its present form) does hardly present an alternative vision. All of the characters are equally victims of gender-construction. Thus the play creates a gap which remains to be filled, an absence which is made present by the evocation of the pre-existing gender images without providing the reassurance of an identifiable role model. This "iconoclastic urge"[42] is reflected in what Robert Brustein called Churchill's "inchoateness of style"[43], namely the disruption of history and narrativity, which has been recognized as a characteristic feature of plays by a number of contemporary women playwrights:

> Narrative (and through it, history) invades their stages, interrupting the dramatic present with intimations of the past, forcing the audience to understand female identity as a historical and cultural construction whose causes and consequences constitute the drama being enacted.[44]

Of the four plays discussed, *Top Girls* represents the most radical dramatic deconstruction of the individualized life story and its constitutive elements, identity and narrativity. The very choice of top girls in the play – Pope Joan, Lady Nijo, Dull Gret, Griselda, and Isabella Bird – is a comment on culturally constructed images as part of a web of historical, biographical, fictional, even pictorial texts. The consciousness of this all-encompassing textuality, however, does not – as we have seen – stifle the creative impulse, but rather stimulates it, and leads to a further "breaking out of [the] bounds" of the conventionalized and tamed imagination which Elizabeth Barrett Browning's *Aurora Leigh* experienced back in the nineteenth century.

Notes

1 Browning, Elizabeth Barrett: *Aurora Leigh*. New York, 1857, pp. 5f.
2 Miller, N.: "Emphasis Added: Plots and Plausibilities in Women's Fiction". *PMLA* 96, 1981, 36–48, here: 37.
3 Ibid.
4 Culler, J.: *The Pursuit of Signs. Semiotics, Literature, Deconstruction*. New York, 1981, p. 103. See also G. Ecker: „'A Map for Rereading': Intertextualität aus der Perspektive einer feministischen Literaturwissenschaft". – In Broich, U., Pfister, M. (Eds.): *Intertextualität. Formen, Funktionen, anglistische Fallstudien*. Tübingen, 1985, pp. 297–311.
5 Kristeva, J.: "Women's Time". – In *The Kristeva Reader*. Ed. T. Moi. Oxford, 1986, pp. 187–213, here: p. 210.
6 Ibid., p. 209.
7 Keyssar, H.: *Feminist Theatre. An Introduction to Plays of Contemporary British and American Women*. London, 1984, p. 1. See also S.-E. Case: *Feminism and Theatre*. New York, 1988, J. Dolan: *The Feminist Spectator as Critic*. Ann Arbor, 1988, and R. K. Curb: "Re/cognition, Re/presentation, Re/creation in Woman-Conscious Drama: The Seer, the Seen, the Scene, the Obscene". *Theatre Journal* 37, 1985, 302–316.
8 *Aurora Leigh*. – In *Plays by Women*. Vol. 1. Ed. M. Wandor. London, 1982, pp. 105–133.
9 Gilbert, S. M., Gubar, S.: *The Madwoman in the Attic. The Woman Writer and the Nineteenth-Century Literary Imagination*. New Haven, 1979, p. 580.
10 Stone, M.: "Genre Subversion and Gender Inversion: *The Princess* and *Aurora Leigh*". *Victorian Poetry* 25, 1987, 101–127, here: 123.
11 Wandor, M.: Afterword to *Aurora Leigh*. – In *Plays by Women*. Vol. 1, pp. 134–136, here: p. 136.
12 Blau DuPlessis, R.: *Writing beyond the Ending. Narrative Strategies of Twentieth-Century Women Writers*. Bloomington, 1985, p. 87.
13 David, D. "'Art's a Service': Social Wound, Sexual Politics, and *Aurora Leigh*". *Browning Institute Studies* 13, 1985, 113–136, here: 134.
14 Cf. R. L. Goldemberg's different use of the same compilation technique in dramatizing Sylvia Plath's *Letters Home* (R. L. Goldemberg: *Letters Home*. – In *Plays by Women*. Vol. 2. Ed. M. Wandor. London, 1983, pp. 29–75).

15 Gilbert/Gubar: *The Madwoman in the Attic*, p. 575.
16 Wandor: Afterword to *Aurora Leigh*, p. 134.
17 Gilbert/Gubar: *The Madwoman in the Attic*, p. 580.
18 Ibid.
19 Stone: "Genre Subversion", 126.
20 Wandor: Afterword to *Aurora Leigh*, p. 134.
21 According to Wandor this is true to the spirit of the original (M. Wandor: *Carry On, Understudies. Theatre and Sexual Politics.* London, 1986, p. 189).
22 "If there is a weakness to *Aurora Leigh* it is in the sufficiency of the words which suggest the pleasure but not the necessity of performance." (Keyssar: *Feminist Theatre*, p. 140).
23 *Blood and Ice.* – In *Plays by Women.* Vol. 4. Ed. M. Wandor. London, 1985, pp. 81–116. The 1986 revised edition of the play is not considered here.
24 The common fate of women between childbirth and death is stressed through the use of two nightmarish twin dolls, confining Mary and Elise as well as Mary and Claire to one doll's body respectively, thus serving not as a means to advocate a mystical union of women in motherhood, but rather as an emphasis on the frightening aspect of being "born a slave" (*BL*, p. 114) to biological necessity and – by implication – of being made a slave to cultural gender-construction.
25 Cf. M. Poovey: "My Hideous Progeny: Mary Shelley and the Feminization of Romanticism". *PMLA* 95, 1980, 332–347.
26 *Queen Christina.* – In *Plays by Women.* Vol. 5. Ed. M. Remnant. London, 1986, pp. 13–46.
27 "We [women] have our own history to create, and to write. [...] there will be brilliant women playwrights. I think the form suits us. Women are very funny, coarse, subversive. All good qualities for drama, and for the achievement of progress by the deployment, not of violence, but of subtlety, love and imagination." (P. Gems: Afterword to *Dusa, Fish, Stas and Vi.* – In *Plays by Women.* Vol. 1, pp. 71–73, here: p. 73).
28 Gems' portrayal of Piaf, for instance, turns against romancing the singer, and functions as "a subversion both of female stereotype and of theatrical expectations", achieved through the use of vulgarisms and drastic scenes (Keyssar: *Feminist Theatre*, p. 130).
29 Gems, P.: Afterword to *Queen Christina.* – In *Plays by Women.* Vol. 5, pp. 47–48.
30 Remnant, M.: "Introduction". – In *Plays by Women.* Vol. 5, pp. 7–11, here: p. 8.
31 The power of gender-construction is further emphasized by the portrayal of other women characters in the play. Christina's mother is presented as a victim of an oppressive system viewing women as breeding machines. But her victimization has made her a hysterical creature, constantly knitting and eating chocolates in compensation for a lack of emotional attachment. The suffragettes of the play try to establish an equally oppressive counter system, built on hatred and inconsiderateness. The beautiful Ebba, finally smoothly fits into and takes advantage of the existing system, thus revealing her lack of interest in personal or structural changes.
32 Cf. G. Klotz' analysis of Gems' plays as "VIP-stories" in „Zwischen enttäuschenden Erfolgen und Zerreißproben kultureller Traditionen: Eindrücke vom Theater in Britannien jetzt". *Englisch Amerikanische Studien* 8, 1986, 388–401, here: 395.
33 Pam Gems uses the stage effect of cross gender dressing in *Queen Christina*, where the heroine dresses as a man, and again in her later play about two transvestites *Aunt*

Mary, where the protagonist dresses as a woman. In both cases the device emphasizes the discrepancy between the biological sex and the forcefully imposed or playfully invented gender. Caryl Churchill takes this attack on gender-construction one step further, using cross gender casting in her play *Cloud Nine* in order to radically undermine the distinction between natural and acquired signification (cf. M. Selman: "Reshuffling the Deck: Iconoclastic Dealings in Caryl Churchill's Early Plays". – In Randall, Ph. R. [Ed.]: *Caryl Churchill. A Casebook.* New York, 1988, pp. 49–70, here: p. 60). Whereas Gems uses men's clothes for Christina to stress her transformation into a man, Churchill uses a male actor to portray the internalization of male views about womanhood in a female character. Both playwrights, however, share a common criticism not only of forms of cultural gender-construction, but also of bourgeois feminist ideology.

34 Churchill, C.: *Top Girls.* London, 1982.
35 Keyssar, H.: "Hauntings: Gender and Drama in Contemporary English Theatre". *Englisch Amerikanische Studien* 8, 1986, 449–468, here: 466.
36 Marohl, J.: "De-realised Women: Performance and Identity in *Top Girls*". *Modern Drama* 30, 1987, 376–388, here: 380.
37 Brown, J.: "Top Girls catches the Next Wave". – In Randall (Ed.): *Caryl Churchill*, pp. 117–130, here: p. 127.
38 Fitzsimmons, L.: "'I Won't Turn Back For You or Anyone': Caryl Churchill's Socialist-Feminist Theatre". *Essays in Theatre* 6, i, 1987, 19–29, here: 21.
39 Marohl: "De-realised Women", 382f.
40 Ibid., 386.
41 For example, patient Griselda, homely Jeanine and 'emancipated' Nell are played by the same actress.
42 Selman: "Reshuffling the Deck", p. 53.
43 Cf. R. Brustein: "The British Conquest", review of *Top Girls* in *New Republic*, 14. 2. 1986, 26–28.
44 Diamond, E.: "Refusing the Romanticism of Identity: Narrative Interventions in Churchill, Benmussa, Duras". *Theatre Journal* 37, 1985, 273–286, here: 277.

VERBAL/VISUAL CROSSINGS 1880 - 1980

Edited by Theo D'haen. Amsterdam/ Atlanta GA 1990. 384 pp.

ISBN: 90-5183-198-6   Paper Hfl.   49,50/US-$ 24.75

Bound Hfl. 140,—/US-$ 70.00

Contents: Theo D'haen: Introduction. Robert Druce: Colorless Green Signifieds Sleep Furiously: Reconciling the Image and the Word. Robert M. Levine: Historical Writing and Visual Imagery: Photographs as Documents. Shelley Hornstein-Rabinovitch: Art Nouveau as Surface Described. Patricia Vervoort: Reinforcing the Image: Ensor's Use of Signs in Works between 1886-1896. Willard Bohn: Marking Time with Apollinaire. Albert Cook: Space, Time, and the Unconscious in the Collage Novels of Max Ernst. Cees de Boer: Max Ernst: La Petite Fistule Lacrymale qui dit Tic Tac. Seeing the Poetic Possibilities of Freud's Metapsychology. Stamos Metzidakis: Graphemic Gymnastics in Surrealist Literature. Jacques van der Elst: Theo van Doesburg and Concrete Poetry. Eric Vos: On Concrete Poetry and A 'Classification of the Visual in Literature'. E.M. Beekman: Let it Be. The Ergatic Mode of Netherlandic Poetry and Art. Monique Yaari: Ironic Architecture: The Puzzles of Multiple (En)coding.

FABRICS AND FABRICATIONS
THE MYTH AND MAKING OF WILLIAM AND MARY

Edited by Paul Hoftijzer and C.C. Barfoot. Amsterdam/ Atlanta GA 1990. 314 pp. (DQR Studies in Literature, 6) ISSN: 0921-2507

ISBN: 90-6203-990-1   Bound Hfl. 140,00/US-$ 70.00

ISBN: 90-5183-182-X   Paper Hfl.   49,50/US-$ 24.75

C.C. Barfoot and Paul Hoftijzer: Introduction. Jonathan Clark: 1688: Glorious Revolution or Glorious Reaction? J. van den Berg: Religion and Politics in the Life of William and Mary. Rosemary van Wengen-Shute: The English Church in The Hague during William and Mary's Time. Frans Korsten: The Eve of the Glorious Revolution: The Catholic Threat. Paul Hoftijzer: "Such Onely as Are Very Honest, Loyall and Active": English Spies in the Low Countries, 1660-1688. L. van Poelgeest: The Stadholder-King William III and the University of Leiden. C.C. Barfoot: "Hey for Praise and Panegyric": William III and the Political Poetry of Matthew Prior. Cornelis W. Schoneveld: "How Lov'd She Liv'd, and How Lamented Fell": Congreve and Prior on the Death of Queen Mary, and their Dutch Translator Willem Sewel. Peter J. de Voogd: William III, the Siege of Namur, Prior and Sterne. W. Troost: William III and Ireland. J.Th. Leerssen: Skeletons in the Cupboard: The "Glorious" Revolution and Ireland. Uta Janssens-Knorsch: From Het Loo to Hampton Court: William and Mary's Dutch Gardens and Their Influence on English Gardening. H. Bots and M. Evers: Book News in Locke's Correspondence (1683-1692). Notes on Contributors.

USA/Canada: Editions Rodopi, 233 Peachtree Street, N.E., Suite 404, Atlanta, Ga. 30303-1504, Telephone (404) 523-1964, only USA 1-800-225-3998, Fax (404) — 522-7116
And Others: Editions Rodopi B.V., Keizersgracht 302-304, 1016 EX Amsterdam, Telephone (020) —22.75.07, Fax (020) — 38.09.48

Andreas Höfele, München

The Writer on Stage. Some Contemporary British Plays about Authors

I

The plays I am going to discuss in this paper were not all written and first performed in the 1980s. In fact, the – in my opinion – more important ones are from the seventies, which I hope justifies my including works from the previous decade. Plays about authors continue to be written in considerable numbers – witness the 1989 Edinburgh Festival, which included at least three productions presenting poets as dramatis personae: John Cargill Thompson's *Julius Caesar – The Alternative Version*, Alison Atkin's *Pre-Raphaelite Seeds* and Charles Barron's *Byron. The Road to Missolonghi.*[1] Not all stage works about authors show the structural and thematic autonomy implied by the term 'play'. Many could be best described as collages of texts by the portrayed author arranged to form a running commentary on his or her life. "The man, or woman, behind the work" emerges in a stage presentation whose modest scenic requirements are ideally suited to the small fringe company or travelling oneman show. The texts referred to in this paper, however, are full-fledged plays, even though some of them contain passages from the work of the author-protagonist. The plays are: *Bingo*, Edward Bond's portrayal of Shakespeare during the last few months of his life, leading up to his (fictitious) suicide; *The Fool* by the same author, a condensed version of John Clare's progress from farm labourer to poetical prodigy to inmate in a lunatic asylum; Tom Stoppard's *Travesties*, an encounter between James Joyce, Lenin, and Tristan Tzara in Zurich in 1917 taking place in the memory of a former British consulate employee whom Joyce had persuaded to act the part of Algernon Moncrieff in an amateur production of *The Impor-tance of Being Earnest*; Christopher Hampton's *Total Eclipse*, a play about the tragi-comical relationship of the two poets Paul Verlaine and Arthur Rimbaud: the same author's *Tales From Hollywood*, in which Ödön von Horváth, instead of being struck dead by a falling tree branch in Paris in 1939, emigrates to Cali-fornia where he observes the German emigré writers scene from the inside; Michael Hastings' *Tom and Viv*, the story of T. S. Eliot's first and unhappy marriage to Vivienne Haigh-Wood, a play assembled from those pieces of bio-graphical information which the administrators of Eliot's estate forgot to sup-press; *Futurists* by Dusty Hughes, which follows the fortunes of the Russian literary avantgarde from the high hopes of the early post-revolutionary days into the increasingly repressive political climate of the 1920s; Howard Brenton's

Bloody Poetry, a portrayal of the Byron-Shelley entourage at various stages of their European exile, ending with Shelley's death and cremation on the Viareggio beach.[2]

II

Maurice Beebe introduces his well-known study of "The Artist as Hero in Fiction from Goethe to Joyce"[3] – the subtitle of the book – by quoting a passage from Aldous Huxley's *Crome Yellow* in which Denis, the hopeful young author, having confessed that he is writing a novel, is shocked by his new acquaintance's ability to give a devastatingly correct plot summary.

> 'Little Percy, the hero, was never good at games, but he was always clever. He passes through the usual public school and the usual university and comes to London, where he lives among the artists. He is bowed down with melancholy thought; he carries the whole weight of the universe upon his shoulders. He writes a novel of dazzling brilliance; he dabbles delicately in Amour and disappears, at the end of the book, into the Luminous Future.' Denis blushed scarlet. Mr. Scogan had described the plan of his novel with an accuracy that was appalling. He made an effort to laugh. 'You're entirely wrong,' he said. 'My novel is not in the least like that.' It was a heroic lie. Luckily, he reflected, only two chapters were written. He would tear them up that evening when he unpacked.

Beebe comments:

> Mr. Scogan is not clairvoyant; he is simply well read. The story of Percy could be that of several hundred sensitive young heroes of novels, for by 1921, when *Crome Yellow* was published, both the artist and the adolescent had become hackneyed subjects of fiction. The tradition of artist fiction, which had developed steadily for more than a century, reached a crest in the first two decades of the twentieth century.

I have chosen this passage as a starting point because it establishes unmistakably what the plays I want to discuss are not. They are not dramatizations of the kind of fiction Beebe analyzes in his book, not, in other words, theatrical equivalents of the *Künstlerroman* or *Künstlernovelle* whose focus is on the artist's inner life, the emergence of his talent and his realization of his vocation through a decisive experience – usually happening near the end of the book: a 'conversion'[4], initiation, or 'epiphany'. The creation of a work of art by the protagonist is the telos towards which all such artist's stories move.[5] Joyce's *Portrait of the Artist* is the classic example of this pattern. A look at more recent fiction, however, shows that there has been a change of paradigm. As Lee T. Lemon observes:

Between the generation of James Joyce and the generation of John Fowles, the fictional portrait of the artist changed notably. Essentially, the Byronic gave way to the Wordsworthian. In the years before World War II, our best novelists saw their artists as isolated rebels [...]. Each is larger than life; each has drives that lesser mortals cannot fathom and dare not imitate; each sees himself tragically alone, a Gulliver among pygmies, [...]. The Wordsworthian artist [...] is [...] primarily an ordinary human being trying to live in a world peopled with individuals as important as himself. [He] is likely to have a sense of what he is doing but, unlike the historical Wordsworth, is also likely to recognize his own fuzziness about the place his work occupies in the grand scheme of things [...]. Compared to the Byronic artist, the artist-hero of most contemporary fiction is very much an anti-artist, in the same sense in which many contemporary fictional protagonists are anti-heroes.[6]

Even though Lemon's use of the term "Wordsworthian" may not strike one as particularly apt, the characteristics he lists under this heading all apply to our plays about authors. None of them has a protagonist even remotely resembling the isolated rebel of the Byronic tradition. Ironically, not even Byron "himself", when appearing on stage in Brenton's *Bloody Poetry* and Charles Barron's memory-play *The Road to Missolonghi*, is endowed with any of the demonic charisma of the rôle model which is the historical Byron's legacy to the literary imagination of Europe. Rather than focussing on the lonely struggle of creation, the plays present the writer in situations highlighting his dealings with the world outside, examining an issue first dramatized in Goethe's *Torquato Tasso*: the highly problematic relationship between the artist and society.

The introspective approach characteristic of the typical *Künstlerroman* accounts for these novels' strong affinity to the autobiographical mode. As Ursula Mahlendorf points out: Drama, by its very nature a public genre, is concerned with the external aspect of the hero's life, his relation to other people, his place in the world. The artistic process itself is hardly presentable in dramatic form. It is not to autobiography, then, but to biography and history – or, to be more precise: biography as a specific mode of the writing of history – that we must turn for a conceptual framework suited to our subject.

III

We are faced with – at least at first sight – a paradoxical state of affairs. The concept of history as a consistent, teleologically streamlined process has broken down under the onslaught of deconstructionist theory proclaiming an era of "posthistoire", and the notion of the self as a clearly defined ontological entity has dissolved under the dissecting lens of psychoanalysis and rôle theory, yet we find a conspicuous flourishing of the historico-biographical element in contemporary English literature. A far from comprehensive catalogue of examples would include novels such as Peter Ackroyd's *The Last Testament of Oscar Wilde* and the same author's *Chatterton*, Julian Barnes' *Flaubert's Parrot*, Amanda Prantera's *Conversations with Lord Byron on Perversion, 163 Years after his Lordship's Death*, as well as Jeanette Winterson's *The Passion*, Rose Tremain's *Restoration*, Graham Swift's *Waterland*, William Golding's *Rites of Passage* and his *Close Quarters*, John Fowles' *A Maggot* and, perhaps the pioneering work in the field, his *French Lieutenant's Woman*. One explanation for this peculiar coexistence which readily suggests itself would be the assumption that these works express a sense of nostalgia, that they are symptoms of a retrogressive desire, an attempt to stem the tide of disintegration and fragmentation, with a possible undercurrent of that insular hostility to international avantgarde trends which characterized much English literature of the 1950s.[7] Scholarship on biography has, in fact, often stressed this function of the genre: solace for a bourgeois readership that has lost its philosophical bearings.[8] This is, for instance, the standard explanation for the international vogue of biographical writing after World War I: the consoling wholeness of the written life soothed the shock of displacement.[9] It was precisely during those years, however, that a new kind of 'debunking' biography with an emphasis on the cracks in the monumental public façade of the protagonist and a characteristic preference for the dry mock made its highly successful début in the works of Lytton Strachey.[10] This early 20th-century precedent should alert one to the fact that harmony regained may not be the only or not necessarily even the predominant impulse behind the literary evocation of past lives. Subversion of a hitherto unchallenged public image sets a process of disintegration going simply by making a second sharply contrasting version available whose effectiveness increases proportionally with the degree of deviation from the previously unchallenged old version. And even though both versions may maintain the unity of their subject (Strachey certainly does not question the concept of character as such), the mere fact of their coexistence suffices to undermine that unity. The biographical writing of the twenties may thus be said to contain first hints of a literary use of historico-biographical material not in opposition to, but in accord with the disintegrative powers eroding the traditional ideas of history and personality. That "deeper complicity with things falling apart" which Ihab Hassan[11] lists among the distinguishing traits of a postmodern attitude may express itself precisely by utilising history and biography as quarries for an aesthetics of play whose aim is not the restoration of an irretrievably lost single truth, but a very self-conscious act of composing variations on the theme of epistemological uncertainty.

Needless to say, what one might call the 'deconstructive' mode on the one hand and the 'reconstructive', historicist approach on the other are by no means mutually exclusive. The same double-strategy – an artistic way of having one's cake and eating it too – that determines the use of parody in, say, Nabokov, Thomas Mann and Max Beerbohm is also at work in a treatment of the past which is both deconstructive and reconstructive. Just as parody, while undermining the validity of established modes or canonized literary models, nevertheless partakes – albeit ironically – of their original evocative power[12], even the most fragmented or wilfully distorted presentation of historical persons and events will still generate some kind of coherence, a version of a life or character. Tom Stoppard's *Travesties*, with its obvious artificiality and its intertextual acrobatics, clearly marks the deconstructive end of the scale, while in Michael Hastings' *Tom and Viv*, with its impetus to uncover the human suffering behind the poetry, the far from perfect life that Eliot submerged in the dogma of perfect, impersonal art, the reconstructive element clearly dominates. Christopher Hampton's *Total Eclipse* is closer to Hastings, while the later *Tales from Hollywood* is similar to *Travesties*. It is characteristic of both the more documentary and the more openly fictitious plays to insist on their factual basis. In fact, this insistence tends to be, if anything, more pronounced in the deconstructive variant, witness the scene in *Tales from Hollywood* in which Tarzan shakes hands with the most famous of the German emigrants ("Me Johnny Weismuller, you Thomas Mann"), Chico interrogates Harpo Marx about a tennis match Harpo has lost to Arnold Schönberg, and Horváth walks arm-in-arm with Greta Garbo. The scene ends with Horváth's comment:

Well. Thomas Mann did know Johnny Weismuller. Schoenberg did play tennis with Harpo Marx. And I did meet Garbo. But I need hardly say the reality was very different.[13]

The factual is stressed here only in order to underline how completely it is at the author's disposal; a further implication being that all factual evidence can only be grasped or communicated as fiction. It follows that history is no more than an image generated in the audience's mind: scraps of information blend past and present in the viewer's imagination and create what Botho Strauss has called "a multiple consciousness" („ein mehrfaches Bewußtsein").[14]

Unlike *Travesties* or *Tales from Hollywood*, Edward Bond's two plays about authors lack the more obvious pointers to the fictitiousness of their rendering of history. Yet *Bingo* and *The Fool* are no less marked by their author's determination to recreate history according to his own vision. If anything, Bond's grip on his source material is even tighter, one might almost say: more relentless, than that of Hampton, Stoppard, or any of the other playwrights I have mentioned. In his singleminded concentration on the artist's rôle in a capitalist society, Bond imposes the strongest thematic unity on his sujet. *Bingo* and *The Fool* stand out among contemporary plays about authors as the most probing examinations of the writer's dilemma and are therefore – in the Shavian sense of the word – the most 'unpleasant'. When Dusty Hughes concludes the introduction to his play on the poets of the Russian Revolution with the statement:

> *Futurists* is finally about the indestructability of poetry. It is a musical which has poems for songs, and in which poetry is the main character[15]

this indicates a willingness to hand the play over to the poets and let them use it as a podium from which to speak for themselves in their own words. Bond offers no such opportunity to Shakespeare or Clare. More than any of the other playwrights considered here, he yokes the authors he is writing about to his own purpose with an unflagging insistence on the writer's moral responsibility. His creation of Shakespeare, especially, brings to mind Harold Bloom's concept of 'misreading': a kind of literary battle of wills in which a 'strong poet' as 'strong reader' bends his canonised predecessor into a shape he can make use of, or control.[16] Nevertheless, Bond introduces his writer-protagonists in a most unobtrusive fashion, with Shakespeare, the "divine Bard", the undisputed grandmaster of poetic eloquence sitting in brooding semisilence through much of *Bingo*; and John Clare, introduced as one of a group of farm labourers, emerging as the centre of interest only after the fourth of the eight scenes of *The Fool* is almost over.

This strategy points to a question all plays about authors must find an answer to: how can the writer on stage be portrayed convincingly as a writer if the act of creation itself is not shown? Kings, princes, politicians, the heroes of the traditional history play, are identified by the events whose course, to a greater or lesser degree, they have determined. The presentation of these events on stage constitutes the action of the play. The poets of the past can only be identified by their language. It is the essence of their significance in history. Yet trying to capture this essence in a play by letting a Shelley, Byron, Rimbaud or Shakespeare intersperse their everyday speech with immortal lines from their masterpieces would surely lead to embarrassing results. Except, of course, in a play that discards the conventions of psychological realism for an openly parodistic approach to its characters. A James Joyce who is not only a famous novelist but also a stage Irishman addicted to limericks and a parodic understudy for Oscar Wilde's Lady Bracknell may talk like a walking compendium of his own work without raising any question of plausibility. The writer as caricature in Stoppard's play is naturally also the writer as text, locked in an intertextual debate with other texts. Psychology does not come into this. It is, however, a major consideration in plays with no parodic intent. Conveying a sense of brilliance without resorting to quotation or pastiche is the crux of any such play. While the attempt to out-Shakespeare Shakespeare is doomed to failure, suggestive laconism also has its dangers. Hampton's portrayal of Rimbaud, for instance, tends to overstate the adolescent prodigy's taciturn self-assurance, thereby making him appear, at times, more like a puffed-up brat than the young genius who stocked and mesmerized everyone he met. Howard Brenton's *Bloody Poetry*, on the other hand, by presenting very eloquent versions of Byron and Shelley manages to bring out the two poets' youthful iconoclasm and exuberant vitality, but hardly convinces us that these men were capable of anything weightier than undergraduate witticisms in verse or prose. Edward Bond, faced with the formidable task of reincarnating the most awe-inspiring of culture heroes, succeeds in doing so by avoiding not only the obvious pitfalls of 'high-sounding' pseudo-Elizabethan rhetoric but also the temptation to make every remark resound with deep meaning. Present but almost-speechless during the first scene of the play, Bond's Shakespeare becomes the centre of attention not by virtue of any self-assertive rhetoric but through silence that becomes all the more conspicuous through the other characters' continual attempts to make him break it. Bond does not block our vision with his own invention of Shakespeare, the artist. Instead, he leaves enough space for us to fill in the Shakespeare world we know from *Hamlet, The Tempest,* or *King Lear*. This universe of experience and imagination is never questioned, nor is it inadvertently diminished by futile attempts to prove its existence. Treating Shakespeare's artistic supremacy as given, Bond can concentrate his whole effort on the question of how *King Lear* could be written by a man who shared the acquisitiveness of the new landowning class in the early days of the enclosure movement.

V

Nobody in their right mind is going to expect a great writer to be a great man.[17]

These words from Michael Hastings' introduction to *Tom and Viv* express the basic consensus of all the plays considered here. The term "artist-hero", so readily labelling the protagonist of the *Künstlerroman*, does not apply to the artist on stage. He is no hero. His story does not follow the optimistic pattern encapsulated in the German word *Bildung*. There is no overcoming of obstacles and final triumph of self-realisation. Where the play covers a longer span of the writer's life, as it does in *The Fool, Total Eclipse, Tales from Hollywood,* and *Tom and Viv*, it presents the obstacles he has to contend with, but no final triumph. In *Tales from Hollywood* we follow the progress – or rather: regress – of the writer from artistic integrity to total subjugation under the dictates of commercialism. In *The Fool*, the reversal of the teleogical pattern is even more radical.

Far from enabling him to transcend the limitations of his working-class world, the talent which Bond's John Clare is gifted with turns out to be more of a burden than a blessing, propelling him out of his old life with no chance of finding a footing in a new one. Virtually 'disabled' for any 'normal', bread-winning work, he ends up in the limbo of the asylum. This Clare is a relative not of Stephen Dedalus but of Woyzeck: archetypal anti-hero, maltreated fool, not of Fortune but of society. And Bond's Shakespeare, though safely out of pen-ury's reach on the other side of the class barrier and, in bourgeois terms, a success, is no less at the mercy of his creative gift – a retired Prospero in the peaceful seclusion of his garden, yet unquiet, constantly under attack by his memory as well as new encroachments of the world outside. He is not the Shakespeare of Keats' famous letter, "the cameleon Poet" who "has as much delight in conceiving an Imogen as an Iago"[18], but more like the Teiresias of Eliot's *Waste Land*, an old man cursed with a comprehensive vision of evil and suffering, whose only wish is for oblivion; one of the living dead whose insight is yet no safeguard against corruption and the weakness of self-interest. Guilt – an insistent subtext of *The Waste Land*'s indictment of the squalor of modern metropolitan life – is the focal point of Bond's portrait of Shakespeare as an old man. As the author writes in his introduction to *Bingo*:

> Shakespeare created Lear, who is the most radical of all social critics. [...] But how did he live? His behaviour as a property-owner made him closer to Goneril than Lear. He supported and benefited from the Goneril-society – with its prisons, workhouses, whipping, starvation, mutilation, pulpit-hysteria and all the rest of it.[19]

Being fully aware of this contradiction, the Shakespeare of Bond's play has no choice but suicide. Bond's rigorism allows the artist no escape route to a morally indifferent, autonomous realm of aesthetic values. His position is diametrically opposed to the view held by Stoppard's James Joyce:

> An artist is the magician put among men to gratify – capriciously – their urge for immortality. [...] What now of the Trojan War if it had been passed over by the artist's touch? Dust. [...] A minor redistribution of broken pots. But it is we who stand enriched, by a tale of heroes, of a golden apple, a wooden horse, a face that launched a thousand ships – and above all, of Ulysses, the wanderer [...].[20]

For Bond's Shakespeare, however, the achievement of a lifetime as an artist counts for nothing when measured against his acceptance of – and profiting from – a system whose cruel injustice he sees more clearly than anyone else. "Was anything done?"[21] Coming from Shakespeare, a writer who, by universal agreement, reached the summit of human achievement, this anguished question shows how precarious the artist's position becomes if his claim to be judged by the quality of his work alone is challenged or even denied outright. A sense of this precariousness, most oppressive in *Bingo* or *The Fool*, is common to all of the plays under discussion. *Tom and Viv*, for instance, besides being the story of an unhappy marriage with disastrous consequences for the wife, could also be described as a reckoning up of human losses against the gains of perfect poetry. On one level, the play is a piece of literary criticism, a reading of *The Waste Land* earmarking those references to the poet's life which Eliot, the critic, had declared off limits.

'My nerves are bad to-night. Yes, bad. Stay with me.
'Speak to me. Why do you never speak. Speak.
'What are you thinking of? What thinking? What?
'I never know what you are thinking. Think.'

I think we are in rats' alley
Where the dead men lost their bones.

'What is that noise?'
                            The wind under the door.
'What is that noise now? What is the wind doing?'
                            Nothing again nothing.
                                                            'Do
'You know nothing? Do you see nothing? Do you remember
'Nothing?'[22]

Hastings finds the key to the poem's understanding in passages like this, which he sees as a reflection of Eliot's exasperated withdrawal from his increasingly 'unmanageable' disturbed wife. Although the play does not make the sensational disclosures nervously anticipated by the guardians of Eliot's reputation, its sympathies lie clearly with the loser, Vivienne, who spent the last twelve years of her life in a mental institution. A remark by Edith Sitwell serves as the play's motto: "At some point in their marriage Tom went mad, and promptly certified his wife." The poet finds sanity and peace of mind by surrounding himself with a shield of respectability, exiling his wife and distancing himself from his personal chaos by inventing the doctrine of impersonal art. Yet he does so, according to the play, only at the cost of an impoverishment of both his life and his art. Eliot emerges – to use the term Bond applies to Shakespeare – as a "corrupt seer".[23]

Quoted out of context, Joyce's plea for the autonomy of art would seem to indicate that the author of *Travesties* does not share the other playwrights' uneasiness about the artist's rôle. Joyce's opinion, however, is counterpoised by statements from Lenin, Tristan Tzara, and the narrator, Carr. These range from Lenin's "Today, literature must become party literature" (ironically coupled with a sentimental infatuation with the *Appassionata*) to Tzara's iconoclastic Dada-manifestoes demanding, among other things, "The right to urinate in different colours", and Carr's bourgeois "It is the duty of the artist to beautify existence." While some critics have taken Joyce's message to express Stoppard's own view, I agree with those[24] who see *Travesties* as the most perfect example of what the playwright himself describes as follows:

> What there is, is a series of conflicting statements made by conflicting char-acters, and they tend to play a sort of infinite leap-frog. You know, an argu-ment, a refutation, then a rebuttal of the refutation, then a counter-rebuttal, so that there is never any point in this intellectual leap-frog at which I feel *that* is the speech to stop it on, *that* is the last word.[25]

VI

For all its playfulness, *Travesties* offers a more probing discussion of the oppos-ing claims of art and life, aesthetics and morals than, for example, Brenton's *Bloody Poetry*, Hampton's *Tales from Hollywood*, or Hughes' *Futurists*, plays which also raise the issue but put more emphasis on the atmospheric or even picturesque aspects of their historical sujets. Is it by chance – or a question of quality – that the plays by Bond and Stoppard, all three of them written in the seventies, address the question of the writer's rôle in society with an intensity that seems to have become somewhat blunted in plays about authors written during the eighties? A more historicist, descriptive conception seems to have gained ground at the cost of a more analytical, more probing approach. Has the writer's position become more secure, then? Has his situation, especially in Britain, improved? Hardly. But whereas writers during the late sixties and seventies used to question not only the traditional bourgeois notion of art, but their own rôle in society as well, the eighties, together with Thatcherism, have brought pressure on the arts that no longer comes from self-questioning, but from without.

A play about a writer's fight for survival in a world dominated by a purely profit-oriented entertainment industry on the one hand and fascism on the other (I am referring to *Tales from Hollywood*, of course) may not be intended as a direct political comment but it fits the present situation well enough. And so does Brenton's presentation of the two rebel poets Byron and Shelley and their commune-like entourage, exiled from the England of the repressive Castlereagh administration. The most revealing reference to current conditions seems to be contained in Hughes' *Futurists*. Huddled together under the roof of the bohe-mian Straw Dog Café, Mayakovsky, Mandelstam, Akhmatova, and the other poets of the avant-garde squabble over which of them is the true poet of the revolution, while the revolution has already begun to take a direction that will make Futurism a thing of the past and the Futurists casualties of history.

While Bond and Stoppard ask whether art which is deeply corrupted by its ornamental rôle in the inhuman status quo of society has any right to exist at all, Hughes shows it to be an invaluable asset to be defended at all costs against the encroachment of an all-powerful and fundamentally hostile state authority.

VII

According to Michel Foucault, a future is thinkable in which "the author-function will disappear", leaving "all discourses" to "develop in the anonymity of a murmur".[26] It would be foolish to argue that the playwrights we have been considering share Foucault's or Roland Barthes' views on 'the death of the author'. Yet their portrayals of writers are marked by the conspicuous absence of two of the most essential elements of the Romantic or 'high modern' image of the author: authority and telos. When Stephen Dedalus realizes his artistic vocation in an ecstatic vision of his mythical namesake – "the hawklike man flying sunward above the sea, a prophecy of the end he had been born to serve"[27] – the two elements form the nucleus of his epiphany. No such vistas of glowing promise ever open up to the writer in our plays. Never does he achieve that godlike position of power and detachment which, according to Stephen Dedalus, defines the relation between the author and his work:

> The artist, like the God of creation, remains within or behind or beyond or above his handiwork, invisible, refined out of existence, indifferent, paring his fingernails.[28]

"Universal History", says Carlyle,

> is at bottom the History of the Great Men who have worked here. They were [...] the modellers, patterns, and in a wide sense creators, of whatsoever the general mass of men contrived to do or to attain; all things that we see standing accomplished in the world are properly the outer material result [...] of Thoughts that dwelt in the Great Men [...].[29]

These basic assumptions of the traditional, idealistic writing of history and biography also inform the traditional historical drama. The lectures *On Heroes, Hero-worship and the Heroic in History* from which the quoted passage is taken not surprisingly name Shakespeare as the prime example of "The Hero as Poet". Our contemporary plays about authors endorse a diametrically opposed view. *Bingo*, *The Fool*, *Futurists*, *Tales from Hollywood*, even *Travesties*, where Lenin and Joyce are turned into the puppets of a farcical 'pre-text', all show how man as the subject *in* history becomes the subject *of* history in the sense of becoming subjected *to* history. Instead of shaping its course, he is shaped by it. What we see is life determined by the relentless grinding of the reality principle. In view of this, Carlyle's assertions of the rôle of the "Great Men" in history ring hollow. "History is a nightmare from which I am trying to awake", says the disillusioned Stephen Dedalus of the "Nestor" episode in *Ulysses*.[30] His words apply to any of the plays about authors discussed here. They, like Ulysses, make it clear that waking up is impossible.[*]

Notes

1 Cf. also Terry Eagleton's new play about Oscar Wilde: *Saint Oscar*. Derry: Field Day, 1988.

2 The editions used are:
E. Bond: *Bingo. Scenes of Money and Death*. [First performed: November 1973] London, New York: Methuen, 1984.
–: *The Fool. Scenes of Bread and Love*. [November 1975] London: Methuen, 1987.
T. Stoppard: *Travesties*. [June 1974] New York: Grove, 1984.
Ch. Hampton: *Total Eclipse*. [September 1968] London: Faber, 1981.
–: *Tales from Hollywood*. [March 1982] London, Boston: Faber, 1983.
M. Hastings: *Tom and Viv*. [February 1984] Harmondsworth: Penguin, 1985.
D. Hughes: *Futurists*. [March 1986] London, Boston: Faber, 1986.
H. Brenton: *Bloody Poetry*. [October 1984] London, New York: Methuen, 1985.
Two more plays about authors are dealt with in Beate Neumeier's paper: Liz Lockhead's *Blood and Eyes*, and Michelene Wandor's *Aurora Leigh*. Another play about a woman author is Hugh Whitmore's *Stevie. A play from the life and work of Stevie Smith*. [March 1977] Oxford: Amber Lane, 1984, while Simon Moss's *Cock-Ups* deals with the life and death of Joe Orton.

3 *Ivory Towers and Sacred Founts*. New York, 1964, p. 3f.

4 Cf. A. Hornung: "Reading One/Self: Samuel Beckett, Thomas Bernhard, Peter Handke, John Barth, Alain Robbe-Grillet." – In Calinescu, M., Fokkema, D. (Eds.): *Exploring Postmodernism*. Amsterdam, Philadelphia, 1987, pp. 175–198.

5 Cf. Ursula R. Mahlendorf, *The Wellsprings of Literary Creation*. Columbia/S. C., 1985.

6 *Portraits of the Artist in Contemporary Fiction*. Lincoln/Neb., London, 1985, pp. IX–XIII.

7 Cf. R. Rubinovitz: *The Reaction against Experiment in the English Novel. 1950–1960*. New York, London 1967.

8 Cf. F. Sengle: „Zum Problem der modernen Dichterbiographie". *DVjs* 26, 1952, 100–111, here: 111.

9 Cf. J. Romein: *Die Biographie*. Bern, 1948, p. 28.

10 Cf. H. Scheuer: *Biographie. Studien zur Funktion und zum Wandel einer literarischen Gattung vom 18. Jahrhundert bis zur Gegenwart*. Stuttgart, 1979, pp. 151–158.

11 *Paracriticisms*. Urbana, 1975, p. 59.

12 Cf. A. Höfele: *Parodie und literarischer Wandel. Studien zur Funktion einer Schreib-weise in der englischen Literatur des ausgehenden 19. Jahrhunderts.* Heidelberg, 1986, pp. 62f., 209, 224–231.

13 Hampton, Ch.: *Tales from Hollywood*, p. 16.

14 *Der junge Mann.* München, 1984, p. 11.

15 *Futurists*, pp. 11f.

16 *A Map of Misreading.* New York, 1975.

17 *Tom and Viv*, p. 46.

18 Letter to Richard Woodhouse, Tuesday 27. Oct. 1818. – In *The Letters of John Keats.* Ed. M. B. Forman. Oxford, ³1947, pp. 226–228, here: p. 228.

19 Bond, E.: *Plays: Three.* London: Methuen, 1987, pp. 4–6.

20 *Travesties*, p. 62.

21 *Bingo*, p. 51.

22 *The Waste Land*, ll. 111–120 (Eliot, T. S.: *Collected Poems 1909–1962.* London, 1963, p. 67).

23 Dieter A. Berger uses this label as a title for his interpretation of *Bingo*; „'The Corrupt Seer': Zur Shakespeare-Rezeption Edward Bonds". *Arbeiten aus Anglistik und Amerikanistik* 4, 1980, 65–78.

24 Cf. B. Neumeier: *Spiel und Politik. Aspekte der Komik bei Tom Stoppard.* München, 1986, p. 157.

25 "Ambushes for the Audience: Towards a High Comedy of Ideas". *Theatre Quarterly* No. 14, 1974, 3–17, here: 6f.

26 Foucault, M.: "What is an Author?" – In Harari, J. V. (Ed.): *Textual Strategies. Perspectives in Post-Structural Criticism.* Ithaca/N. Y., 1979, pp. 141–160, here: p. 160.

27 Joyce, J.: *A Portrait of the Artist as a Young Man.* London, 1958, p. 173.

28 *A Portrait of the Artist*, p. 215.

29 *On Heroes, Hero-worship and the Heroic in History.* Ed A. Herrmann. Bielefeld, Leipzig, 1934, pp. 1f.

30 *Ulysses.* Harmondsworth, 1969, p. 40.

* Finally, a word of thanks to Dr. Rolf Eichler and Dr. Michael Raab for directing my attention to some plays about authors previously unknown me.

SPRACHWISSENSCHAFT

ALFRED BAMMESBERGER (Hrsg.)

Die Laryngaltheorie

und die Rekonstruktion des indogermanischen
Laut- und Formensystems
2. Teil: Register
1990. 67 Seiten, 1 Frontispiz. Kartoniert DM 30,-
(Indogermanische Bibliothek. 3. Reihe)

JOHANNES FRIEDRICH

Hethitisches Wörterbuch

Kurzgefaßte kritische Sammlung der Deutungen
hethitischer Wörter
1990. 2., unveränderte Auflage. 477 Seiten.
Kartoniert ca. DM 75,-. Leinen ca. DM 100,-
(Indogermanische Bibliothek. 2. Reihe.
Wörterbücher)

ALFRED BAMMESBERGER –
ALFRED WOLLMANN (Hrsg.)

Britain 400–600: Language and History

1990. 485 Seiten, mit 6 Karten u. mehreren Abb.
Kartoniert DM 116,-. Leinen DM 146,-
(Anglistische Forschungen, Heft 205)

WILHELM KESSELRING

Dictionnaire chronologique de la langue française

[Continuation du dictionnaire chronologique
du vocabulaire français, le XVIᵉ siècle, du même
auteur]
Le XVIIᵉ siècle. Tome I: 1601–1606
1989. XXIX, 417 Seiten mit 2 Faksimiles.
Kartoniert DM 78,-. Leinen DM 110,-

FRANS VAN COETSEM

Ablaut and Reduplication in the Germanic Verb

Alfred Bammesberger (Hrsg.): Untersuchungen
zur vergleichenden Grammatik der germani-
schen Sprachen. 3. Band
1990. 144 Seiten. Kartoniert DM 56,-.
Leinen DM 76,-
(Indogermanische Bibliothek. Erste Reihe:
Lehr- und Handbücher)

REINHARD KIESLER

Sprachliche Mittel der Hervorhebung in der modernen portugiesischen Umgangssprache

1989. XVIII, 370 Seiten. Kartoniert DM 90,-.
Leinen DM 120,-
(Sammlung romanischer Elementar- und
Handbücher. 5. Reihe. Untersuchungen u. Texte,
Band 16)

PAUL DIELS

Altkirchenslavische Grammatik

I. Teil: Grammatik. II. Teil: Ausgewählte Texte
und Wörterbuch
1989. Unveränderter Nachdruck der Ausgabe
von 1963. Beide Teile in einem Band.
XVI, 430 Seiten. Leinen DM 125,-
(SLAVICA. Sammlung slavischer Lehr- und
Handbücher)

AUGUST LESKIEN

Handbuch der altbulgarischen (altkirchenslavischen) Sprache

Grammatik – Texte – Glossar
1990. 10., von Johannes Schröpfer mit
Verbesserung und Ergänzungen versehene
Auflage. XXXVI, 369 Seiten mit 2 Karten.
Kartoniert DM 48,-
(Indogermanische Bibliothek. 1. Reihe)

CARL WINTER · UNIVERSITÄTSVERLAG · HEIDELBERG

Armin Geraths, Berlin

Bemerkungen zum britischen Musical der achtziger Jahre mit einem skeptischen Seitenblick auf *Blood Brothers* und Marilyn Monroe

I

Die Seriosität wissenschaftlicher Beschäftigung mit dem Musical wird noch immer stark in Zweifel gezogen. Einige Vertreter der anglistisch-amerikanistischen Zunft machen zwar mitunter vorsichtige Anstrengungen, dies zu ändern. Kontinuierliche Forschungsaktivität jedoch ist nirgends festzustellen. So bleibt nur der Weg zum flinken Fachjournalismus, und es wäre unziemlich, ihm den Respekt zu versagen. Ähnlich wie bei der Rock- und Pop-Musikforschung scheint sich eine zielstrebige Musicalforschung nicht etablieren zu können, weil noch immer ungeklärt ist, wer für dieses Unterhaltungsgenre eigentlich verantwortlich zeichnet. Die spezifischen Bedingungen des Dreispartentheaters machen es bis heute auf deutschen Bühnen nur möglich, mit einem hohen Aufgebot an ausländischen Darstellern die Zusammenführung von Sprechtheater, Musiktheater und Ballett praktisch zu bewerkstelligen; und analog dazu will es deshalb hierzulande auch nur ansatzweise gelingen, ein neuartiges Know-how zu entwickeln, das einen einzigen Wissenschaftler dazu befähigt, Libretto, Musik, Choreographie und Bühnenbild sowie das Zusammenwirken der unterschiedlichen Zeichensysteme in gleich kompetenter Weise zu beschreiben. Theater- und Musikwissenschaftler, vorwiegend aber Feuilletonisten haben dabei immer noch die wenigsten Skrupel und repräsentieren bis heute im wesentlichen den Forschungsstand zum Musical.

Nicht alle Gründe für die Berührungsangst mit dieser ständig wichtiger werdenden Bühnengattung sind so honorig, daß es die Sorge um mangelnde Fachkompetenz ist, die vor der Auseinandersetzung mit der Gattung zurückschrecken läßt. Das Musical dient traditionell anspruchsloser Unterhaltung und ist wissenschaftlich immer noch nicht hoffähig. In der Hierarchie der schönen Künste nimmt es einen unteren Rang ein, hat ein breites, niemals elitäres Publikum (wie etwa Alban Berg oder Bernd Alois Zimmermann) und stellt in der Regel geringe Ansprüche an die Rezeptionsaktivität des Zuschauers. Das Rock-Konzert, die Revue, die Show sind enge Nachbarn, und auch zu diesen Genera findet der Fachwissenschaftler – wie gelegentlich selbst noch zum Film – allenfalls zögernd Zugang. Wer sich häufig mit peripheren Kunstformen befaßt, deren Erstrangigkeit aus der Perspektive einer ‚Höhenkamm-Kunst' nicht grundlos in Zweifel gezogen wird, weiß um ein unumgängliches Dilemma. Entweder wirkt sich die bescheidene Qualität des anscheinend Zweit- und Drittrangigen (wie wirkungsmächtig es in quantitativen Kategorien auch immer sein mag) auf die Qualität der kritischen Bemühungen aus und prägt schließlich dem Kritiker selbst das Siegel mäßiger Güte auf; oder man bringt anspruchsvolle Analysekriterien, die an ‚Höhenkamm-Kunst' gewonnen wurden, auf dünnblütige Werkchen mit ihrer essentiellen Oberflächlichkeit zur Anwendung, – erntet damit aber bestenfalls zwiespältiges Lob. Die Analyse sei zwar trefflich, doch erheblich besser und gewichtiger als das federgewichtige Opus der leichten oder seichten Muse selbst: insofern zwar ein rührender Rettungsversuch, doch eher verlorene Liebesmüh', ein Unterfangen, wo Scharfsinn und Energie zum Analysegegenstand in einem kaum angemessenen Verhältnis stünden. Wen wundert es also, daß große Fachvertreter dort lieber nicht investieren, wo man sich aufgrund immer noch deutlich vorherrschender Wertnormen einer vor-demokratischen Ästhetik allzuleicht aufs Glatteis begibt.

Indes, bei einem so durch und durch vom Angelsächsischen her geprägten Phänomen wie dem Musical sollte sich der Anglist/Amerikanist für zuständig erklären. Das gleiche gilt für die Rock- und Pop-Musik, die enge Berührungspunkte mit dem vielleicht wichtigsten Teil des modernen Musicals, dem Rock-Musical, aufweist, da die rock- und pop-musikalischen Register auf dem Musiktheater ein Novum bedeuten und im Gegensatz zu Registern der europäischen Musiktraditionen Argumenten einer strengen vergleichenden Wertung entzogen sind. Genaue sprachliche und landeskundliche Kenntnisse sind häufig vonnöten und bei Musikwissenschaftlern, die sich inzwischen bei der Behandlung von Rockmusik und Musical am mutigsten vorgewagt haben, oft nur begrenzt vorhanden. Daß man sich allerdings gegenwärtig immer noch besser der Musikwissenschaft anvertraut als der Anglistik, zeigt das erst kürzlich erschienene Buch der Hamburger Musikwissenschaftler R. Flender und H. Rauhe mit dem Titel *Pop-Musik. Geschichte, Funktion, Wirkung, Ästhetik*.[1] Es dokumentiert in vorbildlichem Maße interdisziplinäres Arbeiten und bietet in gemeinverständlicher, niveauvoller Darstellung Information und theoretischen Zugriff, so daß nunmehr eine solide Forschung in Gang gesetzt werden kann, auch wenn bisweilen allzu glatt mit Kategorien der marxistischen Nach-Achtundsechzigerjahre, etwa den Begriffen einer trivialisierenden Warenästhetik gearbeitet wird. Die gelegentlichen Niveaueinbrüche, insbesondere da, wo es um detaillierte Analysen der *lyrics* geht, kehren hervor, daß komparatistisch-interdisziplinäres Arbeiten unvermeidbare Schwachstellen hat. Doch dies scheint der Preis dafür zu sein, daß man breit angelegte Forschung zu einer Gattung in Bewegung bringt, die wahrscheinlich zur zentralen theatralischen Gattung überhaupt avancieren dürfte, sofern die Künste auch weiterhin ernstmachen mit dem Bemühen, eine demokratische Ästhetik zu verwirklichen und die Quadratur des Kreises zu vollziehen, die darin angelegt ist, daß egalitäre und elitäre Wesensmerkmale ihre Gegensätzlichkeit verlieren. Trivialität und Raffinement zugleich, Rezipierbarkeit auf beiden Ebenen ohne essentiellen Verlust ließen sich als Ziele der Gattung des neuen Musicals ins Auge fassen. Daß diese Idealvorstellung überhaupt ernsthaft geäußert werden darf, gründet sich auf einige wenige Exemplare der Gattung Musical, die diesen utopisch klingenden Annäherungswert erreichen. *Hair* und *West Side Story* gehören dazu ebenso wie *Cabaret*, *Chorus Line* und alle Musicals von Rice/Lloyd Webber, in vorderster Linie aber *Evita*, dessen Werbeslogan "a giant among musicals" ausnahmsweise keine Übertreibung ist. Hier wurden Standards gesetzt und Erwartungen fundiert, an denen das Musical der achtziger Jahre gemessen werden muß.

II

Über das britische Musical des auslaufenden Jahrzehnts informiert am umsichtigsten das 1987 erschienene Buch eines Journalisten, des britischen Theaterkritikers Sheridan Morley, das den Untertitel trägt *The First Hundred Years of British Musical*. Ein implikationsreicher Titel, der voller Stolz auf Grund einer höchst positiven Gegenwartsdiagnose und einer nicht minder eindrucksvollen Bilanz mit Blick über ein Jahrhundert hinweg der Gewißheit Ausdruck verleiht, daß eine unterschätzte Gattung inzwischen so recht in Schwung gekommen sei und das Bisherige einen Aufbruch zu noch größeren Taten verheiße. Das Musical ist die Gattung der Zukunft; was bislang an Erfolgen vorliegt, wird zur vielversprechenden Vorleistung. Ferner aber ist eine verschmitzte Polemik im Untertitel angelegt. Denn daß das britische Musical bereits hundert Jahre währt, will manchen doch verwundern, der bisher auf der Binsenweisheit beharrte, das Musical sei keineswegs eine britische, sondern im Gegenteil eine ganz und gar US-amerikanische Gattung. Die Staaten, der Broadway und sein Musical gelten bis heute als Synonyma vor allem in der nicht-angelsächsischen Welt, die so eigentümlich musical-arm ist und sich von der genannten Synonymität nur mühsam freimachen kann. In einer Quiz-Sendung des ZDF wurde vor einiger Zeit über *Evita* und *Chess, Jesus Christ Superstar* und *Les Misérables, Cats, Joseph* und *Starlight Express* berichtet, kommentiert und examiniert. Dabei wurden die genannten Werke wiederholt als Broadway-Musicals apostrophiert, die man auch in Wien, London, Sydney und Berlin aufführe. Keiner der Experten, Testkandidaten oder Moderatoren sah eine Notwendigkeit darin hervorzuheben, daß diese Stücke zwar tatsächlich am Broadway in Szene gesetzt wurden, aber allesamt britischen Ursprungs sind. Der Kenner weiß seit Ende der siebziger Jahre, daß die nationale Anbindung der Gattung des Musicals an die Vereinigten Staaten überholt ist und daß man wie Morley mit nationalem Stolz sehr wohl vom britischen Musical sprechen darf. Dies ist aber auch in einem engeren Sinne als dem der Welterfolge, die auf britischem Boden entstanden, eine Charakterisierung mit einer nationalistischen Beimischung. *Englishness* ist ein Kriterium, das in letzter Zeit auch als wissenschaftliche Kategorie wieder häufig bemüht wird und nicht selten eine bewußte Neudefinition der englischen Kultur mit dem Ziel der Abschottung vom Allzu-Kosmopolitischen (dem alles Englischsprachige im Zuge einer sich anbahnenden Weltkultur ausgesetzt ist) zum Ziel hat. Morley gibt neben dem Stolz auf die Internationalität, die das britische Musical in phänomenaler Weise gewann, seine Wunschvorstellungen zu erkennen, daß ein Wandel eintreten und essentielle *Englishness* die Verwechslung mit dem Broadway-Musical unmöglich machen möge. Ein nationalbritisches Musical müsse Abstand nehmen von einer Entwicklung, die immer stärker auf Sensationen ausgerichtet sei und spezifische Qualitäten der britischen Kultur zugunsten einer eingeebneten und abgeschmackten Allerweltskultur zurücktreten lasse. Was ein solch elitärer Musicaltypus leisten soll, verrät der bisher hier verschwiegene Haupttitel des Morleyschen Buches. Er lautet: *Spread a Little Happiness*. Der Aktionsradius der Gattung wird darin beängstigend eng gezogen, in diesem Titel viel enger als Morley es in seinem Buch dann gottlob tatsächlich durchhält. Doch der nostalgische Grundtenor, die der Gattung zudefinierte Minimalfunktion, das sanfte Glück einer verflossenen Epoche, die so peinlich genau in die Thatcher-Ideologie paßt, verkürzt das Musical um die subversive Dimension, die es seit *Hair, Cabaret* und *West Side Story*, vor allem aber seit *Evita* hinzugewonnen hat. Dabei ist erstaunlich, daß Morley als Favoriten des ihm vorschwebenden idealen britischen Musical-Typs zwei Werke nennt, die alles andere als eskapistisch, oberschichtenspezifisch und alltagsfern zu sein scheinen. Er favorisiert zum einen ein den wenigsten bekanntes und zum anderen ein inzwischen nahezu weltweit bekanntes Musical; zum einen *The Hired Man* von 1984 und zum anderen *Blood Brothers* von 1983. Willy Russells *Blood Brothers* wurde 1988 neu inszeniert, ist gegenwärtig am Albery Theatre in London ein großer Erfolg, wurde in München und in Hamburg[2] so recht und schlecht aufgeführt und sollte Ende Oktober 1989 seine Broadway-Premiere erfahren, die allerdings bis heute nicht stattgefunden hat. Letzteres, die Broadway-Premiere, müßte Morley mächtig verwundern: denn seiner These zufolge haben die tatsächlich wertvollen, typisch englischen Musicals gar keine Chance, international zu wirken, da sie nicht broadwaygerecht (und das heißt wahrscheinlich nicht welthaltig genug oder auch zu provinziell in ihrem Zuschnitt) sind.

Extrempositionen nehmen für Morley zwei in der Tat qualitativ divergierende Musicaltypen ein. *Starlight Express* steht in Opposition zu *The Hired Man*; das lautstarke, schale Ausstattungsstück hebt sich scharf von einem Musicaltypus ab, der ein niveauvolles Sujet besitzt, einen genau angebbaren Problembestand zu erkennen gibt und dabei mit Hilfe ernstgemeinter Texte und einer in englischen Traditionen verwurzelten Musik rundum Teilhabe am britischen Erbe kundtut, soziales Bewußtsein zum Ausdruck bringt und andere Schichten im Zuschauer anspricht als stupides Amüsierbedürfnis:

> 1984 did [...] bring *The Hired Man*, Howard Goodall's marvellous setting of Melvin Bragg's novel about mining and farming life around the Lake District in the early years of the century. [...] there was the idea here of telling one family's domestic story against a huge background of World War I, pit disasters and the birth of trade unionism. [...] *The Hired Man* triumphed [...] because it took its inspiration not from the usual Broadway sources but instead from a quite different and very local tradition, in this case the choral work of Elgar.[3]

> [...] *The Hired Man* [...] came as a reminder that there remained the countryside music of a nation which can still take the Last Night of the Proms to its heart.[4]

Daß *The Hired Man* ein großer finanzieller Flop war und sich der musicalerfahrene Zuschauer gelegentlich peinlich berührt sah bei soviel Nostalgie, Sozialkitsch, Blut und Boden – eben all den mehr als verdächtigen Symptomen einer regressiven *Englishness* – kann Morley nicht dazu bewegen, sein Bewertungssystem in Frage zu stellen. Die großbürgerliche Elgar-Tradition und die *Last Night Prom Music*, die sich schon Festlandeuropäern schwer vermittelt und allgemein als britisches Kuriosum angesehen wird, soll ein Gegengewicht darstellen zu der Gattungstradition, für die der Name Broadway einsteht. Broadway aber ist alles, was nicht im engsten Sinne sentimentaler *Englishness* einverleibbar ist, sondern weitere Dimensionen im Blick hat, die den globalen Wirkungsradius des Musicals garantieren. Nicht Elgar und nicht die britische *Countryside Music* in Reinkultur, sondern letztere in Verschmelzung mit der Musik- und Körpersprache der nordamerikanischen Schwarzen vermochte diese weltweite Wirkungsmächtigkeit allererst zu leisten.

Es ist geschickt, *Starlight Express* als Gegenposition anzuprangern, denn niemand wird ernsthaft verteidigen wollen, was hinsichtlich der künstlerischen Qualität ganz am unteren Rande operiert. Kindische *lyrics*, etwa die ‚epochale‘ Verszeile "freight is great", und das sensationelle Rollerskating über mehrere Stockwerke hinweg bei einer dröhnenden Disco-Musik lassen keinen Zweifel daran, daß Ausstattung und Akustisches eine Plot-Idee oder gar eine im Text greifbare Konzeption zurückgedrängt haben. Der große Trevor Nunn äußert sich denn auch recht verlegen über seine Mitwirkung an der Show und gibt ironisch zu bedenken, daß man in Kürze wohl ein Unterwassermusical[5] anbieten müsse, wenn man der in *Starlight Express* eingeschlagenen Überbietungsstrategie auch weiterhin folgen wolle. Doch Nunn stieg nicht aus, machte weiter; auch er teilt die Überzeugung, daß gerade im Musical die neuesten technischen

Möglichkeiten der Pop- und Rockkultur einbezogen und zumindest erprobt werden sollten. Und wenn Morley insbesondere auf Dave Clarks von Cliff Richard initiiertes *Time* schlecht zu sprechen ist, hängt dies vor allem damit zusammen, daß der größte Mime des Jahrhunderts, Lord Olivier[6], als holographischer Geistersuperschädel von mehreren Metern Durchmesser bereit war, verblasene Äonentexte zu rezitieren und sich (imposant und gruselig zugleich) dabei in jede Gesichtspore und jede Mundschleimhautfalte schauen zu lassen. Olivier und Nunn widersetzen sich den in beiden Fällen vorwiegend peinlichen Experimenten aus guten, allerdings kaum flugs zu erläuternden Gründen nicht, auch wenn Elgar und der Lake District (Schlüsselreize britisch-nationaler Gemütserregungskunst) hier als Orientierungsmarke aus dem Blick verloren wurden.

III

Im Klartext gesprochen richtet sich Morleys Polemik gegen einen bedeutenden Zeitgenossen, ohne den es überhaupt müßig wäre, im größeren Stil über das britische Musical nachzudenken, es sei denn als eines freundlichen, liebenswürdigen Nebenzweiges der englischen Theaterproduktion, wie er etwa mit dem Namen Noël Coward verbunden ist. So wie ohne Boris Becker deutsches Tennis auch heute noch so nebensächlich wäre wie vor zehn Jahren, wäre das britische Musical ein Mauerblümchen ohne Andrew Lloyd Webber. So heißt denn vom britischen nicht nur, sondern vom internationalen Musical reden: von Lloyd Webber reden. Was ihm Morley von Herzen zugute halten kann, ist die Tatsache, daß der Erfolgskomponist als Produzent *The Hired Man* allererst ermöglichte und daß er dabei eine große finanzielle Schlappe erlitt, die er 1984 noch nicht so leicht verkraftete, wie es ihm heute als stabilem Aktienhalter und Besitzer des Palace Theatre möglich ist. Ginge es hier um das Musical der siebziger Jahre, wäre zwar von Lloyd Webber als dem bedeutendsten Repräsentanten dieses Jahrzehnts zu reden; doch auch *Tommy* von The Who und Richard O'Brians *Rocky Horror Show* boten alternative Stile, die man ebenfalls als repräsentativ ansehen kann. Die achtziger Jahre allerdings stehen in fataler Weise im Banne Lloyd Webbers, und es wäre hier eigentlich vonnöten, seine Zentralposition[7] in aller Sorgfalt Punkt für Punkt auseinanderzulegen und nachzuzeichnen, wie alles übrige im Umfeld des Gegenwartsmusicals stets auf diese überragende Figur zugeordnet ist, was etwa in Stilplagiaten zum Ausdruck kommt. Ohne die generelle Wertorientierung Morleys auch nur ansatzweise gutheißen zu können, muß man seine Skepsis gegenüber Lloyd Webber in den achtziger Jahren teilen.

Dazu wäre thesenhaft festzuhalten: Der Rang Lloyd Webbers als Theaterkomponist ist eng an seine Zusammenarbeit mit Tim Rice gebunden. *Joseph, Jesus*

Christ und *Evita* sind bis heute die wirklich großen Leistungen des begabten Musikers.[8] Vom Rang der Textvorlage hängt der Rang seiner Musik ganz entscheidend ab. Konzeptuell ist Lloyd Webber von nur mäßiger Begabung; allenfalls hat er Instinkt für den Marktwert seiner Produkte. Einblick in die Komplexität künstlerischer Faktoren des Gesamtkunstwerks Musical besitzt er kaum. Allein ist er bestenfalls ein Sullivan ohne Gilbert. Die Trennung von Rice hat die Gattung des Musicals von ihrer Erfolgsbahn abgebracht. Lloyd Webber ist immer nur so gut als Komponist, wie es das Textbuch und das in ihm angelegte Gesamtkonzept der Show ist. Nur zwei der inzwischen zahlreichen musiktheatralischen Werke Lloyd Webbers in den achtziger Jahren können neben dem bestehen, was er zuvor mit Tim Rice gemeinsam geschaffen hatte. Beide Werke sind Vertonungen klassischer Texte. Einmal ist von T. S. Eliots *Cats* die Rede, das als Musical in manchem zu kurz greift, aber *sui generis* wohl als genuine Variante gewertet werden darf; und zum anderen ist es das *Requiem*, zu dem es als Konzertwerke zahlreiche riesengroße Vorbilder gibt, das aber nach Lloyd Webbers Plan auch eines Tages szenisch umgesetzt werden soll. Daß letzteres gelingen könnte, lehrt die Ballett-Version der Bachschen Matthäuspassion von John Neumeier. Beide klassischen Texte indes sind lyrischer Natur; und nur mit einem hohen Aufwand an tänzerischer Umsetzung ließe sich die Metamorphose des *Requiem* in eine quasidramatische Bühnenshow bewerkstelligen. Der Rang der Vorlage inspirierte auch den Komponisten zu im Detail erstaunlichen Leistungen, die man in dem weiteren Œuvre der verbleibenden achtziger Jahre nur noch ganz vereinzelt findet. *Starlight Express, Song and Dance, Phantom of the Opera* und kürzlich *Aspects of Love* sind von den Vorlagen her dem infantilen Geschmack des Komponisten angemessen. Denn schon die Kätzchen-Kinderverse und die Puffpuff-Eisenbahnstory machen ja deutlich, in welchen Phantasiewelten sich Lloyd Webber am liebsten bewegt. Gleiches bezeugt sich in der schlichten Gruseloper mit Neuschwanstein-Pomp *Phantom* und schließlich in der völlig jeder modernen Ausrichtung abgekehrten Bildmoritat aus dem gehobenen Milieu der Späten Georgians, die auf der Basis von David Garnetts eher unbekanntem Text *Aspects of Love* (1955) die hochkultivierte und von der Alltagsrealität weit abgekoppelte Lebensweise der Bloomsbury-Clique und ihrer kostbaren Kunst- und Erosprobleme ungemein prächtig, vom Bühnenbild her eminent kulinarisch ins Werk setzt, musikalisch aber in altbackener, schmachtender Filmmusik oder einem Puccini-/Britten-Verschnitt aufgeht, die es einem Lloyd Webber-Fan und Musiktheaterliebhaber schwer macht, anders als apathisch auf seinem Sessel auszuharren.

IV

Über *Aspects of Love* konnte Morley noch nichts sagen: *Englishness* freilich, im Sinne der alten Klassengesellschaft, ist so wundervoll repräsentiert, daß sein

Werturteil möglicherweise positiv ausfiele. Doch sicher ist dies keineswegs, – schlägt Morleys Herz doch auch für ein Musical, das in einer Außenseiterposition immer mehr Beachtung findet, *The Hired Man* zumindest gleichgestellt wird und nun (wie seit Monaten angekündigt) hoffentlich bald am Broadway beweisen darf, wie ein internationales Publikum auf ein Werk reagiert, das alle die positiven Eigenschaften zu besitzen scheint, die man dem modernen Musical schlechthin attestieren möchte. Morley hatte gegen Rice und Webber argumentiert, mit solch bekannten Stories wie der vom Ägyptischen Joseph, der Passion Jesu Christi und der jedermann vertrauten Polit-Revue von Eva Duarte Peron[9] sei es ein leichtes, international Furore zu machen. Mit einer larmoyanten Provinztragödie aus Liverpool hingegen könne man dies kaum zustandebringen. Nun erweist sich Willy Russells *Blood Brothers* in der zweiten Inszenierung von 1988 nach einer bereits ersten erfolgreichen Phase der Produktion mit Barbara Dickson im Globe von 1983/84 nicht nur als West End-Erfolg, sondern wird auch von *Plays International* seit Monaten an die Spitze der empfehlenswerten Londoner Shows gestellt. Zieht man in Betracht, daß Willy Russell mit *Educating Rita* in der Bühnen- wie der Filmversion große Beachtung fand und sein neuester Wurf, das Ein-Frau-Stück *Shirley Valentine*, nicht nur mehrfach in Großbritannien, sondern auch am Broadway Triumphe feiert, gegenwärtig als Filmversion in die Lichtspielhäuser kommt und auch im deutschen Sprachraum (Berlin, Konstanz) vor entzückten Zuschauern in der Art frauenpolitischen Kabaretts mit hohem Identifikationsangebot abläuft, wird man dem ehrgeizigsten Projekt des Autors Russell bei solch einhelliger Zustimmung einen großen Vertrauenszuschuß gewähren müssen. Ein Stückeschreiber, der sich schon als junger Mann im Song-Schreiben und Komponieren geübt hatte, wagt sich an ein Musical und beschreibt launig in einer gut dreiseitigen Einleitung *I Want to Write a Musical*, wie dornig der Weg dorthin war und wie ungläubig man ihm immer dann begegnete, wenn die Frage aufkam: "'Ah. And who's writing the music?' Feebly, apologetically I'd whisper, 'Me'. 'Pardon?' 'Me … me…'" Daraufhin war die Reaktion stets "a sickly, sympathetic nod" und ein sofortiger Fluchtversuch des Gesprächspartners.[10] In der Tat nimmt Russell hier eine seltene Position ein. Sein eigener Librettist zu sein, ist rar in der Geschichte des Musiktheaters. Monolithisch steht Wagner da. Namen wie Lorenzo da Ponte und Boito sind nicht ganz so umrißgenau an Mozart und Verdi gebunden wie Gilbert an Sullivan. Doch wenngleich die Ästhetik des Librettos in den Anfängen steckt und man immer noch auf die kluge Arbeit von Peter Hacks[11] angewiesen ist, geht soviel aus der Praxis der letzten Jahre ebenso wie derjenigen der Musikgeschichte hervor, daß ein ungeeignetes Libretto und analog dazu schwache *lyrics* unausweichlich zu einer dürftigen Musik führen und man nur über erhöhten Aufwand durch Bühnenbild, Showeffekte und Ballett diese Schwächen mühsam wettmachen kann. *Starlight Express* und *Time* sind dafür in den letzten Jahren der klarste Beweis. Russell indessen schreibt ein

Libretto nach allen Regeln der Kunst; das erkennt man daran, daß es keinerlei Mühe macht, mit ihm nach Professorenart zu verfahren.

Morley nennt *Blood Brothers* eine "folk opera".[12] Die erste Fassung, die sich musikalisch spröder gab als die heutige, hätte man eher eine Rockoper genannt. Das wären sinnvolle Benennungen von Journalisten. Der Literaturwissenschaftler indes geht nicht zu weit, wenn er *Blood Brothers* eine Balladenoper nennt und sie damit in eine Tradition einreiht, die mit Gays *Beggar's Opera* beginnt und im 18. Jahrhundert eine Fülle von Nachahmern findet. Sie wandelt sich im 19. Jahrhundert unter den spezifischen Bedingungen einer bürgerlichen Gesellschaft zur "Savoy Opera" Gilberts und Sullivans (die Ballade als Gattung ist bei Gilbert häufig Vorstufe zum Libretto einerseits und Arien-Matrix in den einzelnen *comic operas* andererseits), stellt in Brecht/Weill auch weltanschaulich und theaterästhetisch teils im Rückgriff auf Gay, teils in Varianten wie *Mahagonny* oder *Happy End* Paradigmata für das Drama der Moderne bereit und schafft schließlich auf textlich, programmatisch und musikalisch noch anspruchsvollere (vielleicht prätentiösere) Weise in dem Gemeinschaftswerk von Edward Bond und Hans Werner Henze *We Come to the River* die proletarisch-marxistische Agitprop-Oper, die paradoxerweise nur an den feinsten Adressen wie der Royal Opera Covent Garden und der Deutschen Oper Berlin vor allererlesenstem Publikum mit Expertengeschmack aufgeführt werden konnte. Auf der Ebene, auf der man heutzutage vernünftigerweise die Balladenoper ansiedeln möchte, scheint sie sich seit Oktober 1989 am Londoner Royal Court Theatre eine neue Chance zu geben. Dort stellt Ian Dury mit *Apples* sich selbst in einem betont bescheiden dimensionierten Rockmusical mit redlichem Text und einer seinen Alben entsprechenden musikalischen Mittellage vor.

Die Balladenoper gehört zu den engagierten Bühnengattungen, sie steht oppositionell zur Haupt- und Staatsaktion der feudalen Mythen- oder Bibeloper, wie sie zur Entstehungszeit der Gattung von Händel und Purcell repräsentiert wurde. Das engagierte Element ist *Blood Brothers* deutlich eingezeichnet; schließlich spielt die Handlung in Liverpool und seinem Proletariermilieu, das ja bereits vor zwanzig Jahren britische Provinzialität mit urbaner und mundaner Subkultur in Verbindung gebracht hatte und mit den Beatles einen vorrangigen Platz in der modernen Musikgeschichte einnehmen konnte. Nur Spezialisten erinnern sich daran, daß Willy Russell zu Anfang seiner Karriere 1975 ein kurzlebiges Stück über die Beatles mit dem Titel *John Paul George Ringo ... And Bert* auf die Bühne gebracht und damit früh am Mythos der Liverpooler Weltstars mitgewirkt hatte. Liverpool als Erfahrungshorizont spielt auch in *Shirley Valentine* eine entscheidende Rolle und scheint einem weltweiten Publikum als Folie für eine sozialanalytische Komödie angemessen zu sein.

Blood Brothers ist bei aller Komik und allem kabarettistischen Charme eher ein Melodrama, die übersteuerte Form der Tragödie, über der der Schatten der

Ausweglosigkeit liegt. Während die Tradition der Balladenoper eher den Triumph des gerissenen Gauners in den Mittelpunkt stellt und mit heiteren Konfliktlösungen arbeitet, die bei Gay gewaltsam durch einen *coup de théâtre*, bei Gilbert und Sullivan durch kühnes *topsyturvy* herbeigeführt werden, macht Russell Ernst mit dem Balladengeschehen, das getreu den berühmten Vorlagen wie *Edward* und *Sir Patrick Spens* in düsterer Tragik endet. Schon im Vorspann wird die tragische Lösung vorweggenommen, so daß über die dumpfe Grundstimmung der präsentierten Vorgänge trotz aller zwischengefügten Fröhlichkeit beim Zuschauer kein Zweifel aufkommt. Die in linken Tagen so vehement geführte Debatte über den Vorrang von Milieu und Vererbung wird abermals zugunsten der Milieutheorie in einem klassischen Laboratoriumsversuch vorgeführt.

Die junge oberflächliche Mrs. Johnston ist bereits Mitte Zwanzig mit einer nicht genannten Zahl von Kindern gesegnet, die sie kaum ernähren kann und die das Jugendamt mit Sorge im Alltag beobachtet, zumal sich der Erzeuger aus der Verantwortung gestohlen und mit einer jüngeren Frau eine neue Liaison begonnen hat. Ein Zwillingspärchen allerdings läßt er vor dessen Geburt als Erinnerungsstück zurück, so daß Mrs. Johnston nun in Panik gerät, trotz des neuen Jobs als Haushaltshilfe, den Mrs. Lyons ihr anbietet. Mrs. Lyons sehnt sich seit Jahren vergeblich nach einem Kind; es entsteht das Psychogramm einer gutsituierten und wohlgebildeten Frau John aus Gerhart Hauptmanns berühmtem Theaterstück *Die Ratten* von 1911. Wie Frau John der polnischen Straßendirne Piperkarcka das Baby abkauft, verfährt auch Mrs. Lyons mit dem einen der beiden Zwillingsbrüder. Was wort- und geschehnisreich in Hauptmanns Stück ausgearbeitet wird, kann der Autor Russell in seinem Genus nur holzschnittartig umreißen, so wie es der Ballade und ihren Schwestergattungen entspricht. Die psychologische Komplexität dieses Konfliktes drängt sich nicht nach vorne, ist aber im ausgehenden 20. Jahrhundert nach der langen Tradition des naturalistischen Theaters und der Kenntnis der Tiefenpsychologie ohnehin für jedermann sofort abrufbar. Der Zwilling Mickey bleibt bei seiner tapferen, leichtfertigen, grob-herzlichen Mutter im Proletariermilieu; Eddie wächst bei der Familie Lyons zu einem liebenswürdigen Musterknaben heran. Gelegentlich treffen die Brüder zusammen und sind voneinander fasziniert. Die Gegenwelten sind für die Jungen jeweils die Traum- und Glückswelten. Die bohrende Schuld beider Mütter kompliziert den Umgang der füreinander anfänglich fremden Brüder, die sich bald jedoch durch ein Blutsbruderschaftsritual instinktiv doppelt aneinanderketten und das in der atavistischen Zeremonie verstärken, was die Natur ohnehin für sie vorgesehen hat. Mrs. Lyons wechselt den Wohnort und hat einstweilen Ruhe vor Verfolgung; Mrs. Johnston tut es ihr unwissentlich irgendwann nach. Die Brüder entdecken sich als Freunde wieder und verleben ein paar erfüllte Teenagerjahre, die vor allem von der aufkeimenden Erotik beider auf ihre Art inhibierten Jungmänner und ihrer gemeinsamen Vorliebe für das gleiche Girl Linda geprägt sind. Oxbridge und ein stupides Arbeitsleben im Betrieb trennen die Jungen sodann nicht nur räumlich voneinander. Mickey wird arbeitslos und gerät unfreiwillig in eine Raubmordgeschichte. Eddie macht als Wirtschaftler und Verwaltungsmann Karriere. Die Statusdifferenz läßt sich immer schwerer überbrücken. Mickey wird im Gefängnis schwermütig und tablettenabhängig; Eddie nimmt ihm Linda, die inzwischen Mickeys Frau geworden war, als zeitweilige Geliebte weg und ruiniert damit den Blutsbruder völlig. Mickey tötet in einem Anfall von Eifersucht Eddie; die Polizei erschießt den verzweifelten Mickey. Ein Tragödienlamento sondergleichen bestimmt das letzte Bild. Am nachhaltigsten haftet beim Zuschauer eine der letzten Sequenzen, die der antik-klassischen Anagnorisis entspricht. Mrs. Johnston eilt zum Tatort und schreit: "Mickey. Don't shoot Eddie. He's your brother. You had a twin brother. I couldn't afford to keep both of you. His mother couldn't have kids. I agreed to give one of you away." [13] Dann kommt der Moment, wo allen im Auditorium (außer denen, die vorher schon aus Selbstschutz mit Kichern begonnen haben) unabweisbar die Tränen in Augen und Kehle drängen (wie ästhetisch legitimiert dies auch immer sein mag): "*Mickey* (something that begins deep down inside him): You! (Screaming) Why didn't you give me away! (He stands glaring at her, almost uncontrollable with rage) I could have been ... I could have been him!" [14] Die Chance, in einem günstigeren Milieu das positive Spiegelbild seiner selbst geworden zu sein, ist auf dem Höhepunkt der physischen Erregung so stark, daß sich beim Herumfuchteln mit dem Revolver der Schuß löst und den Bruder Eddie tötet. Eine andere als die böse Endlösung kann Russell nicht anbieten.

An diesem Punkt fällt *Blood Brothers* wahrscheinlich hinter die Standards der Gattung zurück, indem sich der heillose Balladenschluß der lyrisch-episch-dramatischen Vorbildgattung in der Opernvariante wieder festsetzt. Gay sowie Gilbert und Sullivan arbeiteten mit utopischen Lösungen oder Nonsens- und Scheinlösungen. Die Lösung in *Blood Brothers* bleibt aus, falls die unmittelbar nach dem tragischen Ereignis vorgetragene Überlegung des Erzählers, in zwei Zeilen und im Paarreim verbunden, nicht als Quintessenz verstanden werden soll:

And do we blame superstition for what came to pass?
Or could it be, what we the English, have come to know as class? (S. 158)

Diese hier ganz knapp angedeutete Perspektive, die sich gegen die im Thatcher-England eher verstärkte Klassenstruktur der Gesellschaft wendet und damit ein Thema des Filmemachers Derek Jarman (*The Last of England*) anreißt, verliert sich aber wieder im Balladenton, der ins allgemeine gewendet ist und eher das Fatum der menschlichen Existenz beschwört als gezielte Kritik plaziert und statt auf Heillosigkeit auf Heilung sinnt:

Did you ever hear the story of the Johnston twins,
As like each other as two new pins,
How one was kept and one given away,
How they were born, and they died, on the self same day?

Der *narrator* als Medium des engagierten epischen Theaters, der im Kommentar das Verständnis lenken und Lösungen suggerieren könnte, erschöpft seine Funktion im Gestus des Zeigens, von dem Brecht sprach, obwohl sich das so einfach gehaltene Geschehen selbst expliziert, so daß eine neutrale Zeigefunktion eher redundant wirken muß. Das Lamento der überragenden Gestalt des Musicals, Mrs. Johnston, deren Klage Anfang und Ende wie einen expliziten Rahmen bestimmt, gibt die Charakteristika des Musicals *Blood Brothers* als Balladenoper deutlicher zu erkennen als die über das Stück verteilten Partien des Bänkelsängers. Sie singt:

Tell me, it's not true
Say, it's just a story.
Something on the news
Tell me it's not true.
Though it's here before me,
Say, it's just a dream,
Say, it's just a scene
From an old movie of years ago,
From an old movie of Marilyn Monroe. (S. 159)

Im Angesicht der Fakten wird Trost in der Kunstwelt gesucht, der Welt der Dichter, die von Platon bis Nietzsche dafür getadelt wurde, daß sie zuviel lüge. Stories, Träume, Filmszenen sind schicksalhafte Zuspitzungen ohne lebensweltliches Korrelat: so zumindest ist die Rezeptionsweise von Kunst, höherer oder niedrigerer, speziell da, wo sie eskapistisch eingesetzt und nur unter der Voraussetzung solcher die Welt verschönernden Qualitäten überhaupt angenommen wird. Da das Musical von Russell so angelegt ist, daß keinerlei Lösungsansatz geboten wird, sondern allein Ohnmacht konstatierbar bleibt, Ausweglosigkeit, die sich am natürlichsten und sinnvollsten in Tränen und ein paar tiefen Seufzern Luft verschafft, bleibt nur der Verweis auf die Allgemeinheit des Falles, seine Paradigmenhaftigkeit, die in der *conditio humana* gründet und auch dann nicht erledigt wäre, wenn die britische Klassengesellschaft verschwände und Aberglaube dem Licht der Vernunft wiche. Klage über die Tragik menschlicher Verstrickung statt Erweckung kritischen Potentials, das Lösungen anstrebt, wird zur dominanten Haltung des Musicals *Blood Brothers*.

V

Die Bedeutung, die Marilyn Monroe dabei zukommt, hebt dieses Wesensmerkmal unmißverständlich hervor. Mehrere dutzend Male ist von dem berühmten Filmstar die Rede; ja, sie wird zur Zentralfigur des Stückes, obwohl sie vordergründig mit dem Plot nichts zu tun hat. Das Anschauungsfeld, das die Monroe aufzubauen hilft, ist so stark, daß man glaubt, wie in einem Vexierbild über sie an die geheime Botschaft des Musicals heranzukommen; und es war gewiß kein belangloser Einfall bei der ersten Produktion von *Blood Brothers*, auf einen Gazevorhang, den der Zuschauer vor Vorstellungsbeginn und in der Pause betrachten konnte, das allbekannte Lächeln der Monroe im Großformat auf sich wirken zu lassen. Mrs. Johnston vergleicht zunächst sich selber in ihrer Jungmädchenzeit mit Marilyn. Sodann ist die Geliebte ihres treulosen Mannes der Monroe ähnlich. Mickey, der Beruhigungstabletten schluckt und in Verzweiflung verharrt, wirkt ebenso wie Marilyn Monroe:

> It seems like jail's sent him off the rails
> Just like Marilyn Monroe
> His mind's gone dancing
> Can't stop dancing...
>
> He sits and counts the days to go
> And treats his ills with daily pills
> Just like Marilyn Monroe. (S. 150)

Marilyn fungiert als Analogon für alle Lebenssituationen eines mit den Nöten des Proletariermilieus kämpfenden Einzelwesens, als Mythos des Alltags, der diese Lebenssituation deuten hilft und sämtliche Facetten abzudecken scheint. Auch die Monroe mußte erst aus kleinstem Milieu aufsteigen.[15] Sie war Mickey und Eddie zugleich. Sie war schön, begehrt, weltberühmt, erfolgreich, von großer Intelligenz, aber selbst in luxuriösem Umfeld auch tieftraurig und unglücklich ohne ersichtlichen Grund. Man ist verleitet, Andy Warhols serielle Siebdrucke der Monroe mit hundertfacher Abschattung und divergierender Farbgebung ein und derselben Fotografie als heuristisches Modell der Pop-Art für das Rockmusical *Blood Brothers* heranzuziehen.

Aber was für ein Paradigma gibt sie denn ab, wenn sie von Russell wie der Kehrreim zu jeder Balladenstrophe, sprich Szene, und jeder einzelnen freudigen oder schmerzlichen Zuspitzung im Stück die Quintessenz zu formulieren in der Lage ist? Marilyn überwand ja die Klassengrenzen: sie entkam dem schädigenden Milieu. Und alles Geld dieser Welt und aller Ruhm vermochten sie nicht zu trösten? Hatte sie doch die ganze Welt gewonnen und dennoch Schaden genommen an ihrer Seele? Sozialkitsch und triviale politische Slogans, wie man sie nach 1970 so reichlich parat hatte, fördern die Einsicht im vorliegenden Fall

nicht. Die Monroe als Refrain in Russells Balladenoper widerlegt alles das mit
Macht, was man sich als Sozialreform in den siebziger Jahren blauäugig vor-
gestellt hatte. Sie ist unfreiwillig das Gegenparadigma zu Russells Paradigma
vom menschen- und glücksmordenden Milieu der in sozialer Not lebenden
Mitglieder der Gesellschaft auf der einen und dem Schlaraffenland, das aus
Wohlstand stammt und glückliche Karriere im Anschluß an ein Oxbridge-
Studium garantiert, auf der anderen Seite. Russell bringt hier die Diskussion
ungewollt ein tüchtiges Stück voran. Doch diese täte eher der Bundesrepublik
Deutschland gut. Ob indes die fortschreitende Verelendung großer Bereiche im
Thatcher-England solch differenzierter Lektion schon bedarf, muß eher in
Zweifel gezogen werden.

Anmerkungen

1 Darmstadt, 1989.
2 Vgl. G. Knopf: „Blutsbrüder. Mißglückter Musical-Einstand am Deutschen Schau-
   spielhaus". *Das Musical* H. 19, 1989, 14f.
3 Morley, Sh.: *Spread a Little Happiness. The First Hundred Years of the British Musical.*
   New York, 1987, S. 203.
4 Morley: *Spread a Little Happiness*, S. 210.
5 Vgl. die *Souvenir Brochure* der Londoner *Starlight Express*-Produktion.
6 Morley: *Spread a Little Happiness*, S. 212.
7 Vgl. u. a. G. McKnight: *Andrew Lloyd Webber. A Biography.* London, 1984; J.
   Mantle: *Fanfare. The Unauthorized Biography of Andrew Lloyd Webber.* London,
   1989; M. Walsh: *Andrew Lloyd Webber. His Life and Works.* London, 1989; F.
   Hirsch: *Harold Prince and the American Musical Theatre.* Cambridge 1989, S. 157–
   173 ("The British connection").
8 Vgl. A. Geraths: „Entmythologisierung und Komik: Lernangebote in den Rock-
   Musicals von Tim Rice and Andrew Lloyd Webber, besonders in 'Joseph and the
   Amazing Technicolor Dreamcoat'". *anglistik & englischunterricht. 17. Learning
   English Humour II.* Trier, 1982, S. 51–81.
9 "[...] Rice and Lloyd Webber fell back on such ready-made sources as the Bible
   [...] or the Life of Eva Peron. [...] it was precisely that quality of pre-sold famili-
   arity which made them acceptable [...]." (Morley: *Spread a Little Happiness*, S. 10).
10 Russell, W.: *Educating Rita, Stags & Hens and Blood Brothers.* London, New York,
   1986, S. 73.
11 Hacks, P.: „Versuch über das Libretto". – In ders.: *Oper.* Düsseldorf, 1976, S. 201–
   298.
12 Morley: *Spread a Little Happiness*, S. 202.
13 Russell: *Educating Rita, ...*, S. 157f.
14 Ebd., S. 158.
15 Vgl. u. a. N. Mailer: *Marilyn.* New York 1973.

Therese Fischer-Seidel, Gießen

Mythos und sein Wandel in den Dramen Harold Pinters:
Von *The Birthday Party* zu *Mountain Language*

Da die Einteilung der Literatur in Jahrhunderte und Dekaden bekanntlich eine Erfindung der Kritiker und nicht der Autoren ist, muß man mit aller gebotenen Vorsicht zu Werke gehen, wenn man etwas über das Werk des nach Beckett bedeutendsten englischen Dramatikers in den 80er Jahren sagen will. Nur vorsichtig läßt sich umreißen, was vier Grundtendenzen der Entwicklung zu sein scheinen, die das Werk Pinters in den 80er Jahren genommen hat.

1. Die dramatische Produktion Harold Pinters in den 80er Jahren (d. h. von 1980–1988) scheint von einer Wende zum Politischen geprägt, wie auch Aussagen des Autors selbst nahelegen:[1] *The Hothouse*, 1958 geschrieben, wurde 1980 erstmals zur Aufführung freigegeben. Es geht darin um die Mißstände in einer Nervenheilanstalt. *Other Places*, aus drei Dramen bestehend, wurde 1982 uraufgeführt. Von diesen drei Dramen verweist besonders *Victoria Station* (1982) am Beispiel des Funktaxifahrers und seiner Kommandozentrale auf konkretes politisches Potential, nämlich die wechselseitige Abhängigkeit, die zwischen dem Bestimmer (Controller) und dem Ausführenden (Driver) besteht. In *One for the Road* (1984) geht es, oberflächlich gesehen, um Mord, Vergewaltigung und Folter. Auch die Wiederaufnahme von *The Birthday Party* im Jahre 1987 in einer Fernsehinszenierung, in der Pinter eine Hauptrolle spielte, scheint die „Wiederentdeckung des Politischen" durch Pinter zu bestätigen, da gerade in diesem Drama Machtstrukturen des Totalitarismus, konkret sogar der nationalsozialistischen Gewaltherrschaft, abgebildet gesehen wurden. *Mountain Language* (1988), schließlich, erscheint schon von seinem Ambiente her – es spielt vor und in einem Gefängnis – als die deutlichste Verkörperung der politischen Dimension.

2. Jedoch ist die sogenannte „Wende zum Politischen" – literaturtheoretisch gesprochen – der Versuch, ein Problem zu lösen, das Pinter einmal selbst formulierte, nämlich jenes, daß mit zunehmendem Bekanntheitsgrad die Schwierigkeiten des Schreibens steigen. Die Prägung eines Adjektivs wie "Pinteresque" sei alles andere als hilfreich für ihn. Ein Autor von der Bekanntheit Pinters muß sein eigenes Werk und dessen Rezeption mit ins Kalkül ziehen.[2]

3. Die „Selbstrezeption" ist Teil des Kommunikationsprozesses zwischen Autor und Leser/Zuschauer. In allen Dramen der 80er Jahre finden sich Selbst-

zitate und Referenzen auf Pinters eigenes, früheres Werk. So ist sogar der Titel von *One for the Road* wörtliches Zitat aus *The Birthday Party*.

4. Während die Dramen von *The Birthday Party* bis zu *Betrayal* hauptsächlich Auseinandersetzungen mit den formalen Problemen der Gattung sind und als Ausfaltung eines virtuellen Systems der Gattungsdiskussion zu verstehen sind, findet sich in den Dramen der 80er Jahre wieder deutlicher eine Hinwendung zu Inhalten. Es werden etwa Mechanismen der Macht und der Kontrolle auch durch Sprachregelungen dargestellt. Dies geschieht aber in einer Weise, die sie in einer geradezu archetypischen Allgemeingültigkeit zeigt. Während Mythos in den Dramen bis *Betrayal* als Gattungsstruktur zu verstehen ist, ist Mythos in *Mountain Language* archetypisch-inhaltlich gefaßt.

Meine Ausführungen werden drei Teile haben: Der erste wird sich mit der Mythenkonzeption in den Dramen Pinters bis 1978 (*Betrayal*) beschäftigen, der zweite wird als Folie für die Entwicklung in den 80er Jahren eine etwas eingehendere Betrachtung des mythenparodistischen Verfahrens in *The Birthday Party* liefern und der dritte wird schließlich *Mountain Language* zum Gegenstand haben.

Zunächst gilt es aber den Begriff Mythos, wie er hier gebraucht ist, zu definieren und zu erklären, inwiefern er auf die Dramen Pinters anwendbar ist. *Mythos*, nämlich *plot* oder Handlungsstruktur, wurde von Aristoteles als der wichtigste Bestandteil der Tragödie definiert. Mythos war aber als Inhalt zugleich auch das allen Zuschauern der Tragödie Bekannte, der gemeinsame Erwartungshorizont, der Inhalt der Mythen. Der gemeinsame Erwartungshorizont, den der britische Dramatiker bei seiner Kulturgemeinschaft voraussetzen kann, sind bestimmte Vorstellungen von der formalen Struktur der Gattung Drama. Zu diesen Vorstellungen gehört im aristotelischen Verständnis ein logisch-kausaler Ablauf. Bei Aristoteles ist davon die Rede, daß sich die Handlung mit Wahrscheinlichkeit und Notwendigkeit zu entwickeln habe. Dies bedeutet aber, daß auch die Handlung und die als ihre Funktion verstandenen Charaktere im Rückschlußverfahren verständlich und erklärbar sind.

Dies gilt nicht nur für die klassischen oder auch klassizistischen Formen der Gattung des Dramas, sondern auch für die epigonal aus jenen entstandenen; zu den Epigonalformen gehört das analytische Drama Ibsens ebenso wie das *well-made play*, die beide in der Moderne seit dem ausgehenden 19. Jahrhundert an die Stelle des klassischen Handlungsdramas getreten sind. Auch der Einakter, mit seiner Enthüllungsstruktur und der Betonung der einzelnen Situation anstelle einer Abfolge von Situationen wie im klassischen Handlungsdrama, ist als eine solche Nachfolgegattung zu verstehen.[3] Pinter ruft diese Strukturtypen parodistisch auf, variiert den Typus und macht diese Variation seinem neuen Darstellungsziel dienstbar.

Parodie als charakteristischer Zug der Moderne – wie auch an der darstellenden Kunst sichtbar[4] – ist dabei jenes Darstellungsverfahren, das den Aufruf von Strukturtypen und ihre Variation zur Bildung neuer literarischer Strukturen benutzt, aber nicht zwangsläufig auf die Zerstörung der benutzten oder aufgerufenen Strukturen abzielt. Im Falle des Pinterschen Werks – vielleicht bis zu *Betrayal* (1978) – sind Ziel und Verfahren der Parodie zwar nicht identisch, aber doch deutlich miteinander verknüpft. Die Gattungsmuster, die aufgerufen werden, sind die Mittel, ihre Dementierung ist eines der zentralen Ziele des parodistischen Verfahrens.

I. Mythos im dramatischen Werk Pinters bis zu Betrayal: *Von der christlichen Mythologie zur Gattungsparodie*

Die Dramen Pinters bis zu *Betrayal* sind zu verstehen als eine systematische Auseinandersetzung mit den Formen und Kategorien der Gattung. Aus einem möglichen Gesamtspektrum werden Handlung, Personen, Zeit, Raum, Wirklichkeit als Teilaspekte herausgelöst. Bereits der *Dramentitel* deutet an, welcher Aspekt dies jeweils ist. *The Birthday Party, The Caretaker, The Lover* thematisieren den Charakter und seine Darstellung im Drama. *The Lover* ist ebenso wie *The Collection* eine Parodie des naturalistischen Einakters und seiner Enthüllungsstruktur. *The Collection* hebt den Wahrheits- und Wirklichkeitsbegriff in den Titel. *The Homecoming* konzentriert sich auf die Kategorie der Handlung und bedient sich parodistisch des klassischen aristotelischen Handlungsdramas. Die Kategorie der Zeit wird in *Old Times* zum Thema; *Old Times* ist zugleich als Dementierung des analytischen Dramas zu verstehen. *No Man's Land* greift die Kategorie des Raumes auf und rekurriert in der Selbstparodie auf das neuere, etwa von Beckett und Pinter selbst etablierte, situative Drama als Gattung. Das Spektrum wird mit *Betrayal* vervollständigt. Dieses Drama thematisiert wiederum den Wahrheitsbegriff und weitet die Diskussion diesmal auch auf die Informationsvermittlung auf der Autor-Leser-Ebene aus. Dies wird im Titel angezeigt; *Betrayal* ist auch als Metapher für die Enttäuschung der Zuschauererwartung zu verstehen. Das parodistisch verwendete Gattungsmuster ist hier das *well-made play*, die Eheintrige.

The Homecoming wurde von der Kritik als die Erfüllung der klassischen Form des aristotelischen Dramas begrüßt. Tatsächlich aber verwendet dieses Drama das aristotelische Handlungs- und Aufbauschema nicht in ungebrochener Form, sondern benutzt diese Form lediglich als Vehikel für das neue, das gruppendynamische Geschehensschema. Für den Nachweis, daß die Dramen Pinters bis zu *Betrayal* durch das Primat der Formdiskussion gekennzeichnet sind, ist *The Homecoming* deswegen zentral, weil hier die Überlagerung zweier Schemata zum ersten Mal sehr deutlich auch in der äußeren Struktur des Aufbaus signalisiert ist.

The Birthday Party ist für unseren Zusammenhang doppelt aufschlußreich: an diesem Drama ist deutlicher als an allen anderen die „Absicht" des Autors erkennbar, und dies vor allem im Licht der späteren Dramen und der Revisionen, die Pinter an diesem Drama vornahm; und es ist eine wichtige selbstreferentielle Folie für die Produktion der 80er Jahre, auch für Mountain Language.

Es gibt kein anderes Drama Pinters, das so stark überarbeitet wurde. Und die Revisionen weisen alle in die gleiche Richtung: sie lassen die Strukturidee, das Thema der Identität, hervortreten. So sind in der zweiten Auflage etwa Informationen weggelassen, die zu einer Konstruktion von traditioneller Vorgeschichte (etwa der Goldbergs) verleiten könnten. Wenn man Revisionen als Indikator für Unzufriedenheit mit der Durchführung der Absicht oder auch als Hinweis auf eine Änderung der ursprünglichen Absicht deuten darf, dann liefert die Werkgenese oder auch die Publikationsgeschichte dieses Dramas deutliche Evidenzen. Als zusätzliche Evidenzen können zwei Verfilmungen gelten. Sie stammen aus dem Jahr 1968 und aus dem Jahr 1987. Die neueste, für das Fernsehen eingerichtete Verfilmung ist besonders aufschlußreich. Pinter spielt darin Goldberg, und diese Fernsehfassung kann als *definitive version*, quasi als eine „Ausgabe letzter Hand" gelten.[5]

Nur The Hothouse, 1958, im Jahr nach The Birthday Party entstanden, hat ein für die Autorintention ähnlich aufschlußreiches Schicksal. Pinter hatte das Stück anfänglich völlig verworfen und erst 1980 zur Veröffentlichung freigegeben. Es ist im Nachhinein, als Teil der Schaffensgeschichte Pinters, interessant, sonst vielleicht eines seiner schwächeren Stücke. Beide Dramen, The Hothouse ebenso wie The Birthday Party, greifen den gleichen Mythos, nämlich Geburt und Tod Christi, auf. Beide Dramen wurden von Pinter in den 80er Jahren wieder aufgegriffen und können deswegen Hinweis auf eine Entwicklung sein.

The Hothouse, dessen wichtigster Schauplatz die Nervenheilanstalt ist, satirisiert die traditionellen Methoden der Behandlung Geisteskranker. In diesem Drama wird eine Christusfigur mit dem sprechenden Namen Lamb als Opfer und Täter zugleich gezeigt.[6] Lamb wird an Weihnachten einer Elektroschockbehandlung unterzogen und wird damit vom Komplizen zum Opfer. Während die Christusanalogie in The Hothouse dem Inhaltlichen, etwa der Sozialkritik, verhaftet bleibt, wird der Mythos in The Birthday Party schon deutlicher abstrahiert und als Struktur zur Grundlage des Verfahrens der Autor-Leser-Kommunikation gemacht. Mountain Language folgt in der metaphorischen Abstraktheit des Mythos eher der in The Birthday Party eingeschlagenen Richtung als der satirischen, reale Zustände anprangernden von The Hothouse.

110

Die *ecce homo*-Züge des Protagonisten von *The Birthday Party* – Christus als Opfer –, die in den frühen Fassungen noch deutlicher aufgerufen werden, treten in den Überarbeitungen schließlich zurück. Das Schlußtableau des zweiten Aktes zeigt Stanley in einer Kreuzigungshaltung. In der Filmversion von 1987 fehlt diese. Anders als Lamb in *The Hothouse* ist Stanley in *The Birthday Party* schließlich nicht mehr als Allegorie im inhaltlich gefüllten Sinne, nämlich als die Verkörperung des Opferlamms, zu verstehen. Stanley bleibt vielmehr eine leere, identitätslose Figur, für die Norbert Greiner zu Recht den Begriff „Schwundfigur" geprägt hat.[7]

Die Christusparallele und das Muster des Geburtstages hängen insofern zusammen, als mit der Menschwerdung Christi in der bibelexegetischen Tradition der Typologie auch immer die Geburt des Neuen Adam gemeint ist. In Harold Pinters Geburtstagsfeier gibt es beides, die Geburtstagsfeier im ironisch invertierten Sinne als Todesfeier, als *funeral*, und im eigentlichen Sinne, nämlich als Entstehung einer Figur im Prozeß dramatischer Konstruktion im situativen Drama. Die Etablierung der Figur erfolgt gleichzeitig mit der Dekonstruktion traditioneller Motivationsstrategien.

Traditionelle Motivationsstrategien wären etwa diejenigen, die, den Regeln der Logik folgend, die Vorgeschichte des Charakters als aufdeckbar annehmen und die Motive weiteren Handelns in einer logisch-kausalen – auch psychoanalytisch begründbaren – Charakterkonsistenz suchen. Gegen eine so verstandene Charakterkonsistenz oder auch Charakteridentität im Drama und im Leben hegt Pinter tiefes Mißtrauen. Identität etabliert sich in seinen Dramen viel eher unmittelbar im Geschehen auf der Bühne. Dabei folgt das Verhalten der Figuren den Gesetzmäßigkeiten der Gruppendynamik, denen zufolge sich menschliches Verhalten jeweils neu nach den rollenspezifischen Konstellationen definiert.[8] Diese Konstellationen beruhen auf allgemeineren, geradezu archetypischen Strukturen; die Machtpositionen der Figuren definieren sich z. B. aus der alters- und geschlechtsspezifischen Identität der Gruppenmitglieder.

"There are things I remember which may never have happened, but as I recall them, so they take place." Dieser Ausspruch Annas aus *Old Times* könnte die aphoristische Erfassung der darin entfalteten Zeit- und Wirklichkeitsvorstellung sein und zugleich das Motto der Dramatologie, die der Autor der traditionellen entgegenstellt.

Diese hier programmatisch formulierte neue Dramatologie Pinters beruht statt auf Zeit- und Vergangenheitsvorstellungen traditioneller Art auf einem Konzept der räumlichen Präsenz, des unmittelbar in der Anschauung auf der Bühne Einsichtigen.[9] Dies ist die positive Füllung der Gattung, welche der Auflösung der Gattungskonvention entgegengesetzt wird.

Pinters Drama *No Man's Land* nimmt sich die dramatische Kategorie des Raumes zum Thema, wie die Komponente *Land* des Titels andeutet, und parodiert zugleich das von Pinter selbst und von Beckett initiierte situative Drama, das Drama einer neuen bildhaften Unmittelbarkeit. In Referenzen auf die Zuständlichkeit und den Theaterraum an den markanten Stellen der Struktur und im Spiel mit den auch nichtsprachlichen Mitteln der Gestaltung im Theater – etwa dem Bühnenbild, den Requisiten und der Beleuchtung – wird dieser Gattungsbezug deutlich signalisiert. (In *Mountain Language* – dies sei kurz vorausgeschickt – scheint hier insofern wieder eine Veränderung eingetreten zu sein, als die Sprache als dramatisches Mittel, wie auch der zweite Bestandteil des Titels andeutet, wieder wichtiger wird.)

Nach *No Man's Land*, dem Drama der völligen Handlungsarmut, scheint Pinter mit *Betrayal* zu einem Drama der handlungsreichen Geschäftigkeit zurückgekehrt zu sein. *Betrayal* scheint feingesponnene Intrige, *well-made play* im Sinne Noel Cowards und Terence Rattigans zu sein. Aber der Schein trügt. Mit der Struktur der invertierten Chronologie widerlegt *Betrayal* die kunstvoll gebaute Konstruktion dieses Dramentyps. In *Betrayal* ist es neben dem Titel, der das Verfahren der enttäuschten Gattungserwartung aufnimmt, die so abgewandelte Struktur des Aufbaus, welche auf die Parodie von Mythos hinweist. Der Titel ist zugleich Beweis für das Insistieren Pinters auf dem Primat von Form und Verfahren, das in seinem späteren Werk (von *The Homecoming* an) das wichtigere Thema ist. Von der Parodie des christologischen Bezugs in *The Birthday Party* zur absoluten Gattungsparodie liegt ein Zeitraum von zwanzig Jahren und ein konsequenter Weg der Auseinandersetzung mit dem Drama als Gattung. Die Suche nach Innovation in den zehn Jahren seit *Betrayal* kann nicht ohne das Einbeziehen des bereits Geschaffenen auskommen. Pinter hat mit seinem Mitwirken an der Neuverfilmung von *The Birthday Party* den Hinweis darauf geliefert, daß ihn auch heute noch sein frühes Werk beschäftigt – und sei es auch nur als jene Folie, gegen die er anschreiben muß.

II. Das Thema der Identität in The Birthday Party: *Feier und Geburt als Menschwerdung*

"You'll be a mensch."[10] In diesem Ausspruch Goldbergs wird das zentrale Thema von *The Birthday Party* noch einmal kurz vor Schluß des Dramas prägnant formuliert: Es ist dies Identität und ihre Entstehung als psychologisch-soziologisches, als philosophisches und poetologisches Problem. Und auch das zentrale Verfahren, der parodistische Rekurs auf den Mythos von der Menschwerdung Christi, wird noch einmal deutlich. Auf allen drei Ebenen der Struktur – dem Aufbau- und Handlungsschema, der Textur sowie den Charakteren und ihrer Konstellation – lassen sich Thema und Verfahren von *The Birthday Party*

112

an dieser Textstelle exemplifizieren. Die Versprechung Goldbergs ist Teil eines stichomythischen Dialogs zwischen ihm und McCann, der als *dénouement* die „Wiedergeburt" des Helden beschwört. Auf der Ebene der Autor-Leser-Kommunikation wird aber deutlich, daß das Muster der „Wiedergeburt" nur ironisch invertiert gilt. Die Stelle ist – dramenstrukturell gesprochen – Katastrophe, die Besiegelung des Untergangs des Protagonisten.

Das dramatische Aufbaumuster, das hier strukturell zitiert und funktional abgewandelt wird, verweist deutlich auf den Ursprung der griechischen Tragödie, aber auch des englischen Dramas im Ritual. Beide Traditionen, die griechische ebenso wie die englische, greifen innerhalb der Grundstruktur des „gebändigten", formal verfeinerten Rituals auf die Lebensgeschichte des Helden zurück, im Falle des englischen sogar auf das Leben und Leiden Christi.[11] Was in den Ursprüngen des Dramas als ein Eigentliches zu denken ist, die Feier der „Menschwerdung" des Heroen, wird in *The Birthday Party* zum Uneigentlichen, zur Darstellung. Strukturell ist in Pinters Drama der mittlere Akt, die Geburtstagsfeier, die Peripetie. Sie entspricht auch dem Höhepunkt im griechischen Ritual. Die Geburtstagsfeier ist bei Pinter aber auch Metapher für das Drama insgesamt, für das formal gestaltete Ereignis der Umsetzung der Feier auf der Bühne.

Bei Pinter ist die teleologische Struktur nur als Negativfolie zu verstehen; sie wird ständig in der Lesererwartung aufgerufen, aber nicht oder nur im subjektiven Entwurf der Figuren gefüllt. Die klassische Form des dramatischen Aufbaus mit Exposition, steigender und fallender Handlung und Katastrophe wird in Pinters Drama zwar aufgerufen, aber dem erkenntnistheoretisch-poetologischen Ziel entsprechend umgedeutet. Dieses Ziel ist die Darstellung eines eigenen Identitätsbegriffs.

Die Textur von *The Birthday Party* ist durchsetzt von einer Vielzahl von Hinweisen auf das Identitätsthema, die zum Teil die Christusreferenz mitgestalten. Oft ergeben die Signale – wie am Beispiel *mensch* noch gleich zu zeigen sein wird – auch auf einer Ebene des harmlosen Alltagsgesprächs oder der Alltagssituation noch Sinn. Wenn die Struktur der Identitätsthematik erst einmal bewußt ist, bildet sich über der mimetischen Strukturschicht eine Schicht des Metadiskurses heraus.

Mit *mensch* wählt Pinter ein Wort, das zwar einerseits durch seine Herkunft aus dem Jiddischen die Kohärenz des englischen umgangssprachlichen Alltagsdiskurses durchbricht, andererseits aber auch in eine traditionell mimetisch verstandene „Charakterisierung" Goldbergs als Juden integriert werden kann. *Mensch* liefert sprachlich den Verweis auf die Christusanalogie in der Weise, daß von allen Extensionen der Christusfigur hier nur die *ecce homo*-Natur Christi, seine menschliche Verwundbarkeit, eben seine „Mensch"werdung, angesprochen wird. Die Gottesnatur Christi bleibt hier außer Betracht. Stanley ist der wiedergeborene Adam nach typologischer Vorstellung, der "new man". Äußeres Zeichen seiner Erneuerung ist – auch hier bleibt Pinter in der Metaphorik der Bibel – der neue Anzug. McCann hatte Stanley kurz zuvor (S. 81) in seinem aufgezwungenen neuen Anzug bewundert und Goldberg hatte ihm eine neue Brille verheißen.[12]

In *The Birthday Party* wird auch auf den Garten Eden angespielt und dies nur in einem scheinbar ganz nebensächlichen Zusammenhang, einem kleinen Lied, das McCann auf der Geburtstagsfeier zum Besten gibt und damit das Stereotyp des trinkfesten, sangesfreudigen, sentimentalen *Stage Irishman* bestätigt (S. 61). Tatsächlich aber wird auf der Ebene des Metadiskurses die Schemenhaftigkeit des Musters beschworen, das immer noch wirksam ist. Die Worte des Textes "Oh, the Garden of Eden has vanished, they say, But I know the lie of it still" erhalten eine zweite Bedeutung, die auf das mythenparodierende Verfahren zu beziehen ist.

Zwischen Stanley und seinen beiden „Betreuern" Goldberg und McCann gibt es eine gewisse Ähnlichkeit. Sie kommt zustande durch die Tatsache, daß sie auf der Ebene der Mythenparodie verschiedene Extensionen des gleichen Begriffs oder auch Facetten des gleichen Figurentypus sind. Während Stanley die Menschennatur Christi aufruft, ist es bei McCann und Goldberg eher der gottähnliche Aspekt des mythologischen Typus. Sie werden sogar als Gott selbst in seiner Schöpfereigenschaft gezeigt, als jener Gott, der den Menschen „nach seinem Bild und Gleichnis" erschafft. Eine scheinbar nur komische Stelle im dritten Akt bliebe ohne die mythenparodistische Dimension funktionslos. McCann bläst Goldberg auf dessen Wunsch seinen Atem in den Mund. Im Verständnis als Alltagssituation – Goldberg fordert "One For the Road" (S. 79) – wird hier zunächst nur die Alkoholfahne McCanns thematisiert. Aber auf der Ebene der Mythendiskussion wird hier das Einhauchen des Odems dramatisiert und auf die Gottähnlichkeit der beiden in ihrem eigenen Verständnis verwiesen.

Stanley ist keine Christusallegorie. Allegorese kann bestenfalls nur eine vorübergehende Zuschauerhypothese sein, die dann zugunsten eines anderen Verständnisses aufgegeben werden muß. Die Auflösung der Allegorese gelingt Pinter aber in *The Birthday Party* nicht in dem gleichen, formal bewältigten Maße wie in einem Drama von der Qualität von *Old Times*. Es ist deshalb nicht verwunderlich, daß Pinter in seiner Revision von 1965 einen Hinweis eliminiert, der Goldberg deutlicher zum allegorischen Charakter, zum Vater des Messias, hätte werden lassen können. Es ist dies der Name Emmanuel, den Goldberg noch in der alten Fassung als den eines seiner Söhne erwähnt.[13] In der Filmversion von 1987 sind Stellen, die als Hinweise auf den allegorischen Charakter Stanleys gedeutet werden könnten, verschwunden. Im Text endet der zweite

Akt, die eigentliche Geburtstagsfeier, mit einem Tableau. Stanley wird von einer Taschenlampe angestrahlt, die eingesetzt werden mußte, weil, wie sich im letzten Akt herausstellt, die Münzen im Stromzähler zu Ende gegangen waren. Die Taschenlampe beleuchtet ihn so, daß sein Schatten, übermäßig vergrößert und verzeichnet, ihn wie die Figur des Gekreuzigten erscheinen läßt: "[...] as he flattens himself against the wall" (S. 65/66). Die Gestalten McCanns und Goldbergs werden so auf ihn projiziert, daß auch sie irreal wirken: "Their figures converge upon him." (Ebd.) Dieses Schlußtableau war auch eine der Evidenzen, die in der Kritik für den angeblich allegorischen Charakter der beiden angeführt wurden. Dies ist in der Filmversion von 1987 nicht gestaltet. Der Akt endet mit einer Großaufnahme, die Stanleys Gesicht inhaltsleer, „charakterlos" zeigt. Auch die anderen Figuren sind nur von einer Assoziationsaura umgeben, sind aber nie identisch mit der Füllung des mythischen Musters. Im Schematismus der Allegorie läge die Deutung Megs als Gottesmutter nahe. Immerhin stilisiert sie sich anfänglich Stanley gegenüber als Mutter, nennt ihn "boy". Sie ist es auch, die zum Anlaß wird, die erste Allusion in diesem Drama auf die Geburt Christi auszusprechen. Sie drängt Petey dazu, aus den Gesellschaftsnachrichten in der Zeitung die Information zu verlesen, daß eine Lady *Mary* Spratt ein Kind bekommen habe. Und sie ist es auch, die das mythische Muster vervollständigt. Als sie erfährt, daß es sich bei dem Kind um ein Mädchen handelt, stellt sie fest: "Oh, what a shame. I'd be sorry. I'd much rather have a little boy." (S. 11) Aber dies macht sie nicht zur Gottesmutter; sie ist selbst nur eine verhinderte Mutter und nimmt genauso schnell in ihrem Geplänkel mit Stanley um das Wort *succulent* eine andere Rolle an: Sie sieht sich selbst als Geliebte und wird dann Goldberg und McCann gegenüber wieder zum Kind. Zu diesem Eindruck trägt, zusätzlich zum nostalgischen Dialog über ihre Kindheit und ihren Vater, auch das Abendkleid bei, das in der Verfilmung von 1987 als hellblaues Spitzenkleid Meg als Mischung von Maria, Kind und Verführerin erscheinen läßt.

Der Mythos von der Geburt Christi wird in allen Strukturbereichen, Großstruktur, Textur und auch außersprachlichen Mitteln der Darstellung, den Charakteren und ihrer Konstellation nur erweckt, nie durchgeführt. Er hat die Funktion, auf ein allgemeineres Thema zu verweisen, nämlich auf das Entstehen (und auch Vergehen) von Identität. Man könnte geradezu in Umkehrung des kritischen Klischees, das Pinters Dramen als „Dramen der verlorenen Identität" bezeichnet, *The Birthday Party* das Drama der entstehenden Identität nennen. Es geht in diesem Drama nicht nur um Entstehung von Identität im psychologisch-soziologischen oder im erkenntnistheoretischen Sinne, sondern auch und vor allem um Identität als Formproblem der Gattung Drama. Es geht um das Entstehen und Vergehen von Identitätsbildern als Selbst- und Fremdbilder im individual- wie im gruppenpsychologischen Sinne; es geht auch um die

Macht, die solche Wirklichkeitsentwürfe über das Individuum haben. Es geht auch um Stereotype im national- und geschlechtsrollenspezifischen Sinne. Dies wird gestaltet im Spiel mit Bühnenfiguren, wie dem *Stage Irishman* oder auch *Stage Jew*, und im Spiel mit den technischen Mitteln wie Auftritt, Abtritt, Beleuchtung.

Alle Teile von Mythos als Aufbau, als Handlungsstruktur des Dramas im aristotelischen Sinne sind auf dieses Thema und seine dramatische Gestaltung bezogen. Die Segmente oder Teile von Mythos sind nicht nur als Negierung des Herkömmlichen, etwa der Enthüllung von Vorgeschichte und Situation in der Exposition, zu verstehen, sondern auch als positive Etablierung und Vorführen der Entstehung von Identität. Und dies nicht nur als mimetisches Problem, sondern auch im Verlauf des Dramas, als Spiel mit der Zuschauererwartung, als die mit ins Kalkül genommene traditionelle Struktur.

Die radikale Kompromißlosigkeit Pinters in der Ablehnung traditioneller Motivationsstrategien schlägt sich in der Form seines Dramas nieder: Die markanten Punkte und Teile der Struktur des dramatischen Mythos sind alle umgedeutet zu Stellen, an welchen es um die Entstehung (= Geburt) von Identität geht.[14] Auf den dramatischen Mythos bezogen ist das Segment „Geburt" des Titels nicht negativ, sondern positiv gefüllt, während es auf den christlichen Mythos bezogen, negativ, als Auflösung, gefüllt ist. Wenn „Geburt" als Metapher für Identitätsentstehung zu verstehen ist, so ist der zweite Bestandteil des Titels, „Feier", auf der Ebene der dramatologischen Diskussion Metapher für die Kunst gewordene Gestalt des Rituals.

Das *dénouement* wird umgedeutet. An der traditionellen Stelle des *dénouement* findet sich ein stichomythischer Dialog zwischen McCann und Goldberg (S. 82ff.), mit der die Geburt der neuen Identität Stanleys rituell begangen wird. Goldberg und McCann hofieren ihn nur scheinbar, erweisen ihm nur spöttisch ihre Referenz. "They begin to woo him, gently and with relish." (Ebd.) heißt es in der Regieanweisung. Dieses Muster ähnelt deutlich der Verspottung Christi durch seine Peiniger. In der totalen Betreuung[15], die man ihm verheißt, soll der „Neue Adam" am Ende entstehen. Wenn Goldberg ihm ankündigt, "it's about time you had a new pair of glasses." (Ebd.), so wird darin nicht nur die neue Sicht der Wirklichkeit angesprochen, die man ihm aufoktroyieren will, sondern auch eine neue Sichtweise seiner eigenen Identität. Genannt werden all die kostenlosen ("All on the House") Hilfsmittel ("crutches") vom Babypuder bis zum Sauerstoffzelt, von der Brille bis zum *ear plug*, die dieses Wunder der Reorientierung vollbringen sollen.

Stanley hat diesen Ansinnen keine felsenfeste Überzeugung vom Wert seiner eigenen Person entgegenzusetzen. Er bleibt stumm und bewegungslos. Eigene Identitätsbilder von sich entwirft vor allem Goldberg, der seine eigene Existenz und Vergangenheit, seine kulturelle Identität als Jude zwischen *gefilte fish* (S. 43) und *rollmop* (S. 59) sentimental glorifiziert. Und auch Meg beharrt – ironischer aber charakteristischer Schluß des Dramas – auf ihrem Selbstbild, von dem sie auch Petey überzeugen kann. Sie sei "the belle of the ball" (S. 89) gewesen.

Das *dénouement* von *The Birthday Party* wurde sorgsam vorbereitet durch den Höhepunkt der Glückswende im zweiten Akt, in einer geradezu parallel zum stichomythischen Dialog konstruiertenSzene (S. 47–52). In einer Verhörsituation werden dort von Goldberg und McCann alle Identitätsdeterminanten traditioneller Art abgefragt. Es sind dies zunächst die Fragen nach Herkunft, Beruf, Familienstand, die an die Figuren eines traditionellen Dramas gestellt und in der Vorgeschichte eines solchen Dramas auch beantwortet werden ("When did you last pray?" "What about the Albigensenist heresy?"). Fragen nach der Handlungsmotivation werden im Sinn der Kriminalistik gestellt ("Why did you kill your wife?"), aber auch im Sinne der Psychoanalyse, als Anamnese der Vorgeschichte.[16] Stanley kann diese Fragen nicht oder nur unvollständig beantworten. Das Verhör gipfelt in der zentralen Frage "Who are you, Webber?" Hier wird mit der Frage auch schon die Identität festgelegt, ein Name gegeben. Auch *Mountain Language* beginnt mit der Frage nach dem Namen.

Bei einem Dramatiker, der logisch begründbare und durchschaubare Charaktere ablehnt, kann natürlich die Exposition solche Informationen nicht liefern. Dem Prinzip der Umdeutung der Teile des Mythos zur Konstatierung des Themas folgend, begann *The Birthday Party media in res* mit der Nennung des Themas. Wenn Pinter Meg in der erstenSzene insistieren läßt, "Is that you, Petey", dann wird hinter der Banalität der Alltagssituation bereits das zentrale Thema sichtbar. Und auch die scheinbar banale Konversation wird zum Diskurs über Identität und ihre Bewertung. Mit penetranter Gleichförmigkeit werden die Adjektive "nice" und "good" wiederholt. Der dritte Akt beginnt mit einer parallel zu dieser Eröffnung des Dramas konstruierten Szene, in der Meg diesmal nicht nach Petey, sondern nach Stanley und dessen Identität fragt. Die Adjektive signalisieren nichts anderes als ästhetische (*nice*) und moralische (*good*) Prädikation, die zum Akt der Identitätsfestlegung gehört.

Diese Beispiele mögen als Hinweis auf die Gattungsreflexion genügen. Sie ließen sich ergänzen – etwa auch durch die Beschreibung der Bühnentechniken und nichtsprachlichen Bühnenmittel, wie der Auftritt und die Bühnenbeleuchtung. Die Aufnahme der Bühnenmittel in die Handlung signalisiert in *The Birthday Party* allerdings noch nicht den Kunstmittelcharakter, wie das dann später in *No Man's Land* geschieht.

Die Füllungen von Mythos, einmal als Formalstruktur der Handlung und einmal als Mythologie, sind in *The Birthday Party* noch beide realisiert. In den auf *The Birthday Party* folgenden Dramen bis zu *Betrayal* hat Pinter Mythos als

Mythologie zurücktreten lassen und sich stärker noch als in *The Birthday Party* den Formalproblemen der Gattung zugewandt. In den Dramen der 80er Jahre wird dann wieder auf die inhaltliche Füllung des Begriffs Mythos Bezug genommen. *Mountain Language*, wie auch die beiden Bestandteile des Titels anzeigen, rekurriert zum einen inhaltlich auf den mit dem Begriff "Mountain" assoziierten Mythos, zum anderen aber auch auf Sprache als Herrschaftsmittel und als dramatische Gestaltungskategorie.

III. *Mythos in den Dramen der 80er Jahre*: Mountain Language *als Rückgriff und Innovation*

Mountain Language scheint ein Rückgriff auf das erste abendfüllende Drama Pinters, *The Birthday Party*, in Bezug auf das Thema zu sein. Wie in diesem ersten Drama geht es hier auch um Identität, dies aber zunächst weniger als Problem der dramatischen Form denn als Problem der außerdramatischen Wirklichkeit. Die „Feststellung der Identität" ist Teil des Macht- und Herrschaftsapparates, der in *Mountain Language* in erschreckender Konkretheit vorgeführt wird. Aber obwohl eingekleidet in einen konkreten Zusammenhang – den Besuch in einem Gefängnis oder einem Gefangenenlager –, sind die Ereignisse merkwürdig abstrakt und die inhaltlichen Konkretisationen sind noch deutlicher dem Konstruktionswillen des Zuschauers überlassen.

Diese geradezu paradoxe Doppelnatur zwischen archetypischer Abstraktion und politischer Konkretheit beginnt bereits beim Titel dieses Dramas: Ist der Titel im eigentlichen und damit deskriptiven Sinne zu verstehen oder im uneigentlichen, ironischen? Wenn *Mountain Language* auf *sermon on the mount*, die Bergpredigt, anspielt, dann entsteht ein ironischer, nahezu zynischer Kontrast zwischen dem in der Bergpredigt festgehaltenen christlichen Verhaltenscode, jenem der Friedfertigkeit, Gerechtigkeit und der Versöhnung und dem tatsächlichen Verhalten der Mitglieder dieser offensichtlich christlichen Sozietät, dem Gefängnispersonal und der Gesellschaft, deren Vollstrecker (Exekutive) es ist. – Daß es sich um eine christliche Gesellschaft handelt, erfährt man symptomatischerweise aus einem Fluch "Jesus Christ" (S. 29), der am Ende der dritten Szene von einem Gefängnisaufseher ausgesprochen wird. Dies mag zum einen für die Natur des Mythos wichtig sein, zum anderen aber auch für den konkreten politischen Bezug. Pinter selbst hatte in dem bereits erwähnten Interview mit Nicholas Hern, das er zu *One for the Road* gegeben hatte, darauf hingewiesen, daß es ihm heute nicht mehr nur um die Metapher, sondern um die Darstellung der Fakten gehe, weil es heute viel einfacher sei als 1957, „den Horror dessen zu ignorieren was um uns herum vorgeht". 1957, als er *The Birthday Party* schrieb, seien „die Rampen der Konzentrationslager noch eine offene Wunde gewesen", so daß auf die konkrete Füllung nicht habe hingewiesen werden müssen. Wichtig war ihm auch in diesem Interview darauf hinzuweisen, daß auf beiden Seiten, bei Kommunisten und bei Nichtkommunisten, gefoltert wird.

Die Gewalt, die in *Mountain Language* ausgeübt wird, ist – viel konkreter noch als in *The Birthday Party* – körperliche Gewalt, Körperverletzung und Vergewaltigung, sie wird aber auch im Umgang mit der Sprache deutlich. Tabuwörter wie *fucking, fuck* und *bloody* (S. 25, 37, 47) sind häufig gebraucht[17], was besonders deswegen auffällt, weil so wenig Adjektive verwendet werden. Sie werden von den Sprechern im übertragenen Sinne gebraucht – "Where's the bloody Babycham?" (S. 37) –, ergeben auf der Autor-Leser-Ebene aber eine Aura der Gewalt.

Wenn man den Titel im eigentlichen Sinne versteht, dann nennt er eines der beiden zentralen Prinzipien, die in diesem Drama als gegensätzliche, geradezu unversöhnliche errichtet sind. Der Assoziationsreichtum von *Mountain* ist fast unbegrenzt: Der Ort der Transzendenz, der Verkündigung, der Hilfe ("I lift up mine Eyes unto the mountain from whence cometh my help"; Psalm 90).

Aber durch das Gegenprinzip *Capital* wird es auch wieder eingeschränkt. *Mountain* wirkt in diesem Gegensatzpaar im Drama keineswegs als Metapher, sondern als ganz konkreter Ort, der in der Geistesgeschichte der abendländischen Kulturgemeinschaft bereits als Chiffre fest etabliert ist. *Mountain* ist zum einen Chiffre für einen Zustand der kulturellen Frühe und der Ursprünglichkeit, des Ländlichen ("The Prisoner and the Woman speak in a strong *rural* accent", sagt der Nebentext auf S. 27 [Hervorhebung vom Vf.]), durchaus im positiven Sinne. Zum anderen ist er aber auch – aus der Perspektive derjenigen, die *The Language of the Capital* sprechen, der Bewohner der Hauptstadt (*capital*) – der Ort des Vorzivilisatorischen, der Primitivität. *Mountain* ist vielleicht auch der Lebensraum einer Gesellschaftsform, die noch vor der modernen Tauschgesellschaft liegt und noch nicht den Gebrauch des Geldes kennt, wenn man einmal *Capital* auch als Kapital verstehen will.

Historisch-politisch gesehen – dies jedenfalls im Machtbereich des britischen Empire – ist das Bergland immer der Ort der Freiheit, jener Ort, an dem man auch konkret die Rebellen gegen die Zentralgewalt vermutet hat. Das gilt für Schottland, Irland und auch Indien. Möglicherweise ist der Bezug zu Schottland und Irland als konkreter politischer Hintergrund auch noch dadurch gestärkt, daß die Unterdrückung dieser Völker historisch tatsächlich mit dem Verbot ihrer *Sprache* einherging. – Immerhin hat Pinter dieses Drama seiner Frau, Antonia Fraser, gewidmet, die selbst die Biographin von *Mary, Queen of Scots* ist. Auch zum irischen Umfeld gibt es konkrete, intertextuelle Bezüge. Das Ambiente, mit dem dieses Drama beginnt, die Gefängnismauer von außen, ist auch die Szene von Lady Gregorys bekanntem Einakter *The Gaol Gate*, in welchem es um den Verrat an dem wegen mutmaßlichen Rebellentums einsitzenden irischen Freiheitskämpfer geht. Aber all das greift schon vor auf die Beschreibung der Struktur und des Mythos, die erst noch zu leisten ist. Nur soviel sei noch zum Mythos, der in *Mountain Language* – durch den *Titel* – aufgerufen wird, gesagt. Im Vergleich etwa zu *The Birthday Party* ist er – nur scheinbar paradox – beides: formal abstrakter *und* politisch konkreter. Eine christliche Füllung – *Mountain* als Anklang an das Paradies – ist zwar denkbar, aber nicht explizit gestaltet. *Mountain* ist die Gegenwelt, die durch die Gestaltung ihres Gegenteils im Bewußtsein des Lesers oder Zuschauers nur erweckt wird. Das Negativbild ist sehr konkret gestaltet. Es ist die Welt des Gefängnisses, die Welt der Unfreiheit, der absoluten Willkür, der Rechtsunsicherheit, der Autorität und ihres Mißbrauchs. Angedeutet ist auch, daß es sich bei der Gegenwelt zu *Mountain* um die Welt der Mehrheit handelt, welche die Minderheit, die *Mountain people*, verfolgt. An einer Stelle wird eine Angehörige der *Mountain people*, *a young woman*, von einem Sergeanten sogar als "a fucking intellectual" bezeichnet (S. 25), d. h. als Mitglied jener Gruppe, die *per definitionem* in jeder Gesellschaft Minderheit ist.

Nur an einer einzigen Stelle, die im gedruckten Text noch nicht einmal eine Seite lang ist (S. 41), blitzt eine konkrete Vision der *Mountain people*-Welt auf: sie ist eine Welt des Friedens ("I watch you sleep"), der Harmonie ("And then your eyes open. You look up at me above you and smile" [S. 39]) und aller Attribute des literarischen *locus amoenus*, wie Wasser, Frühling und Wärme. Diese Welt, ebenso wie ihr Gegenbild, die Welt des Gefängnisses, die Welt der *Capital Language*, wird durch Sprache und weniger durch das Bild konstituiert. Wenn es eine dramatologisch deutbare Aussage in diesem Drama gibt, dann ist es vielleicht jene von der wirklichkeitskonstituierenden Kraft der Sprache und dies im Negativen wie im Positiven. Den Titel *Mountain Language* könnte man so in seinem zweiten Bestandteil als Hinweis auf eine Dramaturgie des Wortes sehen, die als Gegenentwurf zur Dramaturgie des Raumes, zum situativen Drama, hier betont ist.

Wenn das Drama Becketts – besonders in seiner späteren Gestalt – vor allem ein Drama der Bildhaftigkeit ist (etwa *Not I*, *Footfalls*, *That Time*, *Quad* und *Catastrophe*), so ist in diesem Drama Pinters die Aufmerksamkeit wieder stärker auf die Sprache auch als dramatisches Mittel gelenkt. In diesem Zusammenhang könnte man den *hooded man*, der im Anschluß an die eben beschriebene idyllische Vision zusammenbrechend gezeigt wird, nicht allein als Gefolterten deuten, sondern auch als intertextuelles Signal. In Becketts *Not I*, in dem die beiden Strukturen des Dramas, Bild und Sprache, thematisiert werden[18], ist der Antagonist, *Auditor*, ebenfalls eine durch die Kapuze unkenntlich gemachte Figur; und in *Quad*, in dem allein der Bühnenraum und das Visuelle (Beleuchtung) strukturkonstituierend sind, tragen alle vier Spieler Kapuzen. Der Verweis auf die Gattung ist in diesem Stück Pinters – ganz im Gegensatz zu seinem ersten, *The Birthday Party* – nicht an den Aufruf einer traditionellen Handlungsstruktur gebunden.

Der Aufbau ist nicht in Akte gegliedert, sondern in vier szenenartige Abschnitte, jeweils durch *Blackouts* getrennt, die I A PRISON WALL, 2 VISITORS ROOM, 3 VOICE IN THE DARKNESS und 4 VISITORS ROOM überschrieben sind. Drei der Szenentitel (I, 2, 4) zeigen den Ort an, der dritte beginnt zunächst ohne Lokalisierung im Dunkeln, zeigt dann einen Korridor. Das plötzliche Aufblenden, das den Blick auf einen Gefängniskorridor freigibt, versetzt den Zuschauer blitzartig in eine alptraumartige Beobachtersituation, in der er sich der Teilhabe an der entsetzlichen Wirklichkeit, dem Blick in die sonst verborgenen Gänge des Gefängnisses nicht mehr entziehen kann. Auch die verharmlosenden Klischees des Sergeanten, "Anyway, in the meantime, what can I do for you, dear lady, as they used to say in the movies?" (S. 39), ändern das nicht. Höhepunkt in einem weiteren Sinne ist diese dritte Szene auch deshalb, weil darin aufs Schärfste die beiden Gegenwelten kontrastiert sind. Und auch ein weiteres Kennzeichen des Totalitarismus, die Banalität der Bürokratie, wird hier enthüllt. Der verbotene Blick auf das Verborgene kommt nur durch das Versagen und die Anonymität der Bürokratie zustande. "A bit of a breakdown in administration, I'm afraid. They've sent you through the wrong door. Unbelievable." (S. 39) und kurz darauf "Yes, you've come in the wrong door. It must be the computer. The computer's got a double hernia." (S. 41) Der Ausdruck *hernia* läßt den Computer geradezu menschlich erscheinen, dies jedenfalls im Vergleich zu dem Menschen, welcher der *young woman* als Informationsquelle avisiert wird. Ihr Angebot, ihm sexuell zu Diensten zu sein – "Can I fuck him? If I fuck him, will everything be all right?" (Ebd.), – erscheint geradezu grotesk.

Identität und Machtausübung durch Festlegen der Identität anderer – *namescalling* – war auch schon zentrales Thema in *The Birthday Party* gewesen, in *Mountain Language* wird dieses Thema ins Groteske übersteigert. Die Eröffnung des Dramas erscheint als absurde Variation zur Eröffnung der *Birthday Party*. Während Megs "Is that you, Petey?" noch durchaus in einen harmlosen Alltagsdiskurs integrierbar war, deckt diese Eröffnung durch das Insistieren die geradezu archetypische Verbindung von Macht und Namensnennung auf:

SERGEANT Name?
YOUNG WOMAN We've given our names.
SERGEANT Name?

YOUNG WOMAN We've given our names.
SERGEANT Name?   (S. 11/12)

Immerhin hatte schon Odysseus sich der Macht des Zyklopen entzogen, indem er die Nennung seines Namens verweigerte bzw. einen falschen nannte – dies nur als Hinweis darauf, daß schon in mythischer Zeit die Verbindung von Macht und Namensnennung bestand.

Ins Groteske übersteigert wird der totalitäre Identifikationswunsch dann, als der Offizier, seinen Unteroffizier scheinbar durch Rechtsstaatlichkeit in die Schranken weisend, nun auch den Namen des Hundes wissen will, der die *elderly woman* gebissen hat:

> OFFICER What was his name?
> *Pause.*
> What was his *name*?
> *Pause.*
> Every dog has a *name!* They answer to their name. They are given a name by their parents and that is their name, that is their *name!* Before they bite, they *state* their name. It's a formal procedure. They state their name and then they bite. What was his name? If you tell me one of our dogs bit this woman without giving his name I will have that dog shot! (S. 17)

Die Anthropomorphisierung des Hundes hat zum einen den tragikomischen Effekt, erlaubt aber auch die Übertragung auf die menschlichen Schergen dieses Staates, der Macht willkürlich, aber mit dem Anschein von Rechtsstaatlichkeit auch durch das Wort, durch Sprachregelungen ausübt. *Mountain language* wird verboten, erlaubt ist nur noch *the language of the capital*. Am Ende des Dramas scheint sich der Bogen zu schließen. Das Verbot scheint aufgehoben.

> GUARD
> Tell her she can speak in her own language. New rules. Until further notice. (S. 47)

Dem Opfer der Verfügung über Sprache, der *elderly woman*, bleibt wie Stanley in *The Birthday Party* aber nur die Sprachlosigkeit. Der Schritt von *The Birthday Party* bis zu *Mountain Language* ist ein Schritt zu größerer Abstraktheit des Mythos und vielleicht gerade deswegen ist *Mountain Language* so unerträglich konkret.

1 Vgl. "A Play and its Politics. A conversation between Harold Pinter and Nicholas Hern". – In *One for the Road*. With production photos by Ivan Kyncl and an interview on the play and its politics. London: Methuen, 1985; ins Deutsche übersetzt von Heinrich-Maria Ledig-Rowohlt im Programmheft der deutschen Erstaufführung im Staatstheater Stuttgart 1986. Die Übersetzung ist bedauerlicherweise unidiomatisch und trifft nicht die für Pinter so typische feine Balance zwischen Sprech- und Schreibstil.

2 Pinter, H.: „Rede anläßlich der Verleihung des Shakespeare-Preises 1970". – In Stiftung F. v. S. Hamburg: *Shakespeare-Preis 1970*. Hamburg, 1970.

3 Als „Krise des Dramas" beschreibt Peter Szondi das analytische Drama Ibsens und stuft den Einakter als Rettungs- bzw. Lösungsversuch ein (P. Szondi: *Theorie des modernen Dramas*. Frankfurt/M., 1956).

4 Vgl. K. R. Maison: *Themes and Variations*. London, 1960; deutsch: *Bild und Abbild. Meisterwerke von Meistern kopiert und umgeschaffen*. München, Zürich, 1960.

5 Als "definitive version" wurde in der Tageskritik die Neuverfilmung von 1987 bezeichnet. Vgl. anon.: "Arts". *The New Statesman*, 15. 6. 1987, 22 und H. Hebert: "At Home for Pinter's Party". *The Guardian*, 22. 6. 1987, 23.

6 Die Komplizenschaft des Opfers glaubt John Ditsky auch als hervorstechendsten Zug Stanleys in *The Birthday Party* zu sehen (J. Ditsky: "Pinter's Christ of Complicity: *The Birthday Party*". –In ders.: *The Onstage Christ*. London, 1980, S. 136–146).

7 Greiner, N.: „Die Figur als Chiffre im modernen Drama. Das Verhältnis von Menschenbild, Figurenkonzeption und Darstellungsmitteln in Pinters 'The Birthday Party'". – In Greiner, N., Hasler, J., Kurzenberger, H., Pikulik, L.: *Einführung ins Drama*. 2 Bde. Band 2: *Figur, Szene, Zuschauer*. München, 1982, S. 47–67, hier: S. 49.

8 Vgl. E. Mengel: *Die Dramen Harold Pinters im Spiegel der soziologischen Rollentheorie*. Frankfurt/M., Bern, Las Vegas, 1978.

9 Als Dramaturgie des Raumes wurden deswegen schon die frühen Stücke Pinters von Hans-Dieter Heitmann bezeichnet (H. D. Heitmann: *Dramaturgie des Raumes. Eine literaturkritische Analyse an Hand von Harold Pinters "comedies of menace"*. Sankt Augustin, 1982).

10 *The Birthday Party*, S. 83; hier und im folgenden wird durch Seitenangabe in Klammern aus folgender Ausgabe zitiert: H. Pinter: *The Birthday Party*. London: Methuen, 1982. Diese Ausgabe enthält wie alle seit 1965 erschienenen Ausgaben den stark revidierten Text der zweiten Auflage.

11 Zum Ursprung der griechischen Tragödie und den Anfängen des englischen Dramas vgl. H. Patzer: *Die Anfänge der griechischen Tragödie*. Wiesbaden, 1962, bes. S. 96f.; G. A. Seeck: „Geschichte der griechischen Tragödie". – In ders. (Ed.): *Das griechische Drama*. Darmstadt, 1979, S. 155–203, hier: S. 159, 160, 161; H.-J. Diller: „Das mittelalterliche Drama von den Misterien- und Mirakelspielen zu den Moralitäten". – In Nünning, J. (Ed.): *Das englische Drama*. Darmstadt, 1977, S. 1–66, hier: S. 36–37. – Ritual ist in diesen Arbeiten und auch bewußt bei mir anders als bei Katherine Burkman verstanden. Bei Burkman dominiert der umgangssprachliche Gebrauch, etwa im Sinne von „Rituale des Alltags", der ein tiefenpsychologisches Konzept voraussetzt (K. H. Burkman: *The Dramatic World of Harold Pinter: Its Basis in Ritual*. Columbus/Oh., 1971).

12 Beides, die Kleidermetaphorik und die Erlösung von der Blindheit, sind auch Bestandteil der maßgeblichen Bibelstelle. Die bekannte Stelle aus dem Brief des Apostels Paulus an die Epheser (Eph. 4/17, 18 und 24) lautet in der *King James Version* unter der Überschrift *The New Life in Christ*:

17 This I say therefore, and testify in the Lord, that ye henceforth walk not as other Gentiles walk, [. . .] through the ignorance that is in them, because of the b l i n d n e s s *of* their heart: [. . .]
24 and ye put on the n e w m a n which after God is created in righteousness and true holiness. [Hervorhebung vom Vf.]

Deutlich bezieht sich diese Stelle in typologischer Manier auf die Schöpfungsgeschichte (Mose 1/26), in der von der Menschwerdung Adams die Rede ist, seiner Erschaffung nach dem Bild und Gleichnis Gottes. Auch das im Bild des Sehens gestaltete Thema der Erkenntnis findet sich dort bereits. Der Verzehr der Früchte des *tree of knowledge* (Mose 2/17) soll dem Menschen „die Augen öffnen" (Mose 3/5).

13 Vgl. H. Pinter: *The Birthday Party*. London, 1962, S. 30.

14 Zu „Punkt" und „Teil" im Aufbauschema der Dramenhandlung bei Gustav Freytag vgl. auch in dem von L. Pikulik verfaßten Band 1 (*Handlung*) von Greiner/Hasler/Kurzenberger/Pikulik: *Einführung ins Drama* S. 182, Anm. 32.

15 Bredella hat die Natur dieser Betreuung als Mischung aus Diktatur und Wohlfahrtsstaat charakterisiert. Als eine solche Mischung sei die „Organisation" zu verstehen, die Stanley angeblich betrogen hat. Vgl. L. Bredella: „Die Intention und Wirkung literarischer Texte: A. Weskers *Chips with Everything* und H. Pinters *The Birthday Party*". *Der fremdsprachliche Unterricht* H. 25, 1973, 34–49, hier: 44.

16 In *Old Times* wird die Situation der Psychoanalyse, Couch und Analytiker, explizit und bildhaft gestaltet. Psychoanalyse und analytisches Drama werden dabei explizit dementiert, wie ich in meinem Aufsatz „Harold Pinter. *Old Times*". – In Lengeler, R. (Ed.): *Englische Literatur der Gegenwart 1971–1975*. Düsseldorf, 1977, S. 132–143, nachgewiesen habe. Der Zusammenhang zwischen der literarischen Gattung des analytischen Kriminalromans und der Psychoanalyse wird neuerlich erhellt durch die erst jetzt durch die Erinnerungen seiner Haushälterin bekannt gewordene Tatsache, daß Kriminalromane die Lieblingslektüre Sigmund Freuds waren. Vgl. D. Berthelsen (Ed.): *Alltag bei Familie Freud. Erinnerungen der Paula Fichtel*. Hamburg, 1987.

17 Hier und im folgenden durch Seitenangabe in Klammern aus H. Pinter: *Mountain Language*. London: Faber, 1988.

18 Vgl. dazu Th. Fischer-Seidel: „Die unausweichliche Modalität des Sichtbaren: Wahrnehmung und Kategorien des Dramas im Theater Becketts". – In Ludwig, H.-W. (Ed.): *Anglistentag 1987 Tübingen. Vorträge*. Gießen, 1988, S. 106–123.

Bernhard Reitz, Gießen

"The act of observing determines the reality" – Die Darstellungskonventionen des *thriller* und die Rolle des Zuschauers in Tom Stoppards *Hapgood*

Das Zitat im Titel ist die Folgerung aus einem physikalischen Experiment, dessen Bedingungen der Physiker Kerner in *Hapgood* ausführlich erläutert. Es geht um die Frage, was Licht ist, ob es aus Teilchen oder aus Wellen besteht. Stellt man zwischen eine Lichtquelle und eine Leinwand ein Hindernis, welches Licht nur durch zwei schmale Öffnungen durchläßt, so ergeben sich widersprüchliche Befunde. "Every time we don't look", doziert Kerner, d. h., jedesmal, wenn wir den Weg des Lichtes durch das Hindernis nicht Schritt für Schritt verfolgen, sondern auf das Ergebnis blicken, erhalten wir ein Wellenmuster. "Every time we look to see how we get a wave pattern, we get a particle pattern. The act of observing determines the reality."[1] Einstein hat hierfür keine Erklärung gefunden, und da es im Publikum stets nur eine begrenzte Zahl von Physikern geben wird, kann man auch nicht erwarten, daß Stoppard von dort eine Lösung erhofft. Seine Rückgriffe auf die Probleme der Quantenphysik sind damit keineswegs erschöpft. Kerner bekommt auch nachfolgend noch mehrfach Gelegenheit, die Implikationen der Quantenmechanik zu referieren. Man darf annehmen, daß ein nicht geringer Teil der Zuschauer auf diese Weise erstmals von Heisenbergs Unschärferelation hört. Für physikalisch weniger beschlagene Zuschauer hat Kerner eine Anekdote aus der Wissenschaftsgeschichte parat. In Königsberg gab es einst sieben Brücken über die Flußarme des Pregels, und die Bewohner scheiterten immer wieder an dem Versuch, alle Brücken zu überqueren, ohne eine davon zweimal zu benutzen. Der Schweizer Mathematiker Leonhard Euler löste das Problem mit einem Stadtplan. Es ist allein nicht zu schaffen. Man braucht zwei Personen (S. 45–46).

Physik und Mathematik, d. h. die kognitiven Probleme der empirischen Wissenschaften, besetzen in *Hapgood* jenen Platz, den in Stoppards früheren Stükken insbesondere Philosophie, Kunsttheorie und Ideologie innegehabt haben. Angesichts der Bedeutung, die der experimentellen Analyse in der Physik zukommt – zumindest nach ihrem klassischen Selbstverständnis –, erscheint es deshalb durchaus folgerichtig, wenn bereits in der Exposition auf die Bedeutung der Beobachtung für den Erkenntnisgewinn hingewiesen wird. Innerhalb eines Dramas muß ein solcher Hinweis jedoch auch sofort den Blick auf den Status der Zuschauer lenken. Denn diesen ist im Theater die Beobachterrolle explizit zugewiesen.

Daß Stoppard die traditionelle Beobachterrolle der Zuschauer thematisiert, ist aus der Kenntnis seiner früheren Stücke heraus zu erwarten. Kerners Experiment, wonach zwei widersprüchliche Befunde durch die Art der Beobachtung bedingt sind, verweist explizit darauf, daß auch in *Hapgood* der Status des Beobachters keineswegs konsolidiert ist. Stoppard führt in *Hapgood* seine Auseinandersetzung mit dem Theater als selbstreflexivem Medium fort, und es läßt sich zeigen, daß die für den normalen Zuschauer nur bedingt nachvollziehbaren Entgrenzungen des Handlungsgeschehens in die epistemologischen Probleme der Kernphysik[2] von Stoppard zur Konsolidierung des eigenen dramen- und kunsttheoretischen Standorts genutzt werden. Um dies zu erhellen, ist es jedoch notwendig, Stoppards Auseinandersetzung mit den Darstellungskonventionen des *thriller* über *Hapgood* hinaus einzubeziehen.

Kerners Lehrbeispiel entstammt der Optik. Doch er entwickelt es innerhalb eines Kontexts, für den der Begriff „Grauzone" angemessener erscheint. Denn Kerner ist nicht nur Physiker, sondern zugleich ein Doppelagent des britischen Geheimdienstes. Angeworben wurde er von der Titelheldin Hapgood, die im Geheimdienst nur "Mother" genannt wird und die von Kerner auch einen Sohn namens Joe hat. Dieser Name ist passend gewählt. Denn "Joes" ist die Bezeichnung für die vom Geheimdienst geführten Agenten. Auch die biblische Anspielung erscheint nicht weit hergeholt. Der biblische Joseph wurde von seinen Brüdern verraten und verkauft. Eben dies müssen auch Agenten stets fürchten. Aufgrund dieser Querbezüge ist es kaum verwunderlich, daß auch der kleine Joe in das Geschäft der Eltern verwickelt wird. Er spielt die Rolle einer Geisel, deren Preis Informationen sind.

Mit *Hapgood* hat Stoppard einen *thriller* geschrieben. Die Welt der Spione, in die er uns führt, ist die Szenerie Smileys, und wie bei John Le Carré bestimmen fragwürdig gewordene Loyalitäten Handlung und Konflikte. Ein hochrangiger Verräter im Geheimdienst muß entlarvt werden. Die CIA übt bereits Druck aus. Sie ist vertreten durch einen farbigen Agenten namens Wates, der in seiner ständigen Besorgnis, aufgrund seiner Hautfarbe benachteiligt zu werden, frappierende Parallelen zu Joseph Conrads Wait in *The Nigger of the Narcissus* aufweist. Hapgoods über lange Zeit unklare Beziehungen zu den Männern im Stück ergänzten die Spionage-Handlung um den "love interest", und in Übereinstimmung mit den Konventionen des Genres sind alle Protagonisten verdächtig. Ebensowenig läßt Stoppard die genretypische "last-act reversal" aus. Bevor Hapgood in einer dramatischen Konfrontation ihren Kollegen Ridley als Verräter erschießt, hat der zunächst besonders verdächtige Kerner gestanden, er habe sich unter Druck wieder den Russen zugewandt. Das aber erweist sich als Trick, um Ridley in Sicherheit zu wiegen. Doch ganz am Schluß erfahren wir, daß die bewußte Täuschung auch die Wahrheit war.

Im *plot* von *Hapgood* löst Stoppard die mit den Konventionen des *thriller* verbundenen Erwartungen ein. Den poetologischen Vorgaben wird bis hin zum vorhersagbaren Ende entsprochen. Dies aber wirft die Frage auf, welche Bedeutung Kerners Entgrenzungen des Handlungsgeschehens in die Problembereiche der Quantenphysik eigentlich zukommt. Vordergründig lenken sie unstreitig von dem deutlich geringer profilierten Ridley ab. Offen bleibt jedoch zunächst, ob damit ein strukturell anspruchsloses Handlungsgefüge nur thematisch aufgewertet oder der Schritt auch zur gattungstheoretischen Reflexion tatsächlich vollzogen wird. Zur Klärung dieses Sachverhalts ist es notwendig, nochmals zur Exposition zurückzukehren und in diesem Zusammenhang Stoppards bisherige Rückgriffe auf die Konventionen des *thriller* auszuleuchten.

Daß Stoppard sich auch in *Hapgood* nicht auf die Darstellungsmittel allein eines Genres beschränkt, wird angesichts seines Œuvres nicht verwundern. Für den größten Teil der Eröffnungsszene bedient er sich der Pantomime. Die Szene spielt in einem Schwimmbad, dessen Umkleidekabinen zur Übergabe von Spionagematerial genutzt werden. Dieser Sachverhalt ergibt sich aus knappen, über Sprechfunk ausgetauschten Informationen der das Schwimmbad überwachenden Geheimdienstbeamten. Sie lenken das Interesse des Publikums darauf, wie sich die Übergabe abspielen wird. Gezeigt wird danach ein Bäumchen-Wechsel-Dich-Spiel, bei dem Aktentaschen deponiert und aus den Kabinen abgeholt und Handtücher als Zeichen des Vollzugs umgehängt werden. Während das Publikum noch amüsiert rätselt, wer da bereits wohl was weitergegeben hat, kommt die Nachricht, daß die Übergabe vollzogen und der Empfänger entkommen ist. Vorbereitet durch Kerners Erläuterung des Experiments liefert aber bereits die zweite Szene die Erklärung. Die Russen setzten Zwillinge bei der Übergabe ein. Doch nur die Regieanweisung offenbart, daß Ridley einer dieser Zwillinge war (vgl. S. 3).

Auch Pantomimen basieren auf optischer Wahrnehmung, und Stoppard nutzt dieses, um sein Publikum recht unverfroren auszutricksen. Er manövriert es in die Situation jener Gutgläubigen, die sich auf das verbotene „Hütchenspiel" einlassen. Bei diesem Spiel, das heute zumeist mit Karten gespielt wird, geht es darum, unter drei auf dem Tisch bewegten Karten die eine rote Karte zu identifizieren. Aber während der gutgläubige Spieler noch setzt, ist die rote Karte schon längst durch eine schwarze vertauscht, und wenn er deren Weg auch richtig verfolgt, so kann er doch nur verlieren. Stoppards Publikum ist in einer vergleichbaren Situation. Es kann das Spiel genau verfolgen und muß doch feststellen, daß es das Richtige und Wichtige nicht gesehen hat. Die Pantomime widerlegt hier die Annahme, daß exakte Beobachtung auch zu einem eindeutig verifizierbaren Ergebnis führen muß. Bestätigt wird, wenngleich auf sehr vordergründige Weise, Kerner, dessen Beispiel ja impliziert, daß das Ergebnis der Beobachtung davon abhängt, was bzw. wie man beobachtet.

Pantomime und physikalisches Experiment konstituieren in *Hapgood* Wahrnehmung als Problem und sind in struktureller Hinsicht zugleich Entgrenzungen der Konventionen des *thriller*. Nur beiläufig sei an dieser Stelle daran erinnert, daß in *Hapgood* die Pantomime nicht zum ersten Mal von Stoppard zur Thematisierung der Wahrnehmung eingesetzt wird. Rosencrantz, der intellektuell etwas beschränkte Zuschauer, der seine "good story, with a beginning, middle and end" einfordert[3], und Guildenstern mit seiner wachsenden Angst vor dem Tod als dem Ende von Leben und Fiktion zugleich sind Stoppards früheste Beispiele für ein Publikum, das zur adäquaten Wahrnehmung nicht fähig ist. Auch ihnen wird eine Pantomime gezeigt. Doch sie vermögen nicht zu erkennen, daß der First Player ihr Schicksal inszeniert hat. Diese Erkenntnisleistung wird in *Rosencrantz und Guildenstern Are Dead* vom realen Publikum erbrcht, dem nun in *Hapgood* allerdings vorgeführt wird, daß gesicherte Wahrnehmung keineswegs selbstverständlich ist.

Indem Stoppard bereits in der zweiten Szene freimütig bekennt, daß er sein Publikum getäuscht hat, nimmt er zugleich die Auseinandersetzung mit den Gattungskonventionen des *thriller* auf. Von allen der Poetik des *well-made play* verpflichteten Genres gelten insbesonders für den *thriller* Faktizität, Kausalität und rational eindeutige Nachvollziehbarkeit des Handlungsgeschehens als konstitutiv. Eine nicht unwesentliche Attraktion des *thriller* liegt gerade darin, daß hier dem Publikum die Gelegenheit zum Mitraten gegeben wird, daß es sich als Detektiv einbringen kann. Im *well-made thriller* ist die Auflösung dann zwar doch unerwartet, aber sie darf niemals unlogisch sein. Angesichts der Bedeutung von Faktizität für die Gattung, einer Faktizität, die nicht erst seit Sherlock Holmes mit dem Schein naturwissenschaftlich-analytischer Akribie umhüllt wird, hat Bernd Lenz für die Prosaformen des Genres den Begriff "factifiction" geprägt.[4] Auf das Drama ist er übertragbar. "[...] the lesson of realism is seen to die hard throughout the thriller", schreibt Bruce Merry in seiner Anatomie des Genres, und er konstatiert, daß "an elemental theology of right and wrong"[5] die Gattung kennzeichne. Eben diesen Anspruch auf Gewißheit, auf eindeutige Unterscheidbarkeit, unterhöhlt Stoppard jedoch gerade dadurch, daß er als Erklärung der rätselhaften Übergabe Zwillinge anbietet. Vordergründig genügt er dem Anspruch auf rationale Nachvollziehbarkeit der Handlung. Aber nach den Maßstäben der Gattung unterbreitet er ein wenig elegantes Lösungsangebot, das schon zum Überdruß eingesetzt wurde und zum Klischee herabgesunken ist. Mit dem Zwillingsmotiv wird, so scheint es, die Erwartung einer intellektuell anspruchsvollen Konfliktlösung unterlaufen.

Angesichts der hochkomplexen *plots*, die Stoppard für seine früheren Stücke entwickelt hat, darf man unterstellen, daß er auch in *Hapgood* mit einer subtileren Erklärung hätte aufwarten können. Sein Rückgriff auf eines der ältesten Klischees des Genres erscheint vielmehr im bewußten Einklang mit jener Einschätzung des *thriller* gewählt, die in den früheren Dramen Stoppards dominiert. Stoppard hat die Darstellungskonventionen des *thriller* immer wieder einbezogen, und insbesondere die Figur des Kriminalinspektors hat er mit Vorliebe entlehnt. Bei Stoppard amüsieren diese Inspektoren das Publikum durch ihre vergeblichen Versuche, Geheimnisse aufzuklären, die über das enge thematische Feld ihres Genres hinausweisen. Inspektor Bones, der romantische Bewunderer Dotties, der unermüdlich nach dem ermordeten McFee sucht, verkörpert in *Jumpers* anschaulich die Aporien positivistischer Lebenspraxis. Bones' Kollege in *Cahoot's Macbeth* ist ein weitaus bedrohlicherer Vertreter des Genres. Doch seine Anstrengungen, die vermutete politische Verschwörung zu entlarven, bewirken zugleich die strukturelle Entgrenzung des Stücks und tragen damit entscheidend zu dessen "theatricality" bei.[6] Denn um sich vor seinen Nachstellungen zu schützen, wird *Macbeth* in "Dogg Language" aufgeführt, und was sich dem Inspektor als unverständlich und als Nonsens darstellt, bietet dem Publikum mehr als die Möglichkeit, Shakespeares "purple passages" zu entschlüsseln. Intellektuell düpiert wird schließlich auch der Inspektor von *After Magritte*. Er wird bei der Aufklärung seines Falls zu immer surrealeren Hypothesen über die Identität des Täters gezwungen und muß schließlich doch erkennen, daß er sich stets nur selbst verfolgte. Was er konfigurierte, waren intellektuelle und imaginativ anschauliche Entgrenzungen. Doch das Genre läßt nur realistische Auflösungen zu.

Diesen realistischen Lösungsanspruch hat Stoppard am konsequentesten in *The Real Inspector Hound* parodiert. Als der „wahre" Inspektor erweist sich hier der vorgeblich an den Rollstuhl gefesselte Magnus, der aber nicht Magnus ist, sondern dessen vermißter Halbbruder Albert, und hinter all diesen Rollenträgern des Spiels-im-Spiel verbirgt sich der dem Rang nach dritte Kritiker Puckeridge, der sich an die Spitze der Kritikerhierarchie seiner Zeitung mordet.[7] Von der *well-made play*-Exposition, welche die Putzfrau am Telefon vorträgt[8], bis zu dem für den Kritiker Moon überraschenden und tödlichen, gleichwohl fiktionsimmanent logischen Schluß folgt Stoppard den poetologischen Vorgaben des *thriller* mit solch unerbittlicher Vordergründigkeit, daß die Mechanismen des Genres unzweideutig zutage treten. Wo die Kunst sich so sklavisch dem Wirklichkeitsanspruch unterwirft, spiegelt sie nicht mehr Wirklichkeit und wird auch nicht Teil von ihr, sondern wird unwirklich.[9]

Auf die aus den poetologischen Vorgaben des Genres bedingten Grenzen verweist in *The Real Inspector Hound* auch der Kritiker Moon, der bereits während der Exposition seine Rezension zu formulieren beginnt:

[...] does this play know where it is going? [...] Does it, I repeat, declare its affiliations? There are moments, and I would not begrudge it this, when the play, if we can call it that, and I think on balance, we can, aligns itself uncompromisingly on the side of life. *Je suis*, it seems to be saying, *ergo sum*. But is that enough? I think we are entitled to ask. For what in fact is this play concerned with? It is my belief that here we are concerned with what I have referred to elsewhere as the nature of identity. I think we are entitled to ask – and here one is irresistibly reminded of Voltaire's cry "Voila!" – I think we are entitled to ask – *Where is God*? (S. 28)

Stoppards Parodie verblasener Kritiker-Rhetorik ist offensichtlich. Aber ebenso auffällig ist auch die Inkongruenz zwischen den von Moon versuchten Anknüpfungen und dem Stück, das er zu besprechen hat. Die Frage nach dem „Anliegen" eines Stücks erübrigt sich beim *thriller*, und die Fragen nach "the nature of identity" und nach Gott bewegen keinen Zuschauer dazu, sich im mittlerweile 38. Aufführungsjahr *The Mousetrap* anzusehen. Moon etabliert mit seinen Fragen das moderne Drama als Referenzsystem. Was bei Pinter und Beckett angemessen ist, erweist sich angesichts der Mechanik des Krimalstücks jedoch auf groteske Weise als inadäquat. Insofern parodiert Moon mehr als nur seinen Berufsstand. *Ex negativo*, indem er ins Bewußtsein ruft, was der *thriller* von seinen Vorgaben her nicht leisten kann, demonstriert er zugleich die Grenzen des Genres.

Die hier skizzierte, *Hapgood* vorausgehende Auseinandersetzung Stoppards mit den Darstellungskonventionen und epistemologischen Möglichkeiten des *thriller* weckt Zweifel an der Annahme, man könnte sein Spionagestück als einen Akt der Wiedergutmachung an einem zuvor genüßlich demontierten Genre rezipieren. Wo Stoppard sich bisher auf die Dramaturgie des *thriller* eingelassen hat, hat er sie zwar befolgt. Aber die vordergründige Weise, in der dies geschehen ist, war stets kontraproduktiv. Denn durch die Art, wie die Erwartungen an den *thriller* eingelöst wurden, wurden dessen poetologische Prämissen zugleich in Frage gestellt.

Es läßt sich zeigen, daß Stoppard in *Hapgood* die Auseinandersetzung mit diesen poetologischen Prämissen des *thriller* weiterführt. Doch an die Stelle der zuvor überwiegend parodistischen Ausbeutung der Defizite des Genres tritt nun der Versuch, dessen immanente Widersprüche ohne karikierende Überzeichnung und mit dem Ziel der Gattungsreflexion bewußt zu machen.

Diese Dimension des Stückes erschließt sich, wenn man sich vor Augen führt, wie Stoppard das Klischee des Zwillingsmotivs ausbaut, bevor Hapgood das genrekonforme Ende herbeiführt. In seiner herkömmlichen Verwendung im *thriller* ist das Zwillingsmotiv durch das Kriterium der Nicht-Unterscheidbarkeit definiert. Weil Zwillinge sich zum Verwechseln ähnlich sind, als „identisch" gelten, sind sie ideale Täter. Zwei autonome Wesen können, wenn sie nicht zusammen wahrgenommen werden, als eines agieren. Daß bei der in *Hapgood* gezeigten Übergabe Zwillinge agierten, erschließt Kerner jedoch dadurch, daß er diese Überlegung umkehrt. Zwillinge konnten am Werk sein, weil – wie sein Experiment besagt – ein als Einheit wahrgenommenes Phänomen, das Licht, nachweislich zwei Erscheinungsformen, Teilchen und Welle, haben kann. Der Geheimdienstchef Blair und Kerner kommen in ihren Analysen der Übergabe somit zwar zum gleichen Ergebnis, aber auf deutlich verschiedene Weise. Blair operiert auf der Ebene der formalen Logik, der realistischen und kausalen Beweisführung, in der alles eine rationale Erklärung findet. Paradoxien können hier zwar nicht ausgeschlossen werden, aber sie werden auch nicht ernsthaft in die Überlegung einbezogen. Kerners Denken dagegen nimmt die Paradoxie zum Ausgangspunkt. Das nach den Regeln der Logik und der Physik nicht erklärbare Experiment ist nicht das Ende, sondern der Ansatz seiner Analyse.

Wenn Moon zu Beginn seiner Rezension faselt,

> Already in the opening stages we note the classic impact of the catalystic figure – the outsider – plunging through to the centre of an ordered world and setting up the disruptions – (S. 19),

so ist in *The Real Inspector Hound* die pintereske Deutung dem Stück ebenso unangemessen wie der Rest seiner Ausführungen. Für Kerner läßt sich dagegen eine katalytische Funktion durchaus feststellen. Als Physiker ist er jenseits seiner persönlichen Verstrickung im Spionagegeschäft ein Außenseiter in der Welt der Geheimdienste, und sein erkenntnistheoretisches Verfahren stellt nicht nur das in dieser Welt praktizierte Denken, sondern auch dessen Prämissen in Frage. Stoppard zeichnet den britischen Geheimdienst als "ordered world", in dem "laboratory standards for reality" gelten (S. 72). Man kennt die richtige und die falsche Seite, und man glaubt deshalb auch, richtig und falsch unterscheiden zu können. Handlungsleitend sind Rationalität und Kausalität. Das akzeptierte Erkenntnisverfahren ist das "grid"-System, der methodische Vollzug von nachfolgenden Analyseschritten, den Hapgood erläutert, als ihr Sohn bekennt, einen wichtigen Schlüssel verlegt zu haben:

> [...] do the grid for me. From getting up, to when you couldn't find it.
> [...] Just do the grid – five minutes for every square, don't leave any out because the key is in one of them [...]. (S. 22)

Bei der Suche nach dem Schlüssel funktioniert das "grid"-System, und auch bei der Suche nach dem Verräter wird es zunächst angewandt. Jeder ist, der Reihe nach, verdächtig. Die Prämissen des fiktionsimmanenten Verfahrens sind identisch mit den Prämissen der Gattung. Sie bestätigen ein mechanistisches Dramenkonzept, von dem Pinter in seiner Kritik des *well-made play* sagte, es komme dem Kreuzworträtsel gleich:

> The audience holds the paper. The play fills in the blanks. Everyone's happy.[10]

In *Hapgood* zerstört jedoch Kerner diese Illusion einer geordneten Welt, in der jeder Schritt von Feld zu Feld ein Erkenntnisschritt ist. Hierzu bedient er sich wiederum eines physikalischen Bilds. Der geordneten Welt entspricht das von Niels Bohr entwickelte Atommodell, in dem, wie in Schulbüchern noch immer dargestellt, die Elektronen um das Atom kreisen wie Planeten um ihre Sonne. Dieses Atommodell, das ja zugleich ein Modell des Aufbaus der Welt ist, wurde nicht zuletzt durch Heisenberg widerlegt. Was Heisenberg als „Unschärferelation" definierte und was mittlerweile als zentrale Kategorie der Quantenmechanik gilt, ist die Einsicht, daß Elektronen sich eben nicht auf geordneten und exakt berechenbaren Bahnen bewegen, sondern „springen". Kerner drückt das so aus:

> [...] an electron does not go round like a planet, it is like a moth which was there a moment ago, it gains or loses a quantum of energy and it jumps, and at the moment of the quantum jump it is like two moths, one to be here and one to stop being there; an electron is like twins, each one unique, a unique twin. (S. 49)

Über die Implikationen der Quantenmechanik für unser Weltbild wie für das Selbstverständnis der Wissenschaften läßt Kerner das Publikum nicht im Zweifel. Wiederum an Einstein anknüpfend, sagt er:

> He believed in the same God as Newton, causality, nothing without reason, but now one thing led to another until causality was dead. Quantum mechanics made everything finally random, things can go this way or that way, the mathematics deny certainty, they reveal only probability and chance, and Einstein couldn't believe in a God who threw dice. (Ebd.)

Auf der Grundlage der aus der Quantenphysik gewonnenen Einsichten mußte das Selbstverständnis der Naturwissenschaften revidiert werden. Determinative Naturgesetze sind nur im Bereich der Makrophysik gültig, hier sind Entwicklungen eindeutig vorausbestimmt und berechenbar. Die Einzelaktionen von Elementarteilchen dagegen entziehen sich dieser Vorausbestimmung, und die hieraus resultierende Ungewißheit ist nicht in menschlicher Unzulänglichkeit, sondern in den Gegebenheiten der Mikrophysik selbst begründet. In der Welt der Makrophysik hat der Kausalitätsanspruch noch Gültigkeit. In der Mikrophysik, in der Welt der Elementarteilchen, muß Akausalität akzeptiert werden.

Angesichts der in der Quantenphysik gewonnenen Einsichten läßt sich ein positivistisches Wissenschaftsverständnis nicht mehr aufrechterhalten. Die im 19. Jahrhundert betriebene Ablösung der exakten Wissenschaften von der Philosophie eliminierte den Indeterminismus aus der Wissenschaft und suchte ihn auch der Philosophie auszutreiben. Damit schien das Ende der Metaphysik absehbar. In der Quantenphysik dagegen kehrt der Indeterminismus als wissenschaftliche Kategorie zurück, und so wird auch der Brückenschlag zur Philosophie und sogar zur Metaphysik wieder möglich. Für die Kunsttheorie bleibt dies nicht ohne Folgen, wie Stoppard demonstriert. Blair, der Geheimdienstchef, hat einen "B. A. first class" als akademischen Grad, verbunden mit, wie Kerner es ausdrückt, "an amusing incomprehension of the sciences" (S. 72). Gleichwohl beharrt er auf den "laboratory standards for reality". Kerner dagegen, der ausgewiesene Naturwissenschaftler, setzt diesem Anspruch die "artfulness" der Wirklichkeit entgegen (ebd.). Wenn aber die Wissenschaft die Viel- und Mehrdeutigkeit der Welt akzeptieren muß, und zwar nicht deshalb, weil sie bislang noch an vermuteten eindeutigen Erklärungen scheitert, sondern weil es diese nicht gibt, dann werden auch alle jene Kunsttheorien desavouiert, welche die Kunst dadurch zu retten suchten, daß sie sie auf ein positivistisches Wissenschaftsverständnis einschwören. Auf der Grundlage der Quantentheorie erweisen sich die ästhetischen Prämissen des *thriller*, die ihre Abhängigkeit von einem positivistischen Verständnis von Wissenschaft und Welt noch eindeutiger als alle anderen Genres des realistischen Theaters erkennen lassen, nicht als das Ergebnis eines objektivierten Erkenntnisprozesses, sondern vielmehr als Konsequenzen einer subjektiven und auch wissenschaftsgeschichtlich abgrenzbaren Setzung.

Daß in *Hapgood* die Auseinandersetzung um die gattungspoetische Situation des *thriller* und des realistischen Theaters insgesamt anders geführt wird als in *The Real Inspector Hound*, zeichnet sich hier ab. Der Eindruck, daß der *thriller* trotz aller prätendierten Kausalität und Rationalität ein höchst irreales, artifizielles Genre ist, resultierte dort aus der parodistischen Offenlegung der genretypischen Mechanismen. *Hapgood* dagegen thematisiert die philosophisch-wissenschaftstheoretischen Fundamente, auf denen sich diese genretypischen Mechanismen entwickeln konnten. Die Erkenntnis der Irrealität und Artifizialität des Genres gründet hier in der Einsicht, daß der *thriller* ein Verständnis von Wirklichkeit fortschreibt, dessen Geltungsanspruch überholt ist.

Hapgood ist als *thriller* konzipiert und durchläuft, wie eingangs dargelegt, die gattungsspezifischen Entwicklungsschritte. Jedoch hat Stoppard die Gattungskonventionen nicht allein durch die pantomimischen Sequenzen der ersten Szene entgrenzt. Geht man von dem für das realistische Drama akzeptierten Handlungsschema Exposition-Konflikt-Konfliktlösung aus, so steht im *thriller* an der Stelle des Konflikts die Suche nach dem Täter, die auf der Bühne – *The Mousetrap* ist hier durchaus Vorbild – vor allem mit den Mitteln der Befragung, des Verhörs betrieben wird. Ziel dieses Verhörs ist, da ein unbekannter Täter überführt werden muß, die Verifizierung bzw. Falsifizierung von Identitätsvorgaben. An diesem Punkt greift Stoppard erneut in das Handlungsmuster ein. An Stelle der nur vordergründigen Erörterung von Identität im *thriller* setzt er die aus der Quantenphysik hergeleitete philosophische Diskussion der Identitätsproblematik und weitet damit den *thriller* zum *play of ideas*. Als in der Tat katalytische Figur bringt Kerner die Frage nach Gott und nach "the nature of identity" ins Spiel und inkorporiert über das *play of ideas* dem *thriller* eben jene Dimension und Thematik der Moderne, die Moon implizit als dem Genre wesensfremd bestimmt hatte. Die Suche nach dem Verräter wird, und dadurch bleibt das Zwillingsmotiv handlungsbestimmend, zur Frage nach der Natur des Täters. Sie wird aber nun als Frage nach der Natur des Menschen und seinen Erkenntnismöglichkeiten gegenüber der Welt und sich selbst gestellt.

Diese in der Exposition vorbereitete und dann bis zum Schluß durchgehaltene Entgrenzung des *thriller* zum *play of ideas* hat in *Hapgood* allerdings zur Folge, daß über viele Szenen hinweg die Suche nach dem Verräter als nur noch dünner Handlungsfaden erscheint.[11] Moon, so muß man glauben, wird doch bestätigt. Die Konventionen des *thriller* und die intellektuellen Ansprüche des *play of ideas* sind faktisch nicht vereinbar, und dies um so weniger, wenn, wie gezeigt, über das *play of ideas* sogar die poetologischen Prämissen des *thriller* demontiert werden. Stoppard demonstriert jedoch in *Hapgood* erneut, daß er seine Fähigkeit, strukturell eigenständige dramaturgische Paradigmen zu integrieren, noch nicht verloren hat. Sein *thriller* erfährt eine gattungskonforme Auflösung. Aber sie wird nur deshalb möglich, weil fiktionsimmanent die aus der Quantenphysik entwickelten Folgerungen für das Verständnis von Identität und Wirklichkeit akzeptiert werden. Mit dem "grid"-System ist Ridley nicht zu überführen. Dies gelingt erst, als Hapgood sich wie das Elektron beim Quantensprung verhält und eine temporär duale Existenz annimmt. Ridley, oder genauer den Ridley-Zwillingen tritt sie sowohl als die penible Geheimdienstbeamtin "Mother" wie auch als deren eher chaotische Zwillingsschwester Celia gegenüber. Daß mit dieser Verdoppelung nicht nur ein Rollenspiel verbunden ist, sondern im Sinne des Quantensprungs eine tatsächliche Duplizität von Existenz, duale Identität, verdeutlicht Stoppard allerdings auf eher handgreifliche Weise. Als "Mother" wehrt Hapgood die sexuellen Avancen des Kollegen Ridley ab; als Celia gibt sie ihnen nach.

Stoppard hat seinem *thriller* einen poetologischen Quantensprung implantiert. Die realistische Auflösung wird erst durch die Preisgabe des verabsolutierten Realismusanspruchs erzielt, Eindeutigkeit erst durch die Akzeptanz von Vieldeutigkeit erreicht. Damit ist es an der Zeit, zur eingangs gestellten Frage nach der ambivalenten Rolle des Zuschauers zurückzukehren. Die Wahrnehmung bestimmt die Wirklichkeit, folgert Kerner aus seinem Experiment. Wir kennen diese These jedoch aus der Philosophie, als Berkeleys *esse est percipi*, und nicht zufällig haben auch Beckett und Pinter – erinnert sei an Ruth in *The Homecoming*[12] – auf Berkeley immer wieder Bezug genommen. Berkeleys Denken verknüpft Idealismus und Empirismus, wodurch bei ihm die Möglichkeit einer logisch eindeutigen, monokausalen und damit die Existenz Gottes einschließenden Erklärung der Welt wenigstens potentiell gegeben bleibt. Bei Stoppard dagegen wird deutlich, daß die Erfahrungswissenschaften uns zur Akzeptanz der Vieldeutigkeit der Welt zwingen. Für die Kunst bedeutet dies, daß es ihr gegenüber ebensowenig einen gesicherten Standort gibt wie gegenüber der Wirklichkeit. Fiktion und Rezeption sind das Ergebnis immer neuer Setzungen und können Endgültigkeit nicht beanspruchen. "You get what you interrogate for", erklärt Kerner; "the experimenter makes the choice" (S. 12).

Für das Theater Tom Stoppards ist dies keine grundsätzlich neue Einsicht. Denn innerhalb der in den früheren Stücken betriebenen Relativierung von Dogmen, Ideologien und Normen stellt Stoppard stets auch verabsolutierte poetologische Prämissen in Frage. Damit zielt er nicht anders als Pinter auf ein Publikum, das zu intellektuellen Auseinandersetzungen auch mit normativen Poetiken befähigt und deshalb bereit ist, seine Rezeptionshaltung im Hier und Jetzt der Aufführung zu reflektieren und neu zu konstituieren. Auch *Hapgood* setzt dies voraus, denn wie gezeigt wird die Auflösung als eine intellektuell komplexe Lösung erst dann einsichtig, wenn man durchschaut, daß die mit dem Genre verbundenen Erwartungen nur über die Aufhebung der Prämissen des Genres erfüllt werden können.

Doch was sich fiktionsimmanent als scheinbar vertrauter Prozeß von Entgrenzung und Relativierung vollzieht, beruht in *Hapgood* auf gegenüber den früheren Stücken veränderten Voraussetzungen. Von *Rosencrantz and Guildenstern* an war die Einsicht des Zuschauers, sich der Reflexion des eigenen Standorts nicht entziehen zu können, das Ergebnis der durch die Stücke vermittelten Erkenntnis, daß es gesicherte Standorte, archimedische Punkte für die Erklärung der Welt nicht gibt. In *Hapgood* wird diese Erkenntnis dagegen zur Prämisse. Die Implikationen der Quantentheorie für unser Weltbild und für die Kunst werden aufgezeigt, aber nicht auch selbst in einer den früheren Stücken vergleichbaren Weise hinterfragt. Kritik läßt sich allenfalls darin erkennen, daß Kerner, der seine wissenschaftlichen Erkenntnisse lebensweltlich umsetzt, von Stoppard als bindungsunfähig gezeigt wird, als jemand, der angesichts der Vieldeutigkeit der Welt weder privat noch ideologisch zu Festlegungen bereit ist.

In *Hapgood* gerät das Publikum in eine paradoxe Situation. Stoppard führt ihm einmal mehr vor Augen, wie fragwürdig der Anspruch auf rational und kausal eindeutige Erklärungen der Welt ist. Aber indem er die philosophischen wie die poetologischen Implikationen der Quantenphysik aufzeigt, ohne diese selbst der kritischen Reflexion zu unterziehen, legt er sein Publikum, das er zur Erkenntnis seiner Freiheit führen will, zugleich und im Gegensatz zu den früheren Stücken auf erkenntnistheoretische Prämissen fest. Gerade durch die Schlüssigkeit, mit der Kerner seine Folgerungen entwickelt und fiktionsimmanent umsetzt, wird der Zuschauer in die Rolle des Nachvollziehenden gedrängt.

Hapgood postuliert seine Autonomie, konsolidiert aber zugleich auch seine Abhängigkeit.

Damit rückt ein letzter Aspekt ins Blickfeld. Auf der Ebene der poetologischen Auseinandersetzung in *Hapgood* widerlegen, wie gezeigt, die Folgerungen aus der Quantenphysik ein realistisches Kunstverständnis, das die Kunst auf die Analysekriterien der exakten Wissenschaften festzulegen suchte. Nicht Eindeutigkeit, sondern Vieldeutigkeit läßt sich aus den Bausteinen der Welt ableiten, und die Quantenphysik wird damit auch zur Legitimation der Freiheit und der Potentialität der Kunst. Indem die Kunst bislang diese Potentialität und Freiheit gegen normative Ansprüche verteidigte, hat sie sozusagen im Einklang mit den Prinzipien des Universums gehandelt. Dem mag so sein. Aber es stellt sich die Frage, ob die Kunst tatsächlich dieser Legitimation bedarf und ob sie hierzu erneut die Naturwissenschaften bemühen sollte. Es ist das Merkmal der Moderne, daß sie die Kunst von wissenschaftlichen, theologischen und philosophischen Rechtfertigungszwängen befreit hat und deren Eigentlichkeit allein aus sich selbst begründet. Dieser Anspruch ist zwar stets befehdet, aber auch noch nicht widerlegt worden, und nicht nur durch Joyce in *Travesties* hat auch Stoppard ihn verteidigt. Mit der Beweisführung von *Hapgood* allerdings hat er diesem Anspruch womöglich einen Bärendienst erwiesen.

Anmerkungen

1 Stoppard, T.: *Hapgood.* London, 1988, S. 12. Nachfolgende Seitenangaben beziehen sich auf diese Ausgabe.
2 Daß die physikalischen Ausführungen Kerners das Publikum überforderten, wurde in zahlreichen Uraufführungskritiken vermerkt. Im *Daily Telegraph* vom 10. 3. 1988 heißt es z. B.: "Those who [. . .] haven't a 'physical bone' in their bodies, will find much of the dialogue, line by line, especially that of the physicist-defector Kerner, thoroughly incomprehensible".
3 Stoppard, T.: *Rosencrantz and Guildenstern Are Dead.* London, [5]1974, S. 58.
4 Lenz, B.: *Factifiction. Agentenspiele wie in der Realität. Wirklichkeitsanspruch und Wirklichkeitsgehalt des Agentenromans.* Heidelberg, 1987.
5 Merry, B.: *Anatomy of the Spy Thriller.* Dublin, 1977, S. 5 und 4. Die poetologischen Gemeinsamkeiten zwischen der dramatisierten und der Prosaform des Genres werden deutlich, wenn Merry ausführt: "[. . .] the well-made story requires a progression of events, often building up in a geometric, rather than arithmetic, ratio. Good 'story-line' demands tangible causation, and the succession of cause-and-effect in popular narrative leads naturally to a visible pay-off, a 'reversal of fortune', a reward for endeavour and a sanction against illegality" (S. 5).
6 Auf *Cahoot's Macbeth* läßt sich beziehen, was Zimmermann zu *Rosencrantz and Guildenstern Are Dead* schreibt: „Das Stück ist sich [. . .] seines Kunstcharakters stets bewußt, streicht seine Fiktionalität heraus und erinnert das Publikum daran,

daß es sich in einer Aufführung befindet, gibt ihm keine Möglichkeit zum Aufbau einer Wirklichkeitsillusion." (Zimmermann, H.: „T. Stoppards Publikumsverwirrung: Zu Rezeption und Sinn von *Rosencrantz and Guildenstern Are Dead.*" *Jahrbuch der Deutschen Shakespeare-Gesellschaft West*, 1978/1979, 191)

7 Stoppard, T.: *The Real Inspector Hound.* London, ⁵1975. Nachfolgende Seitenangaben beziehen sich auf diese Ausgabe.

8 Vgl. ebd., S. 15.

9 Wie Stoppard sowohl Agatha Christies Vorlage *The Mousetrap* als auch die Möglichkeiten des Spiels-im-Spiel nutzt, um dem Publikum die Spannung zwischen dem Wirklichkeitsanspruch des Genres und dessen Artifizialität zu veranschaulichen, verdeutlicht U. Broich: „Dramatische Spiegelkabinette – Zum Motiv des Spiels im Spiel in den Dramen Tom Stoppards". – In Grabes, H. (Ed.): *Anglistentag 1980 Giessen. Tagungsbeiträge und Berichte.* Grossen-Linden, 1981, S. 139–158.

10 Pinter, H.: "Writing for the theatre". – In ders.: *Plays: One.* London, 1976, S. 12.

11 Während Michael Coveney in der *Financial Times* vom 9. 3. 1988 *Hapgood* zubilligte, "[...] the espionage thriller, the abduction and the confusions of identity are resolved in a seamless, climatic triple-headed narrative", schloß sich die Mehrzahl der Rezensenten Milton Shulmans Urteil an, "Stoppard's disarming venture into the world of spies is less a whodunnit than an whothoughtit" (*Evening Standard*, 9. 3. 1988).

12 Vgl. H. Pinter: *The Homecoming.* – In ders.: *Plays: Three.* London, 1978, S. 67–69.

SPRACHWISSENSCHAFT

KLAUS MATZEL
Gesammelte Schriften
Hrsg.: Rosemarie Lühr – Jörg Riecke –
Christiane Thim-Mabrey
1990. XIV, 786 Seiten, 1 Abbildung.
Kartoniert DM 300,–. Leinen DM 340,–
(Germanische Bibliothek. Dritte Reihe:
Untersuchungen)

KLAUS MATZEL – JÖRG RIECKE –
GERHARD ZIPP
Spätmittelalterlicher deutscher Wortschatz aus Regensburger und mittelbairischen Quellen
1989. XL, 384 Seiten. Kartoniert DM 150,–.
Leinen DM 175,–
(Germanische Bibliothek, 2. Reihe: Wörter-
bücher)

MANFRED MAYRHOFER
Etymologisches Wörterbuch des Altindoarischen
1. Band. Lieferung 8
1990. Seiten 557–636. Kartoniert DM 36,–
(Indogermanische Bibliothek. 2. Reihe.
Wörterbücher)

DIETER MESSNER
História do Léxico Português
(com a origem das palavras citadas)
1990. IV, 79 Seiten. Kartoniert DM 50,–
(Sprachwissenschaftliche Studienbücher.
1. Abteilung)

CLAUDINE MOULIN
Der Majuskelgebrauch in Luthers deutschen Briefen (1517–1546)
1990. XXXIII, 462 Seiten, 2 Faksimiles.
Kartoniert DM 160,–. Leinen DM 190,–
(Germanische Bibliothek. Neue Folge. 3. Reihe)

BODO MÜLLER
Diccionario del español medieval
Fasciculo 5 (acabador-acebuche)
1990. S. 275–354. Kartoniert DM 48,–
(Sammlung romanischer Elementar- und
Handbücher. Dritte Reihe, Band 12)

JOHANNES SCHRÖPFER
Wörterbuch der vergleichenden Bezeichnungslehre
Onomasiologie
Band 1. Ausgabe A. Lieferung 5/6 und 7/8
1989. je 160 Seiten. Kartoniert je DM 76,–

KLAUS STEINKE
Die russischen Sprachinseln in Bulgarien
1990. 262 Seiten mit 13 Karten.
Kartoniert DM 86,–. Leinen DM 110,–
(SLAVICA. Sammlung slavischer
Lehr- und Handbücher. Neue Folge)

JÜRGEN UDOLPH
Die Stellung der Gewässernamen Polens innerhalb der alteuropäischen Hydronymie
1990. 364 Seiten mit 6 Karten.
Kartoniert DM 67,–. Leinen DM 96,–
(Beiträge zur Namenforschung. Neue Folge,
Beiheft 31)

MARIA WALCH
Zur Formenbildung im Frühneuhochdeutschen
1990. 96 Seiten. Kartoniert ca. DM 18,–
(Sprache, Literatur und Geschichte. Studien
zur Linguistik/Germanistik, Band 5)

CARL WINTER · UNIVERSITÄTSVERLAG · HEIDELBERG

Rolf Eichler, Konstanz

Caryl Churchills Theater:
Das Unbehagen an der Geschlechterdifferenz

I

Caryl Churchill ist die am häufigsten aufgeführte und publizierte Dramatikerin des zeitgenössischen britischen Theaters. Sie gehört zu jener lockeren Koalition von vage marxistischen Dramenautoren – sie selbst spricht von ihrer "woobly attraction to marxism" –, die in der Mitte der 70er Jahre bekannt wurden. Diese kommen aus der radikalen Theaterbewegung, dem *fringe*, die sich Ende der 60er Jahre gebildet hatte. Wie Bond, Brenton, Hare und andere hat Churchill Stücke geschrieben, die Kritik an der kapitalistischen Gesellschaft und zugleich an den Konventionen der bürgerlichen Bühne mit ihrer angeblichen Privatisierung der Erfahrung üben.

Unter ihnen ist Bond ausführlicher mit Überlegungen zur gesellschaftlichen Situation und zur Aufgabe des Theaters hervorgetreten. Im Vorwort seines *Lear* beispielsweise stellt er fest, daß es keinen Beweis dafür gebe, daß Aggression naturgegeben sei wie etwa Sexualität und Ernährung. Wir seien vielmehr im Laufe der Evolution traumwandlerisch in die gesellschaftliche Situation geschlidert, in der wir uns nun befinden: "As men's minds clarified they were already living in herds or groups, and these would have evolved into tribes and societies. Like waking sleepers they would not know dream from reality."[1] Seit jenen Tagen seien wir mehr und mehr in einem selbststabilisierten System der Aggression und der Gewalt gefangen: "[...] it is an organization held together by the aggression it creates. Aggression has become moralized, and morality has become a form of violence."[2] Die Aggression schließlich sei in Form der Selbstrepression verinnerlicht worden. Soziale Moral sei letztlich korrumpierte Unschuld: "[...] social morality is a form of corrupted innocence [...]".[3] Bei Bond wird deutlich, daß in seiner Utopie marxistischer Provenienz ein Gutteil Nostalgie nach dem Verlorenen Paradies steckt. Hier ist weniger Aufklärung als Mythisierung am Werk.

Von Caryl Churchill liegen keine philosophischen Versuche wie bei Bond vor, doch sie teilt dessen Position, wenn sie sich in der Frage der gesellschaftlichen Gewalt speziell mit der Sexualität auseinandersetzt. Churchill geht von der Annahme aus, daß das Geschlecht (weiblich/männlich) keinen Einfluß haben dürfe auf das Verhalten einer Person. Das, was wir heute an Unterschieden

139

sehen, sei erlernt, sei Rolle und nicht Biologie. Programmatisch will sie diese Unterschiedslosigkeit auf der Bühne ausspielen.

Von ersten Bühnenversuchen wie *Objections to Sex and Violence* (von der Kritik mit Bond verglichen)[4] bis hin zum kakophonischen[5] Theater- und Tanzstück *A Mouthful of Birds* zeigt uns Churchill: Männer sind Frauen (*Objections*), Frauen sind Männer (*Top Girls*), Frauen und Männer sind das Gleiche (*Mouthful of Birds*).

Eine anthropologische oder psychologische Diskussion mit Churchills Annahmen zu führen ist hier nicht der Ort. Das Interesse kann allein darin bestehen, festzustellen, inwieweit ihre Stücke im Rahmen der Kunst, näherhin des Theaters, imstande sind, die Defizite der philosophischen, anthropologischen und psychologischen Diskurse zur Geschlechterproblematik aufzudecken, zu bilanzieren und günstigenfalls mit einer neuen Qualität fortzusetzen.[6] – Zur Analyse dienen jene drei Stücke, die am stärksten experimentellen Charakter haben: *Cloud Nine, Top Girls* und *A Mouthful* of *Birds*.[7]

II

Cloud Nine wurde von Caryl Churchill mit der Joint Stock Theatre Group produziert. Deren Arbeitsmethode basiert auf enger Zusammenarbeit zwischen Schauspielern, Autor und Regisseur. Die Gruppe beginnt mit einem Workshop, der gemeinsam Recherchen zu einem Thema durchführt, das im Verlaufe der Arbeiten und Überlegungen durchaus eine andere Gestalt annehmen kann. So wurde beispielsweise der Plan für ein Stück, das über die Emigration handeln sollte und in der ersten Hälfte in Europa und in der zweiten Hälfte in Amerika spielen sollte, aufgegeben zugunsten des Themas über Sexualpolitik, die im viktorianischen und heutigen England zu verdeutlichen war. – Das eigentliche Schreiben folgt bei Caryl Churchill erst nach dem Workshop, der Text selber wird bei den Proben noch verändert.

Die Schauspieler, die am *Cloud Nine*-Workshop (im August 1978) teilnahmen, wurden nicht nur aufgrund ihrer künstlerischen Fähigkeiten ausgewählt, sondern auch aufgrund ihrer unterschiedlichen sexuellen Disponiertheit. Das Thema sollte von innen nach außen entwickelt werden. Man begann mit dem Austausch von Erfahrungen des eigenen Sexuallebens und ging dann über zu einer Diskussion sexueller Stereotypen und schließlich ganz allgemein zum Verhältnis von Geschlecht und Status.

Diese Vorgehensweise zeigt deutlich, daß sich das individuelle Subjekt der Autorin zurückzunehmen trachtet, um eine Pluralität von Ansichten zu Wort kommen zu lassen. Die nicht vorhandene Parteinahme, die man an Caryl

Churchills Schreiben rühmt, hat ihre Wurzel in der gleichen Gültigkeit aller darzustellenden Phänomene. Der eher kollektive Text entbehrt – zumindest streckenweise – einer Rezeptionssteuerung und führt dadurch – am stärksten in *A Mouthful of Birds* – zu phantastischen Gebilden. An dem Umstand, daß sowohl für *Cloud Nine* wie für *Fen* und andere Stücke die ursprünglichen Themen im Laufe der Gruppenarbeit geändert wurden, läßt sich zudem ablesen, daß ein ‚Basisthema‘ existiert, das an der Oberfläche variiert wird.

Die angestrebte Dezentrierung des Subjekts ist nicht das einzige Mittel, mit dem sich *Cloud Nine* in einen universalen Text einzuschreiben trachtet. Hinzu kommt die Forcierung des Spielcharakters, der die Objekte doppelt, indem er sie im Verfahren des *cross casting* antinomisch codiert und ihre Bedeutung damit einer oszillierenden Interferenz anheimgibt. Kollektiver Text und Unverläßlichkeit der Zeichen sind Strukturelemente in *Cloud Nine*, die zum Zwecke einer produktiven Konfusion eingesetzt werden und deren Tragfähigkeit es zu überprüfen gilt anhand der Aussage, die Churchill mit *Cloud Nine* machen will: das Aufzeigen der Parallele zwischen kolonialer und sexueller Unterdrückung.[8]

Zu Beginn des Stückes stellt Clive, der Chef der Farm, seine Familie und Diener als seinen Besitz vor. Dabei werden die Klischees, derer er sich bedient, noch durch die Reimform seiner Worte unterstrichen. Betty, die Ehefrau, wird als Traumfrau, Joshua, der schwarze Diener, als von weißer Gesinnung und Edward, das Söhnchen, als auf dem Weg zur Mannwerdung vorgestellt. Deutlich ist Clive selbst eine nicht eigenständige Figur, wird er vom Herrschaftsdiskurs viktorianischer Moral gesprochen und ist deren Sprachrohr.

Damit die Figuren nicht gänzlich einem Cartoon gleichen, bringt Churchill eine Störung ein: Betty wird von einem Mann, Joshua von einem Weißen, Edward von einer Frau gespielt. Damit werden Clives Worte optisch durchkreuzt (ein Vorgang, der im Leseakt nur anfänglich präsent ist). Zunächst – so will es scheinen – wird durch die Besetzung der Rollen mit ihrem Gegenteil der Verlust der Eigenständigkeit dieser Figuren betont, sind sie möglicherweise als Projektionen Clives zu lesen und enthüllen im Rückbezug auf ihn dessen Verdrängungen. Diese bestünden dann darin, daß er auf der Welt nichts gelten läßt als den weißen Mann. So wäre dann die Umbesetzung der Rollen zu lesen als der Verlust der Eigenständigkeit als Frau, als Neger, als geschlechtlich ambivalentes Kind. Es fragt sich jedoch, ob Churchill durch die optische Umbesetzung der Rollen die verbalen Klischees aufbricht oder ob sie in deren Falle geht. Leicht geschieht dies bei der Figur Edwards, der von einer Frau gespielt wird. Die sich bei Edward herausbildende Homosexualität mit der Signatur weiblich zu versehen läuft geradewegs in jene Falle des Klischees vom Homosexuellen, das ihn sich als effeminiert vorstellt. Anders liegt der Fall, wenn die Ehefrau durch einen Mann oder der Neger durch einen Weißen besetzt wird. Ist man zunächst geneigt, in der männlich dargestellten Betty Clives Narzismus oder in dem ,weiß' dargestellten Joshua Clives Kolonialismus projiziert zu sehen, gerät man bei weitergehender Analyse der von Churchill gewählten Zeichen zur Einsicht, daß sich am Ende der Zergliederungsarbeit keine geheime Einheit fassen läßt. Die Mühe der Interpretation vermag die Auflösung des Bezeichneten in verwirrende Gegensätze nicht in eine synthetische Form zu bringen. Die erlernte Opposition schwarz/weiß, Frau/Mann wird zerspielt.

Diesen Figuren ,ohne Grund', d. h. ohne Individualität, stellt nun Churchill eine Reihe von konventionellen Figuren zur Seite, mit denen gemeinsam eine bissig ironische Komödie gegen die männliche Vorherrschaft im fernen Afrika auf einem Vorposten Kiplingscher Prägung beginnt:

Hinter der Kulisse der Wohlanständigkeit leben alle Männer, aber nur eine der Frauen, ihre Lust in vielerlei Gestalt aus. Wie ein Abziehbild ihres Zeitalters überwacht und ignoriert zugleich Großmutter Maud dieses ganze Treiben. Ungerührt steht sie hinter Clives Sadismus, die im Namen der Aufrechterhaltung normierten Verhaltens geschehen: das Aufschlitzen von Edwards Puppe, das Auspeitschen von Negern durch Joshua und schließlich die Verheiratung des homosexuellen Harry mit der lesbischen Ellen, um beide „von ihrer Krankheit zu heilen"; Clive: "I feel contaminated". – Die Revolte gegen alle diese Repressionen wird am Ende des ersten Aktes einer Pantomime überlassen: Joshua zielt auf Clive und Edward hält sich dabei lediglich die Ohren zu.

Der zweite Akt spielt hundert Jahre später im heutigen London, doch die Figuren sind nur um fünfundzwanzig Jahre gealtert. Diese Aufhebung der zeitlichen Distanz hat, wie die Theaterkritik bemerkte, die Funktion, die Persistenz scheinbar aufgegebener moralischer Imperative anzuzeigen. Wichtiger scheint mir jedoch, daß Churchill hiermit versucht, ihr gespanntes Verhältnis zu Struktur und Geschichte zu bewältigen, das daraus resultiert, daß sie beide ineins setzt. – Die Rollen aus dem ersten Akt sind neu besetzt und diesmal ohne ,oppositionelle' Doppelung, weitere Rollen kommen hinzu. Die Figuren und ihre Handlungen werden nun zum Nennwert genommen, ihre Permissivität und Promiskuität wird ernsthaft, das heißt ohne jede ironische oder satirische Brechung abgehandelt. Der zweite Teil ist ein Spiegelbild des ersten mit Umkehrung der ideologischen Vorgaben: waren einst die Männer die Unterdrücker, so macht jetzt die – daraus resultierende – Emanzipation der Frauen und Homosexuellen allen Schwierigkeiten. Jedenfalls will sich Glück auch in den heutigen Beziehungen nicht einstellen.

In einem Reigen von Situationen sehen wir Victoria (im ersten Akt als Puppe dargestellt), inzwischen verheiratet mit Martin, auf die Lehrerin Lin treffen und mit ihr ein Verhältnis beginnen; Edward, inzwischen offen homosexuell (und von einem Mann dargestellt), nötigt seinen Liebhaber Gerry zu einem eheähnlichen Verhältnis, zu dem dieser nicht willens und nicht fähig ist. Die Probleme, die die Befreiung von der Moral mit sich bringt, werden in Form von Lebenshilfe gelöst: Edward zieht zu Victoria und Lin, d. h. der Homosexuelle, die Heterosexuelle und die Lesbierin führen eine Ehe zu dritt, Martin, der dominante Mann, hütet Victorias und Lins Kind, Gerry schließlich geht zu Mutter Betty zum Tee. Diese hat inzwischen eine emotionale und ökonomische Selbständigkeit erreicht, die ihr unter Clive verwehrt war.

Daß der zweite Akt bei diesem Inhalt nicht zur *soap opera* einer späten „polymorph perversen" *Flower Power Generation* gerät, dafür sorgen inhaltliche Tabuverletzungen und formale Brüche. Gleich zu Beginn des zweiten Aktes monologisiert Gerry von seinen homosexuellen Abenteuern in Vorortzügen, schildert detailliert seine triebhafte Lust an anonymer Fellatio während der sechsminütigen Tunneldurchfahrt von Victoria nach Clapham. Gegen Ende des Aktes dann berichtet Betty, wie sie sich im Orgasmus der Selbstbefriedigung als Person gefunden und befreit hat:

> [...] I started touching myself. I thought my hand might go through into space. [...] Afterwards I thought I'd betrayed Clive. My mother would kill me. But I felt triumphant because I was a separate person from them. (S. 61)

Regelmäßig entsteht bei diesen beiden Monologen, die als Versatzstücke von Pornographie mißverstanden werden könnten, Unruhe im Publikum, das bei aller Liberalität solche Irritationen noch nicht gewöhnt ist einfach wegzustecken. Die Unparteilichkeit, mit der Churchill diese Passagen präsentiert, das Fehlen jeden moralischen Kommentars jedoch läßt diesen Balanceakt zwischen Pornographie und nötiger Information über das Panorama sexueller Dispositionen gelingen.

Formal wird die konventionelle Darstellungsart durchbrochen, wenn im Verlaufe eines heidnischen Beschwörungsrituals, das die Gruppe betrunken im Park inszeniert, Figuren aus dem ersten Akt auftauchen und hier und jetzt mit den Anwesenden ihre Triebhaftigkeit ausleben. Der hierzu intonierte Song "Cloud 9" (in der deutschen Fassung operettenhaft mit „Der siebte Himmel" übersetzt) ist eine Umschreibung des Orgasmusgefühls und wurde von einer Putzfrau während des Workshops gefunden. Er zeigt Momente des Glücks unter dem Motto "and it's upside down when you reach cloud nine". Hierbei bleibt offen, ob die ‚freie Liebe' trunken macht oder erst im Zustand des Betrunkenseins lebbar ist. Die wichtigste Figur, die Churchill aus der Vergangenheit des 1. Aktes holt, ist die *viktorianische* Betty, die im Schlußbild ihre Nachfolgerin umarmt: "Betty and Betty embrace", so die Regieanweisung.

So schön es ist, wenn das triste Geschehen des 2. Aktes versöhnlich schließt, bleibt doch die Frage, ob die beiden Positionen, für die die beiden Bettys stehen, vereinbar sind. Dann aber bliebe die Emanzipation auf der Strecke. Anders formuliert: die ideologische Stoßrichtung des Stückes wird am Ende psychologisch aufgelöst: die spätere Persönlichkeit ist durch ihren Reifungsprozeß in der Lage, ihre frühere Geschichte zu akzeptieren und zu integrieren. Zugleich ist dieses Schlußbild auf der dramaturgischen Ebene der Versuch, eine Klammer zwischen den beiden Akten zu schaffen. Psychologische Lösung und die Bemühung um formale Einheit am Ende des Stückes aber sind Rückzug auf die Konvention.[9]

"[...] Lady, give us back what we were, give us the history we haven't had, make us the women we can't be" (S. 55) singt Victoria bei der Beschwörung indischer Göttinnen im Park. Nicht geschichtsmächtig also sind die Frauen, wohl aber mythenträchtig. Der Wunsch, sie zu dem zu machen, was sie nicht sein können, generiert hier wie anderswo in Churchills Werk zahlreiche Experimente paradoxalen Charakters; sie setzt ein Spiel der Möglichkeiten in Gang, das sich nicht durchzuhalten vermag, denn letztlich werden die innovatorischen Ansätze von konventionellen überformt. In dem Maße, in dem das von *Cloud Nine* vorgeführte Normensystem in Unordnung ist bzw. im Gegensatz zum „System der Vorstellungen" des Rezipienten steht, wird dessen Psyche versuchen, dieses Phänomen zu verarbeiten. Das per (Bühnen-)Spiel in Bewegung geratene „System der Vorstellungen" des Rezipienten könnte aus sich eine ‚Gestalt der Distanz' zum eigenen System bilden. Eine solche ‚Gestalt' ist jedoch systemtheoretisch formuliert von dissipativer Natur, d. h. ihr müßte ständig neue Energie zugeführt werden, um in ihrer Eigenheit von Bestand zu sein; hierzu jedoch reicht das innovatorische Potential des Stückes nicht aus. Statt Gestalt erscheint ein diffuses Gebilde.

Produktionsästhetisch kritisierend läßt sich behaupten, daß in *Cloud Nine* und besonders deutlich in *A Mouthful of Birds* streckenweise die Metaebene des *workshop*, d. h. die Spiel- und Ausprobiersituationen der Experimentierphase ohne weitere Transformation auf die Bühne gebracht zu sein scheinen. Das was wir zu sehen bekommen läßt jedenfalls – insbesondere in *A Mouthful of Birds* – den Verdacht aufkommen, daß wir der Gruppentherapie des Joint Stock-Ensembles beiwohnen, der Phase ihrer Arbeit am ‚Basisthema', dem Problem von Geschlecht und Rolle.[10]

III

Ein weiteres Stück, das Caryl Churchill internationales Renommee verschaffte, war *Top Girls*, 1982 uraufgeführt. Wieder geht es um die Rolle der Geschlechter, wieder darum, vergangene Geschichte mit gegenwärtiger zu konfrontieren.

In der faszinierend einfallsreichen Eingangsszene gibt Marlene ein Essen aus Anlaß ihrer Beförderung zum leitenden Direktor einer Arbeitsvermittlung für

Frauen. Sie hat illustre Gäste geladen, Frauen, die Exzeptionelles geleistet haben: aus der Legende die Päpstin Johanna, aus der Dichtung die geduldige Griselda, aus der Autobiographie Lady Nijo, eine mittelalterliche japanische Hofdame, sowie Isabella Bird, eine viktorianische Weltreisende, und zuletzt die Dulle Griet, die einem Gemälde von Breughel entstiegen ist. Es zeugt von Churchills Kunst der Informationsvergabe, daß sich die genannten Figuren dem Rezipienten erst allmählich über die Erzählung ihrer Lebensgeschichten zu den Personen verdichten, die sie sind. Erst wenn dieser Prozeß abgeschlossen ist, läßt sie Marlene bei der verspätet zur Gesellschaft stoßenden Griselda die Möglichkeit nutzen, beim gegenseitigen Vorstellen die historischen Rollen der Figuren zu benennen. Churchill schöpft allerdings nicht die Möglichkeiten aus, die sich aus der unterschiedlichen Medienherkunft ihrer Figuren hätten herleiten lassen.

Im Gespräch der Frauen macht Churchill extensiv Gebrauch von der Technik der sich überlappenden Reden. *Top Girls* sieht (wie auch andere Stücke bis hin zu *Ice Cream*) als Regieanweisung drei Modelle der sich kreuzenden Rede vor: 1) eine Figur beginnt zu sprechen, bevor die andere geendet hat, 2) eine Figur fährt fort, durch die Rede einer anderen hindurch weiterzusprechen, 3) eine Figur knüpft nicht an die soeben beendete Rede an, sondern an eine weiter zuvor liegende. – Auf diese Weise entsteht ein kunstvoller Redeteppich, dessen Knoten weitgehend aus Assoziationen gebildet werden. Die Figuren gehen kaum in dramatischer Wechselrede aufeinander ein, sondern knüpfen ihr eigenes Erleben in ein Muster ein, das bestimmte dominante thematische Fäden hat.[11] Diese Art des Redens läßt erkennen, daß das Individualschicksal hinter einem kollektiven zurücktritt; alle Beteiligten weben am gleichen Text. Man könnte geneigt sein, die hier interferierenden Redeinstanzen als intertextuell in der Art einer „Dialogizität im primären Sinne" (Renate Lachmann)[12] zu verstehen, wenn hier ein Dialog zwischen den vorhandenen einander fremden Sinnpositionen der Texte (als da sind: historische Abstände und kulturelle Unterschiede) stattfände. Hierzu kommt es jedoch nicht, weil die erzählenden Subjekte erhalten bleiben, und zwar ein jedes in der Kontur einer *idée fixe* (z. B. Nijo fixiert durch ihren Kleiderkodex). Die thematischen Linien, die erkenntlich werden, sind: Flucht vor der Häuslichkeit, Abhängigkeit von männlicher Herrschaft, Verlust der Kinder, Krankheitsgeschichten und der Kleiderkodex. Dieses Muster wie auch jenes zuvor beschriebene Einander-assoziativ-ins-Wort-Fallen liegt nun jedoch in vertrackter Nähe zu jenem Gesprächsverhalten, das man Frauen ohnehin nachsagt, und Frank Rich schreibt anläßlich der New Yorker Aufführung[13], daß der Fehler von *Top Girls* im Inhaltlichen liege. In der Tat können weder gelegentliche Pointen noch humorvolle Momente den Zuschauer über das Scheitern jeder einzelnen Frau hinwegtäuschen. *Repentance* (Nijo), *full of terror and regret* (Johanna) sind die Kosten des Erfolgs in der

Gesellschaft, mit denen sich auch Marlenes Geschichte als belastet herausstellen wird. Vorübergehende Einzelerfolge entpuppen sich immer mehr als kollektiver Mißerfolg dieser Frauen, die versucht hatten, sich in der Männerwelt zu behaupten. Deutlich zeigt sich ihre Abhängigkeit von den Männern, die nicht präsent sind und gerade durch ihre Abwesenheit Schuldgefühle verursachen und wachhalten. Die verlorenen oder nie dagewesenen Väter und Liebhaber bilden den Maßstab, nach dem Churchill das Leben dieser außergewöhnlichen Frauen ausrichtet. Die Mütter sind ausgelöscht, von ihnen ist keine Rede. Als Isabellas Mann stirbt, wurde ihr Leben leer; ebenso wie Nijo, die sich Schuld am Tod ihres Vaters beimißt, nach ihrer Verstoßung durch den Kaiser fühlt, "there was nothing in my life, nothing" (S. 12) und daher Nonne wird, oder wie es für Johanna nach dem Tod ihres Liebhabers Johann nichts mehr gab als ihre Studien. Die usurpierten männlichen Rechte, auf die Marlene bei ihrer Beförderungsfeier anstoßen will, entpuppen sich nach und nach als Ersatzhandlungen für das Eine: den Normalzustand der Frau mit intakter Familie. Renate Klett nennt diese Darstellungsweise Churchills solidarische Kritik an den Frauen[14], männliche Regie hingegen wie die von Walter Adler bei der deutschen Erstaufführung in Köln, die das ,Ersatzhandeln' betont, nennt sie reaktionär. Es will scheinen, als ob hier wie schon in *Cloud Nine* hinter aller Artistik die Klischees lauern, wenn Fehlinterpretationen so nahe liegen.

Wer sich genauer, wie Jutta Thellmann[15], mit den Varianten befaßt, die Dichtung, Historie und Legende zu den einzelnen Frauenschicksalen bereithalten, wird feststellen müssen, daß Churchill die das allgemeine Frauenbild positivierenden Versionen nicht als Prätext genutzt hat. So ist zum Beispiel die Johanna der *Top Girls* – eine wissensbesessene ,Männin', die trotzdem unwissend schwanger wird – die wohl frauenfeindlichste Variante. Thellmann hingegen weist nach, daß die Päpstin Johanna im Mittelalter u. a. auch als Zierde des päpstlichen Stuhls gewertet wurde, da mit der Frau wissenschaftliche Bildung, Weisheit, Beredsamkeit und Schönheit auf den Heiligen Stuhl kamen, was angesichts der sprichwörtlichen Lasterhaftigkeit des Papsttums zu dieser Zeit von Vorteil war. Oder sie verweist etwa auf Achim von Arnims utopische Variante, die in Johanna die männliche und weibliche Komponente amalgamierte und eine Päpstin beschrieb, die Gleichheit vor dem Gesetz sowie sexuelle und emotionale Freiheit anstrebte.

Nur an einer ihrer Figuren arbeitet Churchill eine neue frauengeschichtliche Dimension heraus. An der Bildfigur der Dullen Griet, die keinen Text für sich sprechen lassen kann, setzt Churchill fruchtbar ihre Phantasie frei. Hier überbietet das Stück dann die Ikonographie, die Breughels *Zornige Grete* seit ihrer Entstehung als Muster sexistischer Malerei rezipierte. In der einzigen längeren Redepassage, die ihr das Stück zugesteht, gerät die Dulle Griet zu einer Frau, die ganz persönliches Leid ausdrückt: "My big son die on a wheel. Birds eat him.

My baby, a soldier run her through with a sword. I'd had enough, I was mad, I hate the bastards."[16] Das hat sie zur Revolution angetrieben, hat sie den Dreckskerlen in die Hölle nachziehen lassen, um sie zu verdreschen. Die ursprüngliche Deutung der Dullen Griet als Allegorie auf das flämische Sprichwort „Sie konnte in der Hölle plündern und unversehrt zurückkehren" meinte hingegen damit den Inbegriff des herrschsüchtigen und raffgierigen Weibes, das solche Haare auf den Zähnen hat, daß sie sogar den Teufel das Fürchten lehrt. Caryl Churchills ingeniöse neue Deutung der Höllenallegorie als ein Stück politischer Revolution macht dieses sexistische Verständnis der Figur obsolet und führt die Charakterologie einer angeblich weiblichen Naturhaftigkeit über in eine wesentlich brisantere, geschichtlich-politische Dimension.

Historische Folie und Redeteppich bestimmen die erste Szene. Sie dient als Referenz für den Rest des Stückes, der Marlenes Alltag schildert, der in der Manier Weskers gehalten ist.[17] Nachdem das Stück zunächst diffus eine emanzipatorische Stimmung suggerierte, gewinnt es nun beim plötzlichen und unvermuteten Sprung in die Gegenwart eine andere Qualität. Die Sado-Maso-Spiele, die Angie und Kit als kaputte Großstadtkinder treiben, zeigen Tabuverletzung und affizieren das Publikum stark. Marlene selbst pendelt zwischen Szenen, die sie in ihrer High-Tech-Bürowelt zeigen und solchen in der ärmlichen Küche ihrer verhärmten Schwester Joyce. Sowohl die Interviews in der Stellenagentur wie die langen Gespräche zwischen den beiden Schwestern zeigen Churchills große psychologische Einfühlsamkeit. Zwischen den beiden Schwestern steht Angie, das Kind Marlenes, das diese – getreu ihren historischen Vorbildern der ersten Szene – ihrer Schwester Joyce zur Betreuung überließ, um in London Karriere zu machen. Marlene hat wie ihre historischen Schwestern einen hohen Preis für ihre Männerrolle gezahlt.

Während in den Erzählungen der Agenturgirls noch das – von den Frauen selbst unbefragte – Bild der Wochenendgeliebten verheirateter Männer vorgeführt wird, werden in Joyces Wohnküche immerhin zwei Positionen des Feminismus aufgerufen. Marlene steht für den bürgerlichen Feminismus, der die Chancen für die Frauen darin sieht, daß sie es den Männern gleichtun. Joyce wäre in der Nähe eines sozialistischen Feminismus anzusiedeln, insofern sie die Notwendigkeit erkennt, daß Frauen sich autonom organisieren müssen. Jedoch ist sie von Churchill dergestalt als *downtrodden serf*[18] gezeichnet, daß sie aus dieser Position nicht mit Stärke argumentieren kann.

> MARLENE. And for the country, come to that. Get the economy back on its feet and whoosh. She's a tough lady, Maggie, I'd give her a job. [...]
> JOYCE. What good's first woman if it's her? I suppose you'd have liked Hitler if he was a woman. Ms Hitler. Got a lot done, Hitlerina. / Great adventures.

MARLENE. Bosses still walking on the workers' faces? Still Dadda's little parrot? [...] (S. 83/84)

Margaret Thatcher wird hier als das Top Girl par excellence zitiert, die Schwester Joyce, an der das Leben vorbeigegangen ist, als rückständige Klassenkämpferin gezeichnet.

Auch nach Durchgang durch den Alltagsteil des Stückes wird der Zuschauer feststellen müssen, daß er wie zuvor im historischen Teil keinen Entwurf auf ein neues Frauenbild hin gesehen hat, sondern die Beschreibung eines Zustandes, der Marlene einmal zu dem Ausruf veranlaßt: "Oh God, why are we all so miserable?"[19]

IV

A Mouthful of Birds (1986) ist eine Gemeinschaftsarbeit von Caryl Churchill und David Lan, die einen hohen Anteil tänzerischer Darstellung enthält. Anders als die beiden vorgenannten Stücke ist es nicht spiegelbildlich in Vergangenheit und Gegenwart gehälftet, sondern besteht aus drei Teilen[20], von denen der mittlere Archaisches in das Heute hereinholt. Der erste Teil zeigt Personen in Momentaufnahmen von Alltagssituationen des "Defended Day" wie Telefonieren, Gewichtheben und anderes, denen jedoch surrealistische Elemente beigefügt sind. Im zweiten Teil erfahren die Figuren im "Undefended Day" und seinen entkonventionalisierten und daher schutzlosen Situationen eine radikale Transformation.[21] Thema dieses mittleren Teils ist die Grenzüberschreitung, die Nähe von Rausch und Wahn, Lust und Gewalt, höchstem Glück und Tod, die Verschmelzung existentieller Gegensätze.[22] Vom Ergebnis dieser Transformation berichten die Monologe des dritten Teils: Sie sind Variationen über die Aufhebung der Geschlechterrollen. So z. B. arbeitet Lena, die zu Beginn als Hausfrau kein Kaninchen häuten konnte, nun im Schlachthof; oder Derek, der gelernt hat, die Frau in sich zuzulassen: "I have almost forgotten the man who possessed this body."[23] Nur Doreen hat den Umwandlungsprozeß verweigert. Ihr bleibt daher die Wahnvorstellung: "It seems that my mouth is full of birds which I crunch between my teeth. Their feathers, their blood and broken bones are choking me. I carry on my work as a secretary."[24]

Die Folie für den Mittelteil des Stückes bildet die archaisch dunkle und sexuell turbulente Tragödie des Euripides. Ihr entlehnen Churchill/Lan die Figuren des Dionysos, der Agave und ihres Sohnes Pentheus. Bei Euripides ist Agave die Anführerin der Bakchen/Mainaden, einer Frauenschar, die in Naturverbundenheit und Entrückung lebt, bei Bedrohung durch Männer aber in Raserei und Grausamkeit verfällt. Ihrem Sohn Pentheus, dem ganz auf das Verstandesmäßige gestellten Herrscher Thebens, ist – in seiner Komponente als „lüsterner Tugendwächter"[25] – dieses anarchisch wilde Treiben der Frauen verdächtig. Er läßt sich von Dionysos als Frau verkleiden, beobachtet die Bakchen/Mainaden und wird von diesen zerrissen. – Dionysos ist der schöne Gott, dessen ‚weibisches' Aussehen bei Euripides deutlich herausgestellt wird. Wenn er schließlich Pentheus vernichtet, dann deswegen, weil dieser dem bacchantischen Genußkult abhold ist.

Bei Churchill/Lan erhalten Agave und Pentheus die Aufgabe, Personen des Stückes, z. B. Doreen und Derek, in wahnhafte Besessenheit zu versetzen. Dionysos selbst erhält die Funktion, spielerisch, tänzerisch ein Geschehen zu umkreisen, das er mehr andeutungsweise als konkret ins Werk setzt. Auf diese Weise wird der Prätext genutzt, ein Geschehen zu generieren und zu strukturieren, das in seiner Oberflächenerscheinung wenig mit den *Bakchen* gemeinsam zu haben scheint, tatsächlich aber „Arbeit am Mythos" (Blumenberg) leistet, unter Beibehaltung des hermaphroditischen Mythenkerns. – Während die Frauen im Zustand der Besessenheit ihre Fähigkeit zur Grausamkeit erfahren – Lena etwa ist zum Kindermord bereit, Doreen sticht einer Mitbewohnerin ins Gesicht –, gehen die Männer den Weg in die Friedfertigkeit bei gleichzeitiger biologischer und rollenhafter Transformation. Dan, der Vikar, tanzt in Frauenkleidern, Paul, der Fleischhändler, verliebt sich in ein Schweinchen. Der entscheidenden Transformation jedoch unterliegt Derek. Im 19. Bild (in dem auch Dionysos schweigend anwesend ist) trifft Derek auf eine Frau in französischer Männerkleidung des 19. Jahrhunderts. Der Illusionsraum des Hier und Jetzt vor der antiken Folie wird zusätzlich auf eine nähere Vergangenheit hin vertieft, aus der Herculine davon erzählt, wie sich ihr Leben als Hermaphrodit abspielte: "Was I really Herculine Barbin, playing by the sea, starting school at the convent, nobody doubted I was a girl. Hermaphrodite, the doctors were fascinated, how to define this body, does it fascinate you, it doesn't fascinate me, let it die."[26] Herculine berichtet von ihrer Trauer darüber, daß sie sich im 19. Jahrhundert in ihrer Besonderheit nicht ausleben konnte. In Bildvermischungen von Strand- und Bettszenen, Andeutungen von schmerzhafter Geschlechtsumwandlung entsteht im Rezipienten ein Kaleidoskop erotischer Ahnungen. Die sinnstiftenden Satzstücke sind so organisiert, daß sie Referenzen andeuten, anspielen, aber nicht eigentlich zur Entfaltung kommen lassen. Sie wirken wie eine Sammlung von Filmschnipseln, die vermischt wurden. Am Ende der langen Erzählung Herculines übernimmt Derek den eben gleichen Wortlaut und wiederholt ihre Erfahrung als die seinige. Zugleich beginnt er, die weiblichen Kleidungsstücke, die ihm Herculine überreichte, anzulegen. So gelangt das in Derek angelegte doppelgeschlechtliche Potential in einem Akt magischer Erzählung zur Evidenz. Derek fühlt sich schließlich ebenso befreit wie Herculine, die beglückt ist, in unserer heutigen Zeit akzeptiert zu sein.

Die Aufhebung der Geschlechtsdifferenz im Doppelgeschlecht[27] ist die von Churchill/Lan per Tanz und Text (im 19. wie im 15. Bild) realisierte zentrale Vision. In dem Bemühen, den Mythos des Hermaphroditen zu revitalisieren, liegt jedoch ein nostalgischer Zug[28], eine Rückwendung zu jenem Wesen, das einheitlich vor der Aufspaltung in Mann und Frau existiert haben soll. Dieser Wunsch nach einer Regression der Sexualität korrespondiert mit Bonds Gesellschaftsbild von der Wiederherstellung der „Unschuld", die inzwischen „korrumpiert" worden sei. Beide arbeiten an der Wiederkehr eines glücklichen Urzustandes (Rousseau) und geben ihn als erreichbare Utopie aus. Um die bestehenden, gesellschaftlichen wie sexuellen, Spannungen aufzuheben, bemühen sie – und hierin zeigt sich ihre marxistische Prämisse – den Mythos, um die Geschichte außer Kraft zu setzen.

V

Caryl Churchill hat das Formenrepertoire des Theaters radikal genutzt: mit Zeitsprüngen, Spiegelungen, Vertauschungen, Verschränkungen, Überlappungen, Einblendungen und der Kopräsenz des zeitlich Differenten. Ihre Schreibweise ist phantastisch und didaktisch, humorvoll und grausam, ungewöhnlich und banal. Inhaltlich hat sie sich mit Sexualität als Herrschaftsform befaßt und hierbei näherhin versucht, die Unterscheidung weiblich/männlich hinfällig zu machen.

Bei aller Vielheit des Diskurses jedoch, so will es scheinen, läßt die theatralische Aufbereitung der Problemstellung den Rezipienten letztlich ratlos. Zwar sprechen die meisten *reviews* den Stücken inhaltliche und formale Einfälle zu, bemerken aber auch deren permanente Widersprüche und Unklarheiten ("oddity and obscurity") – auch darin steht sie in der Nähe zu Bond. – Könnte es nicht sein, daß Churchills Programm der Aufhebung der Differenz hierzu geführt hat? Sind nicht ‚Sexualität' und die Komplementärbegriffe Freiheit und Repression im Sinne Derridas ein „unbestimmbares Zentrum", das nur im Spiel der Substitutionen umkreist werden kann? Dies aber kann nur geschehen, wenn die Differenz der Signifikanten nicht aufgehoben ist. Das Verfahren der *différance* (Derrida) als ein nie zur Ruhe kommendes Differieren und Differenzieren und dasjenige des Aufschubs am Ursprung bedingen einander. Wenn es stimmt, daß alles was gedacht werden kann, aufgrund der Differenz gedacht wird, dann läuft der Denkprozeß über die Sexualität nach Aufgabe der Weiblich/männlich-Differenz leer. Caryl Churchills Bemühen, hier den Mythos der Doppelgeschlechtlichkeit einzusetzen, ist eine Rückkehr zum Ursprung. Vielleicht macht dies ihr Theater für viele so attraktiv.

1 Bond, E.: *Lear*. London: Methuen, 1973, S. VI.
2 Ebd., S. VII.
3 Ebd., S. IX.
4 Gilbert, W. S.: "Objections to Sex and Violence". *Plays and Players* 22, vi, 1975, 25.
5 "It's one of those experiences that mystifies, perplexes, aggravates and yanks you clean out of the cosy naturalistic narrative rut that passes for so much contemporary drama." (C. Woddis in *City Limits*, 4. 12. 1986; zitiert nach L. Fitzsimmons [Ed.]: *File on Churchill*. London, 1989, S. 75.)
6 Zur Präsentation von Androgynie, Gynandrie und Hermaphrodismus im zeitgenössischen Theater sowie zur Kritik einschlägiger Literatur vgl. A. Geraths: *„Gay Theater*. Welterfolge zwischen Androgynie-Kult und AIDS". *anglistik & englischunterricht*. 35. *American Theater Today*. Heidelberg, 1988, S. 91–120.
7 In folgenden Ausgaben: *Cloud Nine*. London: Pluto Press, 1979; *Top Girls*. Rev. ed. London, New York: Methuen, 1984 (^{1}1982); *A Mouthful of Birds*. London, New York: Methuen, 1986.
8 "We explored Genet's idea that colonial oppression and sexual oppression are similar. And we explored the feminity of the colonized person." (Zitiert nach Fitzsimmons [Ed.]: *File on Churchill*, S. 46.)
9 Kritisch beurteilt Michelene Wandor (in ihrer Unterscheidung von radikalem, bürgerlichem und sozialistischem Feminismus) die Leistung des Stückes: "*Cloud Nine* is written in two stylistically distinct halves; the first [half] [...] in a very clear socialist-feminist perspective, linking the macro-political dynamic (the public) with the micro-political (the personal). [...] The second half is merely a series of isolated portraits of more libertarian sexual relationships in the 1970s, with no sense of how or why they might link with macro-political ideology. The dynamic, therefore, as far as the women were concerned (this is a mixed play) is to present us with a series of individualised bourgeois feminist life-styles from whom the puritanical constraints of Victorian ideology appear to have been lifted. This implies that while we can analyse the past, we cannot analyse the present, and this actually diminishes the potential of the bourgeois feminist dynamic." ("The Fifth Column: Feminism and Theatre". *Drama. The Quarterly Theatre Review* H. 152, 1984, 5–9, hier: 7).
10 "Like so many improvisation-based efforts, the outcome is jerky and episodic, with mundane natter one moment and frenzied shrieking the next, constantly risking the clichés and bathos which threaten the Method." (O. Taplin, zitiert nach Fitzsimmons [Ed.]: *File on Churchill*, S. 76.) – Daß Banalität und Klischees z. T. unkritisch verwendet werden, gilt für alle drei Stücke. Hierin ein künstlerisches Manko zu sehen, hieße, der Innovation auch heute noch einen Primat in der Kunst einzuräumen.
11 Churchills Eingangsszene ist das theatralische Analogon zu Judy Chicagos Monumentaltisch *Dinnerparty*, der in 39 Gedecken auf ebensoviele bedeutende Frauen einer fünftausendjährigen Geschichte verweist und auf einer Plattform mit 999 Namen steht.
12 „Vorwort". – In dies. (Ed.): *Dialogizität*. München, 1982, S. 8–10, hier: S. 8.
13 *The New York Times*, 29. 12. 1982, C17.
14 „Männliche Exekution. Die deutsche Erstaufführung von 'Top Girls' in Köln". *Theater heute* 25, i, 1984, 23.

15 "Top Girls?" Vortrag vor der Theatergesellschaft Konstanz am 28. 4. 1988, unveröffentlicht.
16 *Top Girls*, S. 28.
17 Vgl. J. R. Taylor: "Plays in Performance, London". *Drama. The Quarterly Theatre Review* H. 147, 1983, 26–28, hier: 27.
18 Vgl. den bereits zitierten Artikel von F. Rich in der *New York Times* vom 29. 12. 1982.
19 *Top Girls*, S. 18. – Die Frauenviten, die Churchill ausgesucht hat, sind bis auf diejenige Griseldas gerade nicht von der ‚Kultur geschrieben', sondern weichen von ihr ab. Lady Birds Weltreisen z. B. sind angesichts von Millionen zeitgleicher "angels in the house" (John Ruskin) aufregendes Novum. Indem Churchill weniger die Gewinne der neuen Existenzformen aufzeigt als vielmehr für sie eine Verlustrechnung aufmacht, werden sie zu Mustern ohne Wert in der Geschichte der Emanzipation.
20 Teil 1: "Dionysus dances" bis "Excuses"; Teil 2: "Psychic Attack" bis "Death of Pentheus"; Teil 3: "Old People" bis "Dionysus dances".
21 Siehe G. Cousin: *Churchill the Playwright*. London, 1989, S. 55ff. über die Vorbereitungen der Joint Stock Company zu diesem Stück.
22 Vgl. U. Kahle: „Ekstase und Besessenheit". *Theater heute* 29, iii, 1988, 15.
23 *A Mouthful of Birds*, S. 71.
24 Ebd.
25 Werner, O.: „Nachwort" zu Euripides; *Die Bakchen*. Stuttgart, 1988, S. 73.
26 *A Mouthful of Birds*, S. 51.
27 Vgl. G. Ecker: „Die verschiedenen Möglichkeiten, die beschritten werden, um dieser Asymmetrie [der Geschlechter] zu begegnen, nämlich sich um den Preis der Selbstentfremdung an ein falsches Ideal von Geschlechtsneutralität anzupassen, sich zu separieren und die Gebundenheit an diese Kultur zu negieren oder sich auf die parallele Suche nach einer eigenen Tradition zu begeben – alle diese Möglichkeiten sind *per se* nicht perfekt und bringen ihre eigenen Probleme mit sich." („ ‘A Map for Rereading'. Intertextualität aus der Perspektive einer feministischen Literaturwissenschaft". – In Broich, U., Pfister, M. [Eds.]: *Intertextualität. Formen, Funktionen, anglistische Fallstudien*. Tübingen, 1985, S. 297–311, hier: S. 297).
28 Vgl. J. Derrida: „Der verlorenen oder unmöglichen Präsenz des abwesenden Ursprungs zugewandt, ist diese strukturalistische Thematik der zerbrochenen Unmittelbarkeit also die traurige, *negative*, nostalgische, schuldige und rousseauistische Kehrseite jenes Denkens [. . .], des Spiels der Welt und der Unschuld der Zukunft, die Bejahung einer Welt aus Zeichen ohne Fehl, ohne Wahrheit, ohne Ursprung, die einer tätigen Deutung offen ist. *Diese Bejahung bestimmt demnach das Nicht-Zentrum anders denn als Verlust des Zentrums*. Sie spielt, ohne sich abzusichern." („Die Struktur, das Zeichen und das Spiel im Diskurs der Wissenschaften vom Menschen". – In ders.: *Die Schrift und die Differenz*, Frankfurt/M., 1972, S. 422–442, hier: S. 441).

Petra Iking, Hagen

"To be hoist with one's own petard": Zur Interaktionsstruktur von Peter Shaffers *Lettice and Lovage*

„Macht kaputt, was Euch kaputt macht!": Dieser modische Spruch aus dem Repertoire jugendlicher Hausbesetzer könnte fast als Motto von *Lettice and Lovage* dienen. Die Protagonisten des jüngsten Stückes von Peter Shaffer, das am 27. Oktober 1987 im Globe Theatre in London Premiere hatte und seither auch an zahlreichen deutschsprachigen Bühnen von Wien und Basel bis Berlin und Hamburg mit großem Erfolg gespielt wurde und wird[1], sind jedoch altersmäßig nicht der Hausbesetzerszene zuzuordnen; es handelt sich vielmehr um zwei gebildete ältere Damen, die als *happy ending* der Komödie beschließen, die zehn häßlichsten Gebäude Londons in die Luft zu sprengen. Um nachvollziehen zu können, warum der Protest von Miss Lettice Douffet und Miss Charlotte Schoen sich nicht in den Bahnen von „Graue-Panther-Aktivitäten" erschöpft, sondern geradezu terroristische Züge annimmt, sei zunächst kurz der Inhalt des Stückes referiert.

Miss Lettice Douffet ist Fremdenführerin in Diensten des Preservation Trust und hat die Aufgabe, Touristen durch Fustian House, einem recht tristen Tudor-Schloß, zu führen. Um nun zu verhindern, daß die Touristen sich langweilen, „würzt" Lettice die mageren und uninteressanten Beschreibungen der Geschichte des Hauses mit spannenden "stories", die sie selber erfindet. Lotte Schoen, Mitglied des Preservation Trust, erfährt von diesen „Ausschmückungen" der historischen Fakten, ist entsetzt ob der Abweichungen von der historischen Wahrheit und entläßt Lettice Douffet umgehend aus den Diensten des Preservation Trust. Nicht zuletzt auch das schlechte Gewissen bewegt sie dann jedoch, Lettice in ihrer mit Theaterrequisiten überfüllten Kellerwohnung – ihre Mutter war Schauspielerin – aufzusuchen, um ihr einen Job als Fremdenführerin auf einem Ausflugsboot auf der Themse zu vermitteln. Bei einem Drink – nach einem Rezept aus der Tudor Zeit – kommen sich die beiden alten Damen näher. Lotte, deren Vater Kunstverleger war und aus Dresden stammte, hat ein abgebrochenes Architekturstudium hinter sich und eine Aversion nicht nur gegen Katzen, sondern auch gegen die ihrer Meinung nach abgrundhäßlichen Neubauten Londons der 50er und 60er Jahre, denen sie ihren eigenen nostalgieseligen Schönheitsbegriff entgegensetzt. Lettice hingegen begeistert sich für historische Begebenheiten, die eine gewisse "grandeur" ausstrahlen.

Diese realitätsflüchtige Vergangenheitsverklärung verbindet die beiden trotz ihrer völlig unterschiedlichen Charaktere: Lotte streng, durchsetzungsfähig und bürokratisch; Lettice hingegen phantasiebegabt, emotional und kreativ. Nach einem Zeitsprung von sechs Monaten erfährt der Zuschauer dann aus einem Gespräch, das Lettice mit ihrem Rechtsbeistand führt, näheres über ihre eigentümliche Beziehung: sie spielen gemeinsam Gerichtsprozesse und Hinrichtungsszenen großer Gestalten der englischen Geschichte nach, wobei es in einem Fall – durch eine unglückliche Koinzidenz – zu einer schweren Verletzung von Lotte kommt. Lettice gerät unter Mordverdacht und könnte nur durch Lottes Aussage, daß alles nur Spiel war, entlastet werden, was zum totalen Reputationsverlust Lottes führen würde; sie kündigt lieber schon im voraus. Lotte und Lettice sind nun beide von beruflichen Zwängen befreit und beschließen, Rache an der Gesellschaft zu nehmen, die der Verwirklichung ihrer Vorstellung von Schönheit und wirklicher Größe entgegensteht. Sie planen, die zehn häßlichsten Gebäude Londons zu zerstören – und zwar mit mittelalterlichen Geschützen, auf deren Bau Lettice spezialisiert ist.

Dieser Schluß erschien Shaffer für eine Aufführung des Stückes am Broadway dann doch wohl zu kühn, und er schrieb für die USA einen weniger schockierenden Schluß, der darauf hinausläuft, daß Lettice und Lotte Führungen zu den zehn häßlichsten Gebäuden Londons veranstalten.[2]

Diese erstaunliche Entwicklung der beiden Damen von unterschiedliche Interessen vertretenden und in unterschiedliche Verpflichtungen eingebundenen Exponenten völlig konträrer Weltsichten zu Verbündeten mit einem gemeinsamen Ziel kann als Exemplifizierung einer Eskalationsspirale begriffen werden, die nicht nur zum Arbeitsplatzverlust beider Damen führt, sondern Lettice auch ins Gefängnis bringt und schließlich in der „ernsthaften" Planung von „Terroranschlägen" endet, als Symbol der "revenge of the ravished past upon the present" (S. 93).[3] Zwar ist diese Entwicklung in den Rahmen einer Komödie gestellt, die mit ihren teils farcenhaften Zügen auch höchst amüsant anzuschauen ist und zumindest auf der Ebene der Beziehung der beiden Damen auch zur Freundschaft (oder zur Zweckgemeinschaft?) und damit zu einem gewissen *happy ending* führt; aber es ist doch gleichzeitig beeindruckend, wie die Interaktion der beiden Damen nicht-intendierte „Nebenwirkungen" zeitigt und letztlich im (komischen) Chaos endet.

An diesem Prozeß ist zweierlei besonders interessant: 1) die Planung von Bombenanschlägen als Problemlösung; 2) die Entwicklung der beiden Damen von Gegnern zu Verbündeten. Um diese spezifische Problemstruktur des Stückes näher zu beleuchten, die mit den Worten von Lotte "to be hoist with one's own petard" (S. 54) treffend umrissen ist, liegt eine genaue Analyse der Struktur der Interaktion der Protagonisten nahe. Damit wird nicht der Anspruch erhoben, alle interpretationsbedeutsamen Perspektiven dieses Dramas zu erfassen; es ist vielmehr eine Blicköffnung für eine oberflächlich nicht sichtbare Struktur des Dramas intendiert. Nicht nur diese Schwerpunktsetzung, sondern insbesondere auch die Tatsache, daß Drama und gesellschaftliche Wirklichkeit in einer unauflösbaren Interdependenz stehen (denn lebensweltliche Probleme gehen – wenngleich in fiktional überformter Gestalt – in das Drama ein), begründen die Wahl eines sozialwissenschaftlichen Analyseinstruments. Als theoretischer Bezugsrahmen wird die sogenannte „pragmatische Kommunikationstheorie" gewählt, wie sie von Paul Watzlawick und seinen Mitautoren in den beiden Werken *Menschliche Kommunikation. Formen, Störungen, Paradoxien*[4] und *Lösungen. Zur Theorie und Praxis menschlichen Wandels*[5] vertreten wird.[6] Unter Rückgriff auf Kybernetik und Systemtheorie untersuchen Watzlawick und seine Mitautoren dort problematische zwischenmenschliche Beziehungen, wobei sie zu einer Kategorisierung von Kommunikationsstörungen gelangen. Im folgenden seien nur die beiden Strukturen gestörter Kommunikation kurz erläutert, die für die Analyse unmittelbar relevant sind, nämlich das sogenannte „Utopie-Syndrom" und die Differenzierung zwischen Inhalts-und Beziehungsaspekt einer Kommunikation.

Mit dem „Utopie-Syndrom" beschäftigen sich Watzlawick et al. in ihrem Werk *Lösungen*, und zwar innerhalb der Fragestellung, wie Probleme entstehen und „wie einige überraschend gelöst werden können, während andere sich bis zur Unlösbarkeit komplizieren."[7] Von besonderem Interesse ist im Zusammenhang der folgenden Analyse jedoch jener Aspekt, der auf die Problementstehung abzielt, und zwar insofern, als der Lösungsversuch einer Schwierigkeit in seinen Auswirkungen schlimmer ist als das ursprünglich zu lösende Problem bzw. ganz neue Probleme erst entstehen läßt. Diese „problemerzeugende Fehllösung" genannten Dynamiken sind dann besonders eindrucksvoll, wenn ihnen ein unerreichbares Ziel oder ein unlösbares Problem zugrunde liegen. Watzlawick und seine Mitautoren subsumieren dieses Phänomen sowie die daraus resultierenden Verhaltensweisen unter dem Begriff „Utopie-Syndrom". Hinsichtlich der anschließenden Dramenanalyse ist die Variante „projektives Utopie-Syndrom" besonders bedeutsam: der von ihm Betroffene glaubt, die Wahrheit, eine endgültige und umfassende Lösung aller Probleme o. ä. gefunden zu haben und fühlt sich demzufolge berufen und legitimiert, alle Mißstände dieser Welt – oder was er dafür hält – zu beheben. Mit missionarischem Sendungsbewußtsein wird er versuchen, den Rest der Welt zu bekehren. Sollten diese Bemühungen jedoch erfolglos bleiben, so sucht er die Ursachen dafür im Verhalten der anderen, die halsstarrig und uneinsichtig sind, jedoch nie in sich selbst oder in der Unerreichbarkeit seiner Ziele. Der radikale Utopist meint, den rechten Weg der Dinge zu kennen, was eine Verunglimpfung – wenn nicht sogar Vernichtung – von Nicht-Bekehrbaren zur Folge hat. Er verabsäumt es, die Grundlagen seiner Überzeugung zu hinterfragen, verabsolutiert seine Ziele und gerät durch die Unfähigkeit, den utopischen Charakter eben dieser Ziele zu erkennen, im Extremfall in existentielle Konflikte.

Das zweite Kommunikationsphänomen, das hier von Interesse ist, nämlich die Unterscheidung zwischen Inhalts- und Beziehungsaspekt einer Botschaft, verdeutlicht die Tatsache, daß eine Botschaft immer untrennbar mit einem bestimmten Kontext verbunden ist, wodurch sich ihr Sinn erst konstituiert. Um es mit den Worten von Watzlawick zu sagen: „Der Inhaltsaspekt vermittelt die ‚Daten‘, der Beziehungsaspekt weist an, wie diese Daten aufzufassen sind."[8] Bei dem Beziehungsaspekt handelt es sich somit um eine Metakommunikation, die ihren Ausdruck in Gestik, Mimik, Tonfall etc. finden kann. Im „Normalfall" gelungener Kommunikation entsprechen Inhalts- und Beziehungsaspekt einander, problematisch wird es jedoch, wenn die beiden Aspekte im Gegensatz zueinander stehen, wenn z. B. die Gestik die verbale Botschaft konterkariert.

Diese kurze Skizzierung des theoretischen Ansatzes soll genügen, um nun auf die bereits erwähnten Worte von Lotte "to be hoist with one's own petard" zurückzukommen, die die Interaktionsstruktur der Protagonisten plastisch charakterisieren. Diese Interaktionsstruktur, die die Planung von Bombenanschlägen impliziert, soll im folgenden als problemerzeugender Fehllösungsmechanismus, dem eine utopische Zielsetzung zugrunde liegt, gedeutet werden.

Trotz aller Unterschiedlichkeit ihrer äußeren Erscheinung und ihrer Verhaltensweisen sind die Protagonisten doch strukturell ähnlich angelegt; beide orientieren sich in gewisser Weise an einem Heile-Welt-Ideal, das seine Konstituenten aus einem idealisierten Bild der Vergangenheit bezieht. Sowohl bei Lettice als auch bei Lotte resultiert diese Fixierung auf eine verklärte Sicht von Historie unmittelbar aus ihrer Erziehung.

Lettice ist wesentlich von ihrer Mutter geprägt worden, die sie als Leiterin einer fahrenden Theatergruppe allein großgezogen hat, nachdem ihr Mann sie drei Wochen nach der Hochzeit sitzen ließ. Besonders bemerkenswert an ihrer Erziehung[9] sind in diesem Zusammenhang zwei Aspekte: einmal die Auffassung, Geschichte und Überlieferung gäben dem Menschen einen Platz, Halt, eine Verankerung in der Gesellschaft und zum anderen das Bekenntnis, es sei ihre Pflicht, den Touristen – als wären es ihre Kinder – eine ähnliche Erfahrung zu vermitteln, wie ihre Mutter sie ihr als Kind vermittelt hatte: "Enlarge – enliven – enlighten them." (S. 25) Hier zeigt sich deutlich, aus welchen Komponenten sich das Selbstverständnis von Lettice zusammensetzt. Das Nachspielen von "stories from our country's past" (S. 25) durch ihre Mutter hat Lettice derartig geprägt, daß sie ihre Identität nur innerhalb derartiger historisierender Spielstrukturen finden kann. Die Überzeugung, diese Kindheitserfahrungen weitergeben zu müssen, ist konstitutiv für ihren Lebenssinn; sie muß aus Gründen der Identitätssicherung an ihr festhalten, wodurch sie in eigendynamische Handlungsketten verwickelt wird, die in einem ersten Schritt zur Zerstörung ihrer materiellen Existenz führen. Die Lösung ihres Lebensproblems, d. h. das Finden einer Identität, ist zugleich das Problem, das sie an den Rand der gesellschaftlichen Existenzfähigkeit treibt: sie verliert aufgrund ihrer Überzeugung, ihrer Begeisterungsfähigkeit und Kreativität freien Lauf lassen zu müssen, nicht nur ihre Stelle beim Preservation Trust, sondern auch ihren Job als Werbedame für Käse in einem Kaufhaus. Ihr Kommentar zu ihrer Tätigkeit im Kaufhaus, die das Wiederholen eines Werbeslogans implizierte, nämlich "There are limits to absurdity, even in the cause of survival" (S. 40), zeigt deutlich, daß der von ihr postulierte Grad an Selbstverwirklichung utopische Züge trägt, denn in einer Gesellschaft des ausgehenden 20. Jahrhunderts kann realistischerweise eine derartige Selbstverwirklichung nicht angestrebt werden, zumindest nicht im Rahmen der Tätigkeiten, die Lettice ausübt. Der projektive Aspekt des Utopie-Syndroms erstreckt sich bei Lettice dabei auf ihre Führungen, d. h. auf die Touristen, die sie begeistern muß, bzw. auf jedes Publikum, dem sie als „Schau-Spieler" entgegentritt. Auch ihr kurzes Intermezzo in den Royal Armouries, das nach dem gleichen Schema ablief, belegt einmal mehr ihre utopische Lebensmaxime.[10]

Während das „projektive Utopie-Syndrom" bei Lettice spielerisch-missionarische Züge trägt, das allerdings für ihre eigene Existenz nicht unerhebliche reelle negative Folgen hat, nimmt es bei Lotte doch erheblich destruktivere Formen an. Im Gegensatz zu Lettice ist Lotte in ihrer Erziehung stark und ausschließlich von ihrem Vater geprägt worden, einem Kunstbuchverleger und Flüchtling aus Dresden, dessen Vorstellung von Schönheit und Stadtgestaltung sich am barocken Glanz des Vorkriegs-Dresdens orientiert. Lotte hat diesen Schönheitsbegriff – trotz ihrer abgebrochenen Architekturausbildung – vollkommen unreflektiert übernommen. Sie führt dazu aus:

I care – I actually care more for buildings than their inhabitants. When I imagine Dresden burning, all I see are those exquisite shapes of the baroque – domes, pediments, golden cherubs going up in flames. Not people at all, just beautiful shapes vanishing forever ... I'm an idolator. That's what my friend called me, and he was right ... If I could save a great baroque city or its people I would choose the city every time. People come again: cities never. (S. 50)

Dieser kaum noch zu überbietende Zynismus zeigt deutlich, daß auch Lottes Verhalten treffend mit dem Begriff „projektives Utopie-Syndrom" umrissen werden kann; mit den Worten Paul Watzlawicks heißt das:

Der von ihr [dieser Form des Utopie-Syndroms] Befallene wähnt sich im Besitz der Wahrheit und damit nicht nur des Schlüssels, sondern auch der moralischen Verpflichtung zur Beseitigung alles Übels der Welt.[11]

Diese moralische Verpflichtung besteht bei Lotte nun darin, ihren Begriff von „schöner Architektur" durchzusetzen bzw. negativ gewendet, was sie für häßlich hält, zu zerstören. Schon als junge Studentin hatte sie zusammen mit einem Kommilitonen geplant, das Shell Building, sozusagen als Symbol der architektonisch-ästhetischen Umweltverschmutzung, in die Luft zu jagen:

'Why should all the bombs just fall on beauty? Why shouldn't one at least be used on ugliness – purely as protest? Witness that someone at least still has eyes!' (S. 51)

Ihr Rachefeldzug erstreckt sich nicht nur auf die Gebäude, sondern insbesondere auch auf die Planer dieser Häßlichkeiten, in ihren eigenen Worten:

'The people who put this up should be hanged in public for debauching the public imagination!' (S. 51)

Ihren studentischen Anschlag auf das Shell Building hatte sie jedoch aus Feigheit nicht durchgeführt, eine Unterlassung, die sie am Ende des Stückes – inzwischen doch einige Jahre älter geworden – unbedingt nachholen will. Somit kommt es zum Wiederaufleben des "Eyesore Negation Detachment", und zwar jetzt zusammen mit Lettice:

It's perfect! Elizabethan weapons attacking modern buildings! The revenge of the ravished past upon the present! [. . .] Let's make the list! The top ten ugliest buildings we want to murder! (S. 93)

Betrachtet man nun diesen Problemlösungsversuch der Damen näher, nämlich den Versuch, ihren eigenen Kulturbegriff mit allen Mitteln durchsetzen zu wollen, so zeigt sich für beide, daß sie hoffnungslos in den Strukturen einer problemerzeugenden Fehllösungsdynamik von der Art des „mehr-desselben" gefangen sind. Für Lettice ist das Zerbomben der zehn häßlichsten Gebäude mit mittelalterlichen Waffen nur ein weiteres Spiel, denn es ist für sie in erster Linie wegen der theatralischen Implikationen von Interesse: "It's sublime! Instead of just *playing* at executions of noble people, we'll be *arranging* them – for *ig*noble buildings which have disgraced our city!" (S. 94) Aber gerade diese Fixierung auf Spielstrukturen als Lösung ihres Problems der Desorientiertheit in der modernen Gesellschaft verschärft das Problem, anstatt es zu lösen. In einer Szene von fast tragischer Größe am Ende des Stückes zeigt sie eine tiefgehende Einsicht in ihre eigene Problemlage:

You're wrong, when you say there's nothing ghosty about me. That's what I *am*. Every day more. [. . .] It grows every day . . . It's like a mesh keeping me out – all the new things, every day more. *Your* things. Computers. Screens. Bleeps and buttons. Processors. Every day more . . . (S. 90)

Ihre Fixierung auf Spielstrukturen erzeugt einen zunehmenden Realitätsverlust, der Lettice umso mehr von der Bewältigung des Entfremdungspotentials, das der modernen Gesellschaft innewohnt, entfernt, je mehr sie versucht, der Entfremdung durch kompensatorische pseudo-authentische Erfahrung in fiktionalen Spielszenen zu entgehen. Doch ihr bleibt keine Handlungsalternative, hilflos ist sie ihrer eigenen Überzeugung ausgeliefert, denn würde sie diese auch noch aufgeben, so würde sie ins Nichts stürzen – mit ihren eigenen Worten:

> You're right. That's the precise word for me. Ridiculous. Ridiculous and useless. (*Pause*) Useless stories. Useless glories. Ridiculous and useless. (*Pause*) I'm sorry. (*Pause*) I haven't got anything else. (S. 91)

Bei Lotte verhält es sich strukturell ähnlich, wenngleich in anderer inhaltlicher Ausgestaltung. So wie Lettice an ihren Prämissen der "stories and glories" festhalten muß, um nicht hoffnungslos unterzugehen, so muß Lotte auch an ihren Grundsätzen von "strictest historical fact" festhalten, kombiniert mit ihrem nostalgisch verklärten Schönheitsbegriff, um nicht der existentiellen Unsicherheit und Orientierungslosigkeit der modernen Gesellschaft anheim zu fallen. Auch sie ist auf der Suche nach festen Maßstäben und Orientierungspunkten, die es in der modernen Welt so nicht mehr gibt; doch dies vermag sie nicht zu erkennen, da auch sie in den Strukturen ihres existenzbegründenden Weltbildes gefangen ist. Sie kann nur innerhalb dieses Weltbildes agieren, kann seine Grenzen nicht überwinden und ist so hoffnungslos dem „Katastrophenrezept des ‚Mehr desselben'"[12] ausgeliefert, was zum zweiten Versuch führt, ihre Vorstellung von geordneter Schönheit mittels Bombenanschlägen gewaltsam zu verwirklichen – ein Unterfangen, das nicht zuletzt auch durch die quasi symbolische Verwendung mittelalterlicher Waffen als "ridiculous and useless" bezeichnet werden kann.

Die Tatsache, daß diese einsichtsvolle Selbstcharakteristik von Lettice auch genau das Problemlösungsverhalten von Lotte trifft, wobei Lotte bezeichnenderweise bei der Wahl der Waffen von dem echten Sprengstoff ihrer Jugendzeit zu Lettices mittelalterlichen Geschützen übergeht, führt zu der Frage, wie sich die Interaktion von Lettice und Lotte genau gestaltet, denn sie beeinflussen sich, wie man unschwer erkennt, gegenseitig ganz erheblich und entwickeln sich dabei von Gegnern zu Verbündeten. Dazu sei zunächst ein Blick auf das erste Zusammentreffen von Lettice und Lotte in dem alten Tudor-Schloß geworfen (Akt 1, Szene 1). Lettice hält einen ihrer unnachahmlichen Vorträge, voller Ausschmückungen und nicht sehr an der historischen Wahrheit orientiert. Lotte hat sich unter die Touristen gemischt, findet die Abweichungen in Lettices Vortrag unerträglich und blamiert Lettice – unmittelbar bevor die Führung zu Ende ist – sozusagen vor „versammelter Mannschaft", indem sie Lettices Vortrag nicht nur als "absolutely intolerable" (S. 13) bezeichnet, sondern die Führung auch abrupt abbricht und ein sofortiges Gespräch unter vier Augen mit Lettice verlangt. Wenn man sich nun diese Situation näher anschaut, so wird unmittelbar deutlich, daß die Rollenverteilung eine von „Vorgesetzte" und „Angestellte" ist. Mit der Begrifflichkeit von Watzlawick kann hier von einer typischen „komplementären Beziehung"[13] gesprochen werden, wobei Lotte die superiore Position einnimmt und Lettice – notgedrungen – die inferiore. In dem unmittelbar folgenden Vier-Augen-Gespräch stellt Lettice jedoch diese Rollenzuschreibung direkt in Frage. Lottes Kritik als Vertreterin des Preservation Trust ist inhaltlich ausgerichtet und wendet sich gegen Lettices "Gross departures from fact and truth" (S. 14). Lettice geht jedoch gar nicht erst auf die von Lotte begonnene Inhaltsdebatte ein, sondern thematisiert sofort den Beziehungsaspekt: "I'm sorry – but I cannot myself get beyond your own behaviour. [...] Is that how you conceive your duty – to humiliate subordinates?" (S. 15f.) Mit dieser Thematisierung der Beziehungsebene, d. h. des analogen Aspektes der Kommunikation, beginnt Lettice eine Metakommunikation und weist damit im Grunde bereits hier die Rollenzuschreibung „Angestellte" zurück. Dennoch fügt sie sich auch auf der rein faktischen Ebene und erscheint am nächsten Tag im Büro von Lotte, wo sie die Kündigung erwartet.

Die zweite Szene des ersten Aktes spielt im Büro von Lotte und zeigt zunächst – in geradezu satirischer Überzeichnung – das Verhältnis von Lotte als resolute Vorgesetzte und Miss Framer als ängstliche Sekretärin. Bereits die Regieanweisung spricht Bände über ihre Beziehung: "The door opens timidly. Miss Framer comes in: a nervous, anxious assistant, frightened, breathy and refined." (S. 19) Dieser Darstellung und satirischen Überzeichnung einer klassischen komplementären Beziehung kommt dabei die Funktion einer Kontrastfolie zu, um die Andersartigkeit der – zwar ebenfalls komplementären – Beziehung Lottes zu Lettice deutlicher hervortreten zu lassen. Wenngleich sich rein faktisch an der Beziehung Lotte – Lettice, d. h. an ihren Rollen als Vorgesetzte und Angestellte, durch die Metakommunikation von Lettice nichts geändert hat, so ist ihr Auftritt in Lottes Büro doch auf der Beziehungsebene höchst signifikant. In der Szene ihrer ersten Begegnung hatte sie sich auf verbale, d. h. digitale Thematisierung ihres Verhältnisses, beschränkt; in dieser Szene stellt sie die Rollenzuschreibung von Lotte auf der Beziehungsebene in Frage, indem sie durch ihre Kleidung die alltägliche Szene in einen grandiosen Auftritt umfunktioniert und somit ihre inferiore Position analog dementiert: "She is wearing a black beret and a theatrical black cloak like some medieval abbot." (S. 21f.) Wenngleich auf der faktischen Ebene für Lettice nichts mehr zu retten ist, denn sie verliert ihre Stelle, so verfehlt ihr Aufzug doch nicht seine Wirkung. Verstärkt wird sie noch durch Lettices furiosen Abgang, bei dem sie in ihrer Kleidung auf die Hinrichtung von *Mary Queen of Scots* verweist, und unter ihrem Mantel ein entsprechendes Gewand zeigt. Mit dem Hinweis "that is strict and absolute fact" (S. 32), mit dem sie die Authentizität dieses „Kleidungszitats" belegt, spielt sie gleichzeitig auf Lottes historische Wahrheitsliebe an, um diese dann erstaunt aber fasziniert zurückzulassen: "She sweeps up her cloak from the floor and walks triumphantly out of the office. Lotte Schoen stares after her in amazed fascination." (S. 32)

Festgehalten werden kann, daß Lettice somit auf der faktischen digitalen Ebene die von Lotte vorgenommene Rollenzuschreibung akzeptiert – ihr bleibt dort auch nichts anderes übrig –, diese Rollenzuschreibung aber zugleich auf der Beziehungsebene desavouiert, indem sie durch ihr Auftreten, ihre außergewöhnliche Kleidung und ihre ganze Erscheinung zeigt, daß sie sich in der superioren Position fühlt. Diese Selbstbehauptung von Lettice auf der Beziehungsebene ist es letztendlich, die Lotte tief beeindruckt und die sie auch veranlaßt, Lettice privat zu besuchen, um ihr einen Ersatzjob zu vermitteln. Bei dieser Gelegenheit initiiert Lettice sozusagen einen Rollentausch, d. h. sie verbalisiert den von ihr auf der Beziehungsebene erhobenen Anspruch auf die superiore Position innerhalb ihrer Beziehung; sie sagt zu Lotte:

> Let me play the interviewer for once: you be the victim. [. . .] It'll be a game! Imagine you are looking for employment and I'm the woman at the agency. (S. 44f.)

Die Tatsache, daß es gelingt und Lotte auf das Spiel eingeht, belegt, daß sich die Struktur ihrer Interaktion geändert hat; sie ist zwar immer noch komplementär, aber da die superiore und die inferiore Position nun abwechselnd von beiden wahrgenommen wird, ist sie auf einer höheren Ebene als symmetrisch zu bezeichnen. Was sich in dieser Szene erst auf sanften Zwang von Lettice ergibt, wird im Verlauf ihrer Beziehung zu einer freien Entscheidung von Lotte; mit den Worten von Lettice:

> We exchanged roles. It was a wonderful moment, if I may say so . . . Lotte – Miss Schoen – elected herself to play the victim. She suggested it, not I. (S. 78)

Und genau in dem Augenblick, als es Lotte gelungen ist, eine symmetrische, d. h. auf Gleichheit beruhende, Beziehung zu Lettice aufzubauen, kommt es zu dem unglücklichen Zufall, daß Lettice Lotte verletzt und unter Mordverdacht gerät. Der bevorstehende Prozeß bringt Lotte nunmehr in die unhaltbare Situation, entweder in aller Öffentlichkeit ihre merkwürdigen Spielgewohnheiten von Hinrichtungsszenen aufdecken zu müssen und sich damit der Lächerlichkeit preiszugeben – was dann auch den Verlust ihres Jobs bedeuten würde – oder aber wider besseren Wissens Lettice einer Mordanklage auszusetzen.

Auf der Ebene der Handlungsstruktur läßt sich aus dieser Interaktionsanalyse folgende Quintessenz ziehen: es zeigt sich eine zunehmende Konzentration auf die Beziehungsebene, auf analoge Strukturen, die hier in Spielstrukturen realisiert werden; in diesen Spielstrukturen entwickelt sich die Beziehung der beiden

Protagonisten zu einer symmetrischen Beziehung. Die Spielstrukturen entwickeln dabei gleichzeitig eine Eigendynamik, die nicht mehr steuerbar auf das Leben der Protagonisten außerhalb des Rollenspiels zurückwirkt. Auf der thematisch-inhaltlichen Ebene ist damit eine Verknüpfung mit der Schein-Sein-Problematik gegeben, wobei durch die Darstellung des Ineinanderwirkens von Spiel- und Realitätsebene die Frage der Konstruktion von Wirklichkeit gestellt wird. Der Wirklichkeitsbegriff wird thematisiert und problematisiert, und damit die Illusion – insbesondere auch des Zuschauers –, zwischen Schein und Sein unterscheiden zu können. Lottes Weltsicht, deren Maxime treffend mit ihren eigenen Worten "Untruth is untruth" (S. 29) umrissen werden kann, wird durch den Handlungsverlauf als zu eindimensional entlarvt, als zu wenig differenziert, um auch mögliche *feed-back*-Effekte von Handlungen miteinkalkulieren zu können. Shaffer greift hier einen Themenkomplex wieder auf, den er schon in früheren Stücken behandelt hat, wie z. B. in dem Einakter *White Lies* (1967), in dem er Probleme von Wahrheit und Lüge, Rolle und Identität behandelt. Aber auch z. B. in seinem großen Stück *Amadeus* steht das Scheitern des Protagonisten Salieri an eigendynamisch eskalierenden Handlungsketten in Zusammenhang mit einem axiomatisch gesetzten eindimensionalen Weltbild im Mittelpunkt der Handlung.

Der entfremdende Einfluß von elektronischen Medien, Video, Computern etc. auf das Individuum stellt ein weiteres charakteristisches Thema der Stücke Peter Shaffers dar. Diese Entwicklungen der modernen Gesellschaft, die für den einzelnen eine Bedrohung seiner Identität darstellen und durch den damit verbundenen Erfahrungsverlust zum Wirklichkeitsverlust führen können, werden in ihren Auswirkungen von Shaffer in seinem jüngsten Stück in den Protagonisten Lettice und Lotte exemplifiziert, wobei die zunehmende Hinwendung zu analoger Kommunikation gleichsam als kompensatorische Gegenbewegung zur Monopolisierung durch die computerbestimmte, digitale Alltagswelt begriffen werden kann. Hier zeigt sich eine deutliche Parallele zu *Equus*, wo dieselbe Problematik in den Protagonisten Alan und Dysart versinnbildlicht ist, wenngleich in sehr viel pathologischeren Dimensionen.

Die Tatsache, daß Shaffer mit *Lettice and Lovage* wieder zum Genre der Komödie zurückkehrt – zuletzt hatte er in den 60er Jahren Komödien geschrieben, allerdings immer Einakter, nie abendfüllende Stücke –, diese Rückkehr zum Genre der Komödie bedeutet nicht, daß seine Inhalte mehr dem Boulevardtheater zuzuordnen wären und damit unkritischer würden. Wie an *Lettice and Lovage* aufgezeigt werden konnte und wie an den deutlichen Parallelen zu früheren – insbesondere auch zu seinen großen – Stücken zu erkennen ist, führt Shaffer mit seinem jüngsten Stück die Tradition der Dramatisierung von Kommunikations- und Interaktionsproblemen fort, wie sie sich insbesondere aus dem Zusammenwirken von individuellen Handlungsversuchen und gesellschaftlichen Zwängen ergeben. Die nicht-linearen zirkulären Handlungsparadigmen, in die die Protagonisten verwickelt sind, erlauben keine Unterscheidung von Ursache und Wirkung. Hierdurch stellt sich die Frage, ob autonomes Handeln überhaupt noch möglich ist; eine Frage, in die der Zuschauer sich einbezogen fühlen muß, nicht zuletzt auch dadurch, daß die beiden Protagonisten am Ende des Stückes ihr mittelalterliches Geschütz auf das Publikum richten.

Anmerkungen

1 Ein Überblick zu den Kritikerreaktionen auf die englische Premiere findet sich in dem Aufsatz von C. J. Gianakaris: "Placing Shaffer's *Lettice and Lovage* in Perspective". *Comparative Drama* 22, 1988, 145–161; vgl. u. a. auch J. Exner: „Einstürzende Neubauten. Peter Shaffers Bombenkomödie *Lettice and Lovage"*. *Frankfurter Rundschau*, 27. 11. 1987, 20; zur deutschsprachigen Erstaufführung vgl. u. a. P. Kruntorad: „Wenn Damen Henker spielen". *Theater heute* 30, ii, 1989, 41.
2 Vgl. dazu auch Kruntorad: „Wenn Damen Henker spielen".
3 Es wird nach folgender Ausgabe zitiert: P. Shaffer: *Lettice and Lovage. A Comedy in Three Acts*. London: André Deutsch, 1988.
4 Bern, ⁵1980 (¹1969). Der Titel der Originalausgabe lautet: *Pragmatics of Human Communication. A Study of Interactional Patterns, Pathologies, and Paradoxes*. New York, 1967.
5 Bern, 1974. Der Titel der Originalausgabe lautet: *Change. Principles of Problem Formation and Problem Resolution*. New York, 1974.
6 Die folgende stark geraffte und damit notwendigerweise verkürzende Darstellung des theoretischen Ansatzes findet sich in ausführlicher Form in P. Iking: *Strukturen gestörter Kommunikation in den Dramen Peter Shaffers*. Essen, 1989, das allerdings *Lettice and Lovage* noch nicht behandelt.
7 *Lösungen*, S. 10.
8 *Menschliche Kommunikation*, S. 55.
9 Vgl. hierzu insbesondere S. 24 f.
10 Vgl. S. 55.
11 *Lösungen*, S. 73.
12 Watzlawick, P.: *Münchhausens Zopf oder Psychotherapie und „Wirklichkeit". Aufsätze und Vorträge über menschliche Probleme in systematisch-konstruktivistischer Sicht.* Bern, 1988, S. 128.
13 *Menschliche Kommunikation*, S. 68 ff.

Englische Textbibliothek

2 **Gay, John:** John Gays Singspiele. Hrsg. v. Sarrazin, Gregor. 1898. XXXII,209 S. Kt 16,- ⟨3-533-01856-3⟩

3 **Keats, John:** Keats' Hyperion. Einl. u. hrsg. v. Hoops, Johannes. 1899. 103 S. Kt 10,- ⟨3-533-01857-1⟩

4 **Fielding, Henry:** Tom Thumb. Hrsg. v. Lindner, Felix. 1899. VIII,111 S. Gb 15,- ⟨3-533-01858-X⟩

7 **Chaucer, Geoffrey:** The Pardoner's Prologue and Tale. A critical edition. Hrsg. v. Koch, John. 1902. LXXII,164 S. Kt 16,- ⟨3-533-01859-8⟩

8 **Die älteste mittelenglische Version der Assumptio Mariae.** Hrsg. v. Hackauf, Emil. 1902. III,XXXIII,100 S. Gb 15,- ⟨3-533-01860-1⟩

9 **Villiers, George:** The Rehearsal. First acted 7.XII.1671, published 1672. Hrsg. v. Lindner, Felix. 1904. IV,111 S. Br 15,- ⟨3-533-01861-X⟩

10 **Garths Dispensary.** Krit. Ausg. mit Einl. u. Anm. v. Leicht, Wilhelm J. 1905. VIII,175 S. Br 17,- ⟨3-533-01862-8⟩
Ln 22,- ⟨3-533-01863-6⟩

11 **Longfellows Evangeline.** Untersuchung über die Geschichte des englischen Hexameters. Kritische Ausg. v. Sieper, Ernst. 1905. VII,177 S. Br 17,- ⟨3-533-01864-4⟩

14 **Shakespeare, William:** Othello. In Paralleldruck nach d. 1. Quarto u. 1. Folio mit d. Lesarten d. 2. Quarto hrsg. v. Schröer, M M. 2.bericht. Aufl 1949. XVI,211 S. Br 20,- ⟨3-533-01866-0⟩

17 **An Enterlude of Welth and Helth.** Eine englische Moralität des 16. Jahrhunderts. Hrsg. v. Holthausen, F. 2. verb. Aufl. 1922. XIX,50 S. Br 14,- ⟨3-533-01867-9⟩

18 **Chaucer, Geoffrey:** Kleinere Dichtungen nebst Einleitung, Lesarten, Anmerkungen und einem Wörterverzeichnis. Neu hrsg. v. Koch, John. 1928. VIII,260 S. Br 25,- ⟨3-533-01868-7⟩

19 **Sire Degarre.** Nach der gesamten Überlieferung und mit Untersuchungen über die Sprache und den Romanzenstoff. Hrsg. v. Schleich, Gustav. 1929. 144 S. Br 20,- ⟨3-533-01869-5⟩

20 **Lee, Nathaniel:** Constantine the Great. Krit. hrsg. u. Einl. v. Häfele, Walter. 1933. 166 S. Br 20,- ⟨3-533-01870-9⟩

21 **Ellwood, Thomas:** Davideis. A reprint of the 1st edition of 1712 with various readings of later edition. Ed. with an introduction and notes by Fischer, Walther. 1936. XXVII,248 S. Br 30,- ⟨3-533-01871-7⟩

CARL WINTER
UNIVERSITÄTSVERLAG
HEIDELBERG

Werner Huber, Paderborn

Irish vs. English: Brian Friel's *Making History*

> To give an accurate description of what has never happened is not merely the proper occupation of the historian, but the inalienable privilege of any man of arts and culture.
>
> (Oscar Wilde)

The English theatre critic Kenneth Tynan once defined the function of the Irish theatre as being that of giving the English theatre a kick up the backside at least once in every generation.[1] A new play by Brian Friel, who is commonly acclaimed as Ireland's leading dramatist, could easily have such a catalytic effect on the English theatre of today, for *Making History*[2] is not just an Irish play, but implicates the English side of the Anglo-Irish dialogue as well. By touching on essentially political issues it somehow concerns Anglo-Irish relations extending beyond the purely literary sphere. On the surface, *Making History* is a 'historical' play about Hugh O'Neill, Earl of Tyrone, who led the Irish rebellion against English rule during the reign of Elizabeth I.[3] The action takes place in Ireland before and after the Battle of Kinsale in 1601, when the Irish and their Spanish allies were defeated. This meant the breakdown of the old Gaelic order and with the plantation of Ulster beginning after 1607 it also marked the beginning of a new chapter in a field where Irish and English (British) history are intricately interwoven. The consequences of all this can still be witnessed today as the "Troubles" in Northern Ireland. Thus, the subject-matter of this play must concern both Irish and English audiences[4] alike as do the central questions of the play, namely, how history is made, how history is written, how history is read and even re-read. The Anglo-Irish dialogue in the widest sense is beset by such problems of modern historiography, which are created by the anatagonism, the simultaneous existence of two different kinds of discourse, i. e., colonial discourse vs. nationalist discourse.

In this paper I will attempt to do at least two things. I will first discuss Friel's play by paying special attention to the meta-historical theme. I will then try to isolate the play's "political relevance", for want of a better term, and its international (Irish vs. English) implications. This will lead me to a thumbnail sketch of Field Day, which as an ideological context is of prime importance to *Making History*.

✳

In 1942, Sean O'Faolain's biography of Hugh O'Neill was published. In his preface O'Faolain sent out a challenge to playwrights of his own and future generations:

> If anyone wished to make a study of the manner in which historical myths are created he might well take O'Neill as an example, and beginning with his defeat and death trace the gradual emergence of a picture at which the original would have gazed from under his red eyelashes with a chuckle of cynical amusement and amazement. Indeed, in those last years in Rome the myth was already beginning to emerge, and a talented dramatist might write an informative, entertaining, ironical play on the theme of the living man helplessly watching his translation into a star in the face of all the facts that had reduced him to poverty, exile, and defeat.[5]

In 1988, Brian Friel responded to this challenge. In fact, Friel drew freely on O'Faolain. The final scene is more or less a dramatisation of the last chapter in O'Faolain's biography. On the whole, Friel is not so much concerned with the exact historical details of Hugh O'Neill's life, nor, as a matter of fact, is O'Faolain, whose general picture of the period sometimes is and has to be that of the imaginative novelist, although he is very strong on the complexities of English colonial policy. Each writer then in his respective genre presents a "study of the manner in which historical myths are created." And one could make the finer distinction by saying that Friel is the more radical of the two in that he wilfully distorts some of the established historical facts to show us all the more clearly the subjective nature of history 'in the making'. Therefore, it may not be a bad idea to recall the exact historical details of O'Neill's life before looking at the play itself.

The life of Hugh O'Neill reveals some almost schizophrenic ambiguities.[6] He was born in Dungannon, Co. Tyrone, in 1540 – or 1550, if we follow O'Faolain. He spent the first years of his life in the care of his Gaelic foster-parents. From 1559 until 1567 he was brought up in the 'New Faith' in the aristocratic households of the Sidneys and Leicesters. He became the second Earl of Tyrone in 1585 with the support of the Government. But more important to him as an Irishman was the Gaelic chieftainship when he was crowned "The O'Neill" in 1593. For most of his life he shifted between English and Irish ways, between being a loyal subject and an Irish Catholic rebel. Thus, he served in or assisted the English army against native Irish clans in 1568 and 1574 and made three major submissions to the Queen. On the other hand, there is a lot of double dealing over much of the same period. O'Neill was in contact with Spain and the Catholic hierarchy (requesting help for a rebellion and the restoration of the Old Faith). He gained a glorious victory over the English in the Battle of the Yellow Ford (1598) and marched all across Ireland to meet the Spanish invasion force only to be trounced by the English at Kinsale (1601). In order to avoid being arrested and completely dispossessed he was forced to make a rather precipitate departure together with the Earl of Tyrconnell and their respective families in what became known as the "Flight of the Earls" (1607). From 1608 until his death in 1616 he made his exile home in Rome where he lived on pensions from the Pope and the King of Spain.

To return to the play: the scene in Act I is laid in O'Neill's home in Dungannon, County Tyrone. The time is August 1591. We find Hugh O'Neill in conference with his personal secretary Harry Hoveden, who, incidentally, is of Old English, i. e. Gaelicized Norman, stock. The arrival of Red Hugh O'Donnell and Peter Lombard triggers a discussion of political business. O'Donnell, the Earl of Tyrconnell, is a rash, hot-blooded, though loyal Gaelic chief, whose immediate concern is with the rivalries among the Gaelic septs. Lombard, the future absentee Archbishop of Armagh, is a church diplomat involved in the international power politics of Rome and Spain. He is engaged on a book vindicating the Irish rebellion of the 1590s as a religious war. Both O'Donnell and Lombard epitomise two of the many forces which make their demands on O'Neill, while he himself is considering his private happiness. O'Neill upstages his interlocutors by his revelation that he has recently eloped with Mabel Bagenal, sister of the Queen's Marshal at Newry. Not only has he chosen for his (third) wife a member of the New English, i. e. Tudor colonist, class, he has also been married according to the Protestant rite.

In Act I, Scene 2, we find Mabel, who has meanwhile converted to Catholicism, defending the Gaelic ways in a discussion with her visiting sister Mary. Mary, who is rooted in the siege mentality of the New English colonisers, extols the advantages of bee-keeping, horticulture, and religion in her culture, while in her view the Gaels have never advanced beyond pastoral farming, cattle-raiding, and superstition. The news breaks that the Pope has issued a Bull of Indulgence (which would give the rebellion the status of a holy war) and that the Spanish are sending an invasion army due to land at Kinsale. O'Neill is suddenly forced to act and take sides. But Mabel, with better political foresight, warns him against "gambl[ing] everything on one big throw" (p. 38), because, as she sees it, there is no real unity in the Irish camp.

> MABEL: You are not united. You have no single leader. You have no common determination. At best you are an impromptu alliance of squabbling tribesmen – [...]
> – grabbing at religion as a coagulant only because they have no other idea to inform them or give them cohesion.
> (Pause.)

O'NEILL: Is that a considered abstract of the whole Gaelic history and civilization, Mabel? Or is it nothing more than an honest-to-goodness, instant wisdom of the Upstart? (p. 38–39)

O'Neill tragically fails to acknowledge Mabel's warning and her essential loyalty to his cause. He feels that he has to give up his policy of sitting out this crisis and letting history march on. As his culture is threatened, he has to abandon his idea of a peaceful rapprochement between the two opposing ways of life, of protecting the time-honoured customs of his people and simultaneously opening them "to the strange new ways of Europe" (p. 40). Mabel breaks away from him when he cruelly taunts her by boasting about his mistresses and illegitimate offspring.

When we see Hugh O'Neill next (in II.1), he is on the run and hiding in the Sperrin Mountains. This is about eight months after the debacle of Kinsale. O'Neill is composing his submission to Queen Elizabeth, thereby following Mabel's advice and hoping to be re-instated eventually. Together with Hugh O'Donnell, who has resigned his title and is about to leave the country, he rehearses the terms of his unconditional surrender, knowing full well that Elizabeth might use him again in order to control the anarchy and rule Ulster through him. Harry Hoveden arrives with news of Mabel's death in child-bed. O'Neill is disconsolate.

The final scene takes place in Rome in the 1610s. Hugh O'Neill, Harry Hoveden and Peter Lombard are united again. It is pension day for O'Neill, and he returns home to his palace, drunk, maudlin, a broken and bitter man suspicious of everyone around him. He discovers Lombard's manuscript of his life and is immediately set to do battle with the Archbishop, who intends his book as a propaganda piece.

LOMBARD: [...] This isn't the time for a critical assessment of your 'ploys' and your 'disgraces' and your 'betrayal' – that's the stuff of another history for another time. Now is the time for a hero. Now is the time for a heroic literature. So I am offering Gaelic Ireland two things. I'm offering them this narrative that has the elements of myth. And I'm offering them Hugh O'Neill as a national hero. A hero and the story of a hero. [...] (p. 67)

O'Neill objects to being transmogrified into a national hero. He wants Mabel to take a central position in the story of his life, although it does not become quite clear what this should be.[7]

In the grand finale Lombard begins to recite the opening lines from his *History of Hugh O'Neill*. He is interrupted and contrapuntally answered by O'Neill himself quoting from his submission to Queen Elizabeth.

LOMBARD: He continued to grow and increase in comeliness and urbanity, tact and eloquence, wisdom and knowledge, goodly size and noble deeds so that his name and fame spread throughout the five provinces of Ireland and beyond –

O'NEILL: May it please you to mitigate your just indignation against me for my betrayal of you which deserves no forgiveness and for which I can make no satisfaction, even with my life –

LOMBARD: And people reflected in their minds that when he would reach manhood there would not be one like him of the Irish to avenge their wrongs and punish the plunderings of his race –

O'NEILL: Mabel, I am sorry... please forgive me, Mabel...

LOMBARD: For it was foretold by prophets and by predictors of futurity that there would come one like him –

A man, glorious, pure, faithful above all
Who will cause mournful weeping in every territory.
He will be a God-like prince
And he will be king for the span of his life.
(O'NEILL *is now crying. Bring down the lights slowly.*) (pp. 70–71)

As Sean O'Faolain had imagined what a play about Hugh O'Neill could be like, we have here the "living man helplessly watching his translation into a star in the face of all the facts that had reduced him to poverty, exile, and defeat".[8]

⁕

Chris Murray has shown that Friel by working with anachronisms and deliberately falsifying some of the established historical facts about O'Neill's life is "using the latest revisionist historical methodology".[9] In fact, Friel is deconstructing history and the O'Neill myth. Through the gap opening up between positive historical facts and legend or myth Friel is making us aware of the pitfalls of historiography. A self-reflexive element is introduced by the characters' discussion of "historical methodology" which surfaces again and again during the first three scenes and which culminates in O'Neill's last stand against his historiographer. This makes the play less a historical drama than a meta-historical drama critical of the ideological uses of history.

From this thematic point of view Peter Lombard is O'Neill's main antagonist in the play. He is embarked upon a history of the life and times of O'Neill.[10] But O'Neill is wary of Lombard's method which discounts 'truth' as a valid criterion (pp. 8–9), for Lombard upholds a principle of unbridled relativity and total opportunism with regard to "the needs and the demands and the expectations of different people and different eras" (p. 16). During his final years in exile in

Rome, when O'Neill has come to the bitter realization that he never came anywhere near being "the Godlike prince" or "a king for the span of his life", as the wording of Lombard's book would have it, he takes Lombard to task for embalming him "in a florid lie", "in pieties" (p. 63).

> O'NEILL: I need the truth, Peter. That's all that's left. The schemer, the leader, the liar, the statesman, the lecher, the patriot, the drunk, the soured, bitter émigré – put it *all* in, Peter. Record the *whole* life – that's what you said yourself. (Ibid.)

What O'Neill wants is not a legend as a national hero, but a modern biography of the *whole* man with Mabel occupying a central place. Lombard, however, is firmly set on transforming the drab events of O'Neill's life into the sublime style of his history. He – and Friel alongside with him – even cites the authority of Ludhaidh O'Cleary, who – and this is not a fiction – wrote a life of Hugh O'Donnell, the loud-mouthed, irascible Gael. O'Donnell is described as "'a dove in meekness and gentleness and a lion in strength and force. He was a sweet-sounding trumpet –'" (pp. 64–65). The discrepancies between fiction and truth, history as fact and history as story, are nowhere made more blatant than in Lombard's retelling of the key events of O'Neill's political life. To Lombard's description of the "legendary battle of Kinsale and the crushing of the most magnificent Gaelic army ever assembled" Hugh can only reply that "Kinsale was a disgrace. [...] We ran away like rats" (p. 65). And what Lombard describes as 'The Flight of the Earls', "that tragic but magnificent exodus of the Gaelic aristocracy" is again perceived and phrased differently by O'Neill: "As we pulled out from Rathmullen the McSwineys stoned us from the shore!" (Ibid.) O'Neill's efforts to debunk Lombard's versions of history are in vain. Lombard is fiercely determined to offer Gaelic Ireland the life of Hugh O'Neill as a story, a myth. He sums up his philosophy thus:

> LOMBARD: [...] People think they just want to know the 'facts'; they think they believe in some sort of empirical truth, but what they really want is a story. And that's what this will be: the events of your life categorized and classified and then structured as you would structure any story. No, no, I'm not talking about falsifying, about lying, for heaven's sake. I'm simply talking about making a pattern. That's what I'm doing with all this stuff – offering a cohesion to that random catalogue of deliberate achievement and sheer accident that constitutes your life. And that cohesion will be a narrative that people will read and be satisfied by. [...] (pp. 66–67)

Compare this with Friel's comments in a programme note to the first production of *Making History*.

> For example, even though Mabel, Hugh's wife, died in 1591 [*sic*], it suited my story to keep her alive for another ten years. Part of me regrets taking

these occasional liberties. But then I remind myself that history and fiction are related and comparable forms of discourse and that an historical text is a kind of literary artifact. And then I am grateful that these regrets were never inhibiting.[11]

On the surface Friel seems to be saying pretty much the same thing as his character Lombard. However, the redeeming factor in *Making History* is the self-reflexive element of writing a historical drama centring round the creation of another historical fiction. This added dimension of a sharpened awareness of the problematic nature of historiography, of history as story, is the salient point and central message. It should be obvious by now that Friel's central theme proceeds from the assumption "that it is not the literal past, the 'facts' of history, that shape us, but images of the past embodied in language" and "that we must never cease renewing those images; because once we do, we fossilize".[12] Those are the words of the character of the hedge-schoolmaster in Friel's play *Translations* (1980). This play is equally "about the tragedy of English imperialism as well as of Irish nationalism".[13] Its context is the mapping and renaming of Ireland by the British Army in the ordnance survey of the 1830s, which followed the Act of Union between Great Britain and Ireland in 1800. As can be imagined, *Translations*, too, makes compelling use of another historical turning-point to explore the themes of the power of language and the clash of two civilizations.

It would not be an understatement to say that Friel in recent times has been preoccupied with the critique of language and myths as fictions created by and embedded in language.[14] The transfer of this critical method to the ideologies conditioning the Anglo-Irish dialogue in the widest possible sense is one of the major hidden "political" messages to be extracted from Friel's play. But in order to fully understand his commitment in this respect a short introduction to the aspirations of Field Day must be inserted here.

*

In 1980, Brian Friel and the actor Stephen Rea founded the Field Day Theatre Company in Derry.[15] Hailed by some critics as the late 20th-century equivalent of the Irish Literary Theatre or – on a more modest scale – the Ulster Literary Theatre, Field Day has continued to commission and produce a new or challenging play every year. With the support of the Arts Councils of both Northern Ireland and the Republic of Ireland alike these productions usually have an opening run in Derry before they are taken on a tour of the whole island – and sometimes on to England. Among the plays produced by Field Day are Friel's adaptation of Chekhov's *Three Sisters* into Irish-English (1981), *Boesman and Lena* (1983) by the Southern African dramatist Athol Fugard, Tom Paulin's version of *Antigone*, significantly entitled *The Riot Act* (1984), Thomas Kilroy's *Double Cross* (1987), *Making History* (1988), and Terry Eagleton's play about Oscar Wilde, *Saint Oscar* (1989). The original impetus for the company and its activities came from a feeling shared by its directors, who also include the poet Seamus Heaney in their ranks, – a feeling "that the political crisis in the North and its reverberations in the Republic had made the necessity of a reappraisal of Ireland's political and cultural situation explicit and urgent".[16] This reappraisal means first and foremost an examination of the various forms of discourse and partisan rhetoric used by all sides concerned in the Anglo-Irish problem. The general idea behind the publications of Field Day and their theatre work is to open up a political and cultural debate by analyzing "the established opinions, myths and stereotypes which had become both a symptom and a cause of the current situation".[17] Fifteen pamphlets have so far been published. "Civilians and Barbarians" (Seamus Deane), "Myth and Motherland" (Richard Kearney), "Anglo-Irish Attitudes" (Declan Kiberd) are just three of the more self-explanatory titles, which sometimes take their myth criticism to a highly abstract level. There is another threesome on emergency legislature and the latest is a trio of pamphlets on "Nationalism, Colonialism and Literature" by such distinguished critics as Terry Eagleton, Fredric Jameson and Edward S. Said. Due any time now is a comprehensive anthology of Irish writing of the last 500 years, which "will have the aim of revealing and confirming the existence of a continuous tradition, contributed to by all groups, sects and parties".[18] Generally speaking, Field Day's main objective is to create an "artistic fifth province"[19], a united Ireland of the mind, which straddles all partisan divisions and which may eventually serve as the groundwork for concrete political solutions, "the basis for a more ecumenical and eirenic approach to the deep and apparently implacable problems which confront the island today".[20]

※

This brief introduction to Field Day should have made clear the context in which Friel's language-centred critique of myth and historiography in *Making History* should be seen. Without becoming overtly political this play works towards a heightened awareness of history and myth. When Hugh O'Neill in the play speaks of trying "to open [his] people to the strange new ways of Europe, to ease them into the new assessment of things, to nudge them towards changing evaluations and beliefs" (p. 40), his words acquire a more than ominous significance. He is suddenly reaching out through the fourth wall and his words could be taken quite literally by any audience on both sides of the Irish Sea – any night. We may well leave it to one of the Field Day pamphleteers to sum up the play's significance and, if you like, missionary gesture:

We must never cease to keep our mythological images in dialogue with history; because once we do we fossilise. That is why we will go on telling stories, inventing and re-inventing myths, until we have brought history home to itself.[21]

The echoes in Friel can hardly be missed.

Notes

1 Quoted in O'Toole: "Competing Voices", 12.

2 *Making History* was first performed by Field Day Theatre Company in the Guildhall, Derry, on 20 Sept. 1988; it then transferred to the National Theatre (Cottesloe), London, where it opened on 5 Dec. 1988. For major reviews, see *London Theatre Record*, Brennan, McKeone, Ridley, Sharkey, and O'Brien, "A Matter of Making". In his recent monograph, George O'Brien also includes *Making History* in his discussion of Friel's œuvre (*Brian Friel*, pp. 117–120).

3 I am indebted to Professor Thomas Kilroy, who kindly lent me the typescript of his play *The O'Neill* (first performed in 1969). There are some astonishing parallels between his play and Friel's: *The O'Neill* is also built around a two-act structure (before and after the Battle of the Yellow Ford) and ends with one of O'Neill's ritualistic submissions to the English Crown. The eponymous hero is a "modern man" drawn between two civilisations. In the words of Chris Murray, Kilroy's play "presented the great Earl as a man baffled and confused by the world he sees breaking up around him. He is a modern figure, like Osborne's *Luther*, unsure of his motives and of his role as saviour of his country: the very opposite of the Yeatsian hero" ("The History Play Today", p. 284). O'Neill is also the subject of a biography by John Mitchel, the Irish nationalist, who is mainly remembered for his *Jail Journal: The Life and Times of Aodh O'Neill, Prince of Ulster* (1846). And there are also a number of historical novels in which O'Neill figures largely, e. g., the anonymous *The Adventurers; or, Scenes in Ireland in the Reign of Elizabeth* (1825); Mrs. James Sadlier: *The Red Hand of Ulster; or, The Fortunes of Hugh O'Neill* (1850); C. Guenot; *Le comte de Tyrone* (1867); P. Dillon: *Earl or Chieftain* (1910).

4 Many English critics failed or refused to see these implications; see, e. g., *London Theatre Record*: "Making History".

5 *The Great O'Neill*, p. VI.

6 For information on the 'historical' O'Neill, see Dunlop: "O'Neill, Hugh", Black: *The Reign of Elizabeth*, Ch. 12: "The Irish Problem", esp. pp. 480–490, and Hayes-McCoy: "The Completion of the Tudor Conquest", pp. 117–137. In the opening chapters of Foster's *Modern Ireland* O'Neill takes pride of place.

7 It may be interesting to note here that the 'historical' Mabel Bagenal broke with O'Neill according to a statement attributed to him in the state papers: " '[. . .] because I did affect two other gentlewomen, she grew in dislike with me, forsook me, and went unto her brother to complain upon me to the council of Ireland, and did exhibit articles against me' " (quoted in Dunlop: "O'Neill, Hugh", p. 1083). O'Faolain thinks there must have been some kind of reconciliation before her death in 1592 or 1593, as she died in Dungannon (*The Great O'Neill*, pp. 117, 121).

8 *The Great O'Neill*, p. VI.

9 "Historical Accuracy", p. 8.

10 Incidentally, this book was never published as such in real life. Lombard's *Commentarius* was completed in 1600, published posthumously in 1632, and suppressed by James I in 1633; it contained a picture of O'Neill's rebellion as a war of religion and national unity. On the 'historical' Lombard, see Foster: *Modern Ireland*, p. 43, and Silke: "The Irish Abroad", pp. 596–598.

11 As quoted in Murray: "Historical Accuracy", p. 2. Compare this, in turn, with one of the central statements in a chapter entitled "The Historical Text as Literary Artefact" in Hayden White's *Tropics of Discourse*, a book which is emblematic of recent trends in historiography: "[. . .] no given set of casually recorded historical events can in itself constitute a story; the most it might offer to the historian are story *elements*. The events are *made* into a story by the suppression or subordination of certain of them and the highlighting of others, by characterization, motific repetition, variation of tone and point of view, alternative descriptive strategies and the like – in short, all of the techniques that we would normally expect to find in the emplotment of a novel or a play" (p. 84).

12 *Selected Plays*, p. 445.

13 Deane, "Introduction", pp. 21–22.

14 On Friel's plays *Faith Healer* (1979), *Translations*, and *The Communication Cord* (1982) as "theatre *about* language" and on their philosophical parallels and sources in Heidegger and George Steiner, see Kearney, "Language Play", and O'Brien, *Friel*.

15 On Field Day as a cultural and political movement, see Binnie: "Brecht and Friel", McGrath: "Introducing Ireland's Field Day", Dantanus: *Brian Friel*, pp. 206–209, Wolf: "Brian Friel's Ireland", and Etherton: *Contemporary Irish Dramatists*, pp. 193–198. For more critical estimates of Field Day's achievements, see Murray: "The History Play Today", pp. 285–286, and O'Toole: "Competing Voices".

16 "Preface" in Field Day Theatre Company: *Ireland's Field Day*, p. VII.

17 Ibid.

18 Ibid., p. VIII.

19 Kearney: "Language Play", 26–27; Dantanus: *Brian Friel*, p. 207.

20 "Preface", p. VIII.

21 Kearney: "Myth and Motherland", p. 80.

Binnie, E.: "Brecht and Friel: Some Irish Parallels". *Modern Drama* 31, 1988, 365–370.

Black, J. B.: *The Reign of Elizabeth 1558–1603*. 2nd ed. Oxford, 1969 (1959).

Brennan, B.: "The Reinvention of Hugh O'Neill". *Sunday Independent*, 25. 9. 1988, 15.

Dantanus, U.: *Brian Friel. A Study*. London, 1988.

Deane, S.: "Introduction". – In *Selected Plays of Brian Friel*. London, 1984, pp. 11–22.

Dunlop, R.: "O'Neill, Hugh". – In *Dictionary of National Biography*. Eds. L. Stephen, S. Lee. 1917; rpt. London, 1968, pp. 1082–1090.

Etherton, M.: *Contemporary Irish Dramatists*. Basingstoke, London, 1989.

Field Day Theatre Company: *Ireland's Field Day*. London, 1985.

Foster, R. F.: *Modern Ireland 1600–1972*. London, 1988.

Friel, B.: *Translations* [1980]. – In *Selected Plays of Brian Friel*. London, 1984, pp. 377–451.

–: *Making History*. London: Faber, 1989.

Hayes-McCoy, G. A.: "The Completion of the Tudor Conquest and the Advance of the Counter-Reformation, 1571–1603". – In Moody, T. W., Martin, F. X., Byrne, F. J. (Eds.): *Early Modern Ireland 1534–1691*. Oxford, 1978 (1976), pp. 94–141.

Kearney, R.: "Language Play: Brian Friel and Ireland's Verbal Theatre". *Studies. An Irish Quarterly Review* 72, 1983, 20–56.

–: "Myth and Motherland". – In Field Day Theatre Company: *Ireland's Field Day*, pp. 59–80.

Kilroy, T.: "The O'Neill. A Play". Unpublished typescript [1969].

Lombardus, Petrus: *De Regno Hiberniae Sanctorum Insula Commentarius* [Louvain, 1632]. Ed. Rev. P. F. Moran. Dublin, 1868.

London Theatre Record, 31. 12. 1988, 1696–1701, s. v. "Making History".

McGrath, F. C.: "Introducing Ireland's Field Day". *Éire-Ireland* 23, iv, 1988, 145–155.

McKeone, G.: "Versions of Irish History". *Drama* No. 171, 1989, 5–6.

Murray, C.: "The History Play Today". – In Kenneally, M. (Ed.): *Cultural Contexts and Literary Idioms in Contemporary Irish Literature*. Gerrards Cross, 1988, pp. 269–289, 349–351.

–: "Brian Friel's *Making History* and The Problem of Historical Accuracy". Paper read at the 2nd Easter Conference on Irish Literature, Antwerp, March 1989. Unpublished typescript.

O'Brien, G.: "A Matter of Making". *Irish Literary Supplement* 8, ii, 1989, 7.

–: *Brian Friel. A Critical Survey*. Dublin, 1989.

O'Clery, L.: *Beatha Aodha Ruaidhi Ui Dhomhnaill/The Life of Hugh Roe O'Donnell, Prince of Tirconnell, 1586–1602*. Ed. Rev. D. Murphy. Dublin, 1893.

O'Faolain, S.: *The Great O'Neill. A Biography of Hugh O'Neill, Earl of Tyrone, 1550–1616*. London, 1942.

O'Toole, F.: "Competing Voices". *Plays and Players* No. 420, 1988, 10–12.

Ridley, J.: "A National Hero". *Times Literary Supplement*, 16. 12. 1988.

Sharkey, P.: "Friel's Latest". *Irish Literary Supplement* 8, i, 1989, 14.

Silke, J. J.: "The Irish Abroad, 1534–1691". – In Moody, T. W., Martin, F. X., Byrne, F. J. (Eds.): *Early Modern Ireland 1534–1691*. Oxford, 1978 (1976), pp. 587–633.

White, H.: *Tropics of Discourse. Essays in Cultural Criticism*. Baltimore, London, 1978.

Wolf, M.: "Brian Friel's Ireland: Both Private and Political". *New York Times*, 30. 4. 1989, sec. 2, 7+.

Neuerscheinungen

ELKE SCHARTMANN
Einsamkeit bei Shakespeare und in der Renaissance-Tradition
1990. VIII, 246 Seiten. Kartoniert DM 35,-.
Leinen DM 65,-
(Forum Anglistik. Neue Folge, Band 3)

IRMELA SCHNEIDER
Film, Fernsehen & Co.
Zur Entwicklung des Spielfilms in Kino und Fernsehen. Ein Überblick über Konzepte und Tendenzen
1990. 255 Seiten. Kartoniert DM 75,-.
Leinen DM 100,-
(Reihe Siegen. Beiträge zur Literatur-, Sprach- und Medienwissenschaft, Band 101)

JOACHIM SCHOLL
In der Gemeinschaft des Erzählers
Studien zur Restitution des Epischen im deutschen Gegenwartsroman
1990. 243 Seiten. Kartoniert DM 60,-.
Leinen DM 86,-
(Beiträge zur neueren Literaturgeschichte. Dritte Folge, Band 105)

NURIT SEEWI
Miami Vice
Cashing in on Contemporary Culture?
Towards an Analysis of a U.S.-Television Series Broadcast in the Federal Republic of Germany
1990. IV, 403 Seiten. Kartoniert DM 72,-.
Leinen DM 98,-
(Reihe Siegen. Beiträge zur Literatur-, Sprach- u. Medienwissenschaft, Band 103)

HANS-MICHAEL SPEIER (Hrsg.)
Celan-Jahrbuch 3 (1989)
1990. 214 Seiten. Kartoniert DM 180,-
(Beiträge zur neueren Literaturgeschichte. Dritte Folge, Band 103)

KATHARINA STAEDTLER
Altprovenzalische Frauendichtung (1150–1250)
Historisch-soziologische Untersuchungen und Interpretationen
1990. XII, 347 Seiten mit 1 Abbildung.
Kartoniert DM 125,-. Leinen DM 150,-
(Beihefte zur Germanisch-Romanischen Monatsschrift, Band 9)

EVA-MARIA THÜNE
Dichtung als Widerspruch
Zur Entwicklung poetologischer Positionen bei Franco Fortini
1990. 285 Seiten. Kartoniert DM 70,-.
Leinen DM 98,-
(Beiträge zur neueren Literaturgeschichte. Dritte Folge, Band 107)

MONIKA UNZEITIG-HERZOG
Jungfrauen und Einsiedler
Studien zur Organisation der Aventiurewelt im 'Prosalancelot'
1990. 184 Seiten mit 8 Abb. Kartoniert DM 50,-.
Leinen DM 76,-
(Beiträge zur älteren Literaturgeschichte)

PETER ZENZINGER (Hrsg.)
Scotland: Literature, Culture, Politics
Mit Beiträgen von: Peter Zenzinger – Christopher Harvie – Allan Macartney – Clausdirk Pollner – Scott Griffith – Richard Kilborn and Peter Meech – Cordelia Oliver – Ian A. Olson – Roderick Watson – Randall Stevenson – Detlef von Ziegesar – Hans-Jürgen Bachorski und Ursula Reichelt – Heinz Kosok – Werner Hüllen
1989. 358 Seiten. Kartoniert DM 50,-
(anglistik & englischunterricht, Band 38/39)

CARL WINTER · UNIVERSITÄTSVERLAG · HEIDELBERG

Publications Received

Antor, Heinz, Ward, Jacqueline: *Getting the Most out of Your Oxford Advanced Learner's Dictionary*. Berlin, Cornelsen Verlag, 1989, 38 S., DM 4,90.

Dieses *workbook* ist speziell auf die Bedürfnisse deutschsprachiger Lernender zugeschnitten. Wie der Titel sagt, will es seinen Benutzern zeigen, wie man den größtmöglichen Nutzen aus der neuen Ausgabe des *OALD* zieht. Eine Vielzahl an phantasievollen, oft spielerischen Übungen führt den Benutzer durch die verschiedenen Bereiche des Wörterbuchs. Die Schüler werden zunehmend vertraut mit dem *OALD* und erfahren nach und nach, daß es kein bloßes Nachschlagewerk, sondern eine Hilfe zum korrekten und idiomatischen Umgang mit der englischen Sprache ist.

Bach, Gerhard, Timm, Johannes-Peter (Eds.): *Fremdsprachenunterricht im Wandel*. Liselotte Weidner zum 65. Geburtstag. Heidelberg, Pädagogische Hochschule/Institut für Weiterbildung, 1989, 120 S.

Inhalt: A. Digeser: Fremdsprachendidaktik im Umbruch. R. Löffler: Bewegung – Körper – Sinne: Ein Beitrag zum ganzheitlichen Lernen im Englischunterricht. J. P. Timm: Wandlungen im Selbstverständnis eines Angewandten Linguisten. G. Bach: Fremdsprachen im Spannungsfeld von Schule, Ausbildung und Beruf. H. Breitkreuz: Kollokationales Lernen im Englischunterricht am Beispiel von group terms und collective nouns. R. Gäßler/K. Wenner-Nogueira: Wer plant den Fremdsprachenunterricht? Praktische Vorschläge zur Überwindung der Lehrbuchdominanz. H. Zeidler: Kulinarisches in Englischlehrwerken der 70er und 80er Jahre. H. Breitkreuz/N. Wiegand: Zur Problematik gemein- und fachsprachlicher False Friends. M. Liedtke: Die Exkursion als hochschuldidaktische Aufgabe im Englischstudium.

Benson, Morton, Benson, Evelyn, Ilson, Robert: *Student's Dictionary of Collocations*. Berlin, Cornelsen Verlag, 1989, XVIII und 286 S., DM 29,80.

Das *Student's Dictionary of Collocations* ist das erste Wörterbuch seiner Art. Selbst in einem einsprachigen Schulwörterbuch finden sich Kollokationen, also nicht Wort für Wort zu übersetzende Wortkombinationen, nicht in dieser Fülle, denn ein solches Wörterbuch hat nicht den Platz dafür. So will das *Student's Dictionary of Collocations* auch nicht ein *learner's dictionary* ersetzen, sondern es ergänzen. Die Kollokationen sind dort verzeichnet, wo man sie leicht findet: in erster Linie unter dem wichtigsten Substantiv der Kollokation. Etwa 13.000 mögliche Kollokationen sind systematisch zusammengestellt. Viele Einträge enthalten zudem grammatische Hilfen und Verwendungsbeispiele. Unterschiede zwischen *American English* und *British English* sind sorgfältig gekennzeichnet, und wo möglich wird eine *Common English*-Variante angegeben. Das *Dictionary* wendet sich an alle, die englische Texte sprechen und schreiben wollen, an Schüler der Sekundarstufe genauso wie Anglistikstudenten, Übersetzer und Lehrer.

Bevan, David (Ed.): *Literary Gastronomy*. Amsterdam, Editions Rodopi, 1988, 113 S., Hfl. 28,–.

Contents: Introduction. N. Thomas: Food Poisoning, Cooking and Historiography in the Works of Günter Grass. S. Ames: Fast Food/Quick Lunch: Crews, Burroughs and Pynchon. B. Knapp: Virginia Woolf's "Bœuf en Daube". G. Bauer: Eating Out: With Barthes. M. Atwood: Introducing *The CanLit Foodbook*. E. Patnaik: The Succulent Gender: Eat Her Softly. R. Boland: Freudian Gastronomy in Mario Vargas Llosa's *La ciudad y los perros*. M. A. Schofield: Culinary Revelations: Self-Exploration and Food in Margaret Laurence's *The Stone Angel*. L. Renders: J. M. Coetzee's *Michael K*: Starving in a Land of Plenty. D. Bevan: Tournier, Bororygmus and Borborology: Reverberations of Eating Each Other.

Britain and America. Tradition and Change. [Schülerbuch.] Eds. Georg Engel, Rosemarie Franke, Armin Steinbrecher, Dieter Vater, Gerhard Weiß, Egon Werlich. Berlin, Cornelsen Verlag, 1989, 320 S., DM 29,80.

Das völlig neu entwickelte Oberstufenlesebuch bietet eine Textauswahl von rund 136 Texten, die der Geschichte der Zielsprachenländer genauso gerecht wird wie dem gesellschaftlichen und politischen Wandel in der jüngsten Vergangenheit. Die zwölf Kapitel des Lesebuchs sind nach dem Prinzip der themenorientierten Textsequenz aufgebaut: Je vier präsentieren Großbritannien und die USA, vier weitere bieten Texte zu länderübergreifenden Themen an, die auch für andere Industrienationen von Bedeutung sind. Bei der Präsentation der Texte geht das Lesebuch einen neuen Weg. Jedes Kapitel bietet das zum jeweiligen thematischen Schwerpunkt notwendige Grundwissen in ein bis drei *Info-Boxes* an, die insgesamt ein kleines Nachschlagewerk ergeben. Rein informative Sachtexte, die Schülerinnen und Schüler erfahrungsgemäß wenig ansprechen, können daher entfallen. Sie erlauben es, sich auf exemplarische, authentische fiktionale und nichtfiktionale Einzeltexte zu konzentrieren. Jeder Text wird durch ein *note* eingeführt und meist durch Arbeitsaufträge ergänzt. Bei einfacheren Texten wurde der Aufgabenapparat im Lehrerbuch untergebracht, um der Leselust nicht entgegenzuwirken. Die problematisierende Auseinandersetzung mit historischen und aktuellen Erscheinungsformen soll den Jugendlichen einen lebendigen Einblick in diese Länder geben. Mit zahlreichen Illustrationen (Photos, Karten, Diagrammen, Cartoons) und je einer physikalischen, farbigen Landkarte der Britischen Inseln und der USA werden die Themen veranschaulicht.

Colvile, Georgiana M. M.: *Beyond and Beneath the Mantle: On Thomas Pynchon's* The Crying of Lot 49. Amsterdam, Editions Rodopi, 1988, 119 S., Hfl. 38,–.

Contents: The Reader's Quest. From Words to Worse. More Mirrors. Metaphor in *CL 49*. Remedios Varo's "Triptych" and "Mise-en-Abyme". On Work and the Workings of Society. Madness, Disease and Death (Within and Without). Woman's Lot and Cry. Pynchon's Alchemy. Conclusion.

Dahl, Erhard, Dürkob, Carsten (Eds.): *Rock-Lyrik.* Exemplarische Analysen englischsprachiger Song-Texte. Essen, Verlag Die Blaue Eule, 1989, 221 S., DM 34,-.

Der Sammelband enthält literaturwissenschaftlich orientierte Analysen mehrerer populärer englischsprachiger Song-Texte, einen historischen Überblick über die Geschichte der Rock- und Popmusik sowie eine umfangreiche Bibliographie der Sekundärliteratur zu dieser Musik und ihren Interpreten. Nicht der Nachweis von Trivialität oder Qualität ist das Ziel der Beiträger, sondern eine möglichst präzise Beschreibung der vorgefundenen Themen, Inhalte, Wirkungsabsichten und der verwendeten sprachlichen Gestaltungsmittel.

D'haen, Theo, Bertens, Hans (Eds.): *Postmodern Fiction in Europe and the Americas.* Amsterdam, Editions Rodopi, 1988, 208 S., Hfl. 49,50.

Contents: Th. D'haen, H. Bertens: Introduction. B. McHale: Some Postmodernist Stories. A. Kibedi Varga: Narrative and Postmodernity in France. A. Linneberg, G. Mork: Antinomies of Nominalism: Postmodernism in Norwegian Fiction of the 1980s. W. Krysinski: Metafictional Structures in Slavic Literatures: Towards an Archeology of Metafiction. I. M. Zavala: On the (Mis-)Uses of the Post-Modern: Hispanic Modernism Revisited. R. Todd: Confrontation Within Convention: On the Character of British Postmodernist Fiction. G. Lernout: Postmodernist Fiction in Canada. A. Mertens: Postmodern Elements in Postwar Dutch Fiction. St. Tani: "La Giovane Narrativa": Emerging Italian Novelists in the Eighties. J. Ortega: Postmodernism in Latin America.

Duytschaever, Joris, Lernout, Geert (Eds.): *History and Violence in Anglo-Irish Literature.* Amsterdam, Editions Rodopi, 1988, 135 S., Hfl. 38,-.

Contents: J. Duytschaever, G. Lernout: Preface. B. Kennelly: Poetry and Violence. J. Leerssen: Táin after Táin: The Mythical Past and the Anglo-Irish. L. Dieltjens: The Abbey Theatre as a Cultural Formation. G. Lernout: Banville and Being: "The Newton Letter" and History. Th. D'haen: Desmond Hogan and Ireland's Postmodern Past. G. Verstraete: Brian Friel's Drama and the Limits of Language. J. Duytschaever: History in the Poetry of Derek Mahon. W. J. McCormack: *Finnegans Wake* and Irish Literary History.

Lambert, Sue: *What to Say.* Ein neuer Reise-Sprachkurs der BBC London. Berlin, München, Wien, Langenscheidt, 1989, 119 S., DM 38,- (mit zwei Audiocassetten).

Dieser BBC-Kurs ist Sprachführer, Konversationsbuch und Mini-Sprachkurs in einem. Er zielt vor allem darauf ab, den richtigen Sprachgebrauch in typischen Alltagssituationen zu vermitteln. Nebenbei liefert *What to Say* auch wichtiges Wissen über Land und Leute; wie man in GB telefoniert, ein Auto mietet, eine Eisenbahnfahrkarte ersteht oder problemlos Reiseschecks einlöst, versucht dieser Kurs zum Großteil per Dialog zu vermitteln. Darüber hinaus werden Schlüsselwörter und Wendungen erklärt und wichtige Satzstrukturen als Nachsprechübungen geboten; wichtige Varianten des amerikanischen Englisch sind ebenfalls im Kurs enthalten.

Lehmann, Elmar: *Ordnung und Chaos*. Das englische Restaurationsdrama 1660–1685. Amsterdam, Verlag B. R. Grüner, 1988, 194 S., DM 75,–.

Die Untersuchung gilt dem kurzen Höhenflug von *comedy of manners* und *heroic play* in der Regierungszeit Karls II. Die Analysen konzentrieren sich auf Figurenkonzeption, Bühnengesellschaft und Handlungsstruktur, auf die theatergeschichtliche Situation sowie auf die gesellschaftliche Stellung und das Selbstbewußtsein der professionellen Autoren im Verhältnis zu den höfischen Mäzenen und Literaten. Es zeigt sich, daß das Restaurationsdrama die aristokratische Existenz preist – aber erstaunlicherweise im Kontext einer aus isolierten, konkurrierenden Individuen bestehenden Bühnengesellschaft. Der Widerspruch zwischen ererbter Privilegierung und individualistischem Konkurrenzkampf, zwischen ständischer Gesellschaft und Eigentumsmarktgesellschaft beherrscht die Dramen in vielfältiger Form. Er wird in der Frühzeit der Restauration überdeckt – durch das Spiel und die strengen Spielregeln, die den Konkurrenzkampf der Komödienfiguren auf die Aristokratie beschränken; durch die gesellschaftlichen Pflichten, mit denen Held und Heldin im ernsten Drama ihre individualistischen Ansprüche disziplinieren. Das drohende Chaos eines allgemeinen, die hierarchische Ordnung untergrabenden Konkurrenzkampfes läßt sich in der politischen Krisensituation um 1680 nicht mehr bändigen. Das Restaurationsdrama, das mit großer Strenge noch einmal die Ordnung der ständischen Gesellschaft beschwört und zugleich mit großer Klarsicht die zukunftsweisenden Entwicklungstendenzen der Gesellschaft darstellt, gerät außer Kurs.

Oxford Advanced Learner's Dictionary of Current English. Fourth Edition. Ed. A. P. Cowie. Oxford, Oxford University Press, 1989, 1579 S.; Vertrieb in Deutschland über Cornelsen Verlagsgesellschaft, Bielefeld; DM 37,80.

This comprehensively revised and greatly expanded new edition of A. S. Hornby's classic and highly acclaimed dictionary for students of English represents a major advance on earlier editions in terms of lexical coverage, ease of use, and the amount of information on meaning, grammar and syntax it provides. It contains: 57 000 words and phrases, over 4 000 new to this edition; 12 700 idioms and phrasal verbs which are fully cross-referenced; 81 500 examples to illustrate usage and collocation, most of them new to this edition; all new illustrations, depicting 1 820 items; 200 new notes on usage, clarifying points of grammatical or semantic difficulty; three new appendices, including a thematically-arranged illustrated appendix; two new guides to using the dictionary; a new, simpler verb classification scheme.

Peeck-O'Toole, Maureen: *Aspects of Lyric in the Poetry of Emily Brontë.* Amsterdam, Editions Rodopi, 1988, 201 S., Hfl. 50,–.

This study attempts to see the poetry as an independent "œuvre" and in order to do so makes use of the differences and similarities between the two kinds of poetry that Emily Brontë composed. One relates to the fictional Gondal world created by Emily and Anne Brontë in childhood and the other to the poet herself. In view of the fragmentary nature of knowledge of the Gondal world (there are no prose chronicles, for example) a plea is made for viewing the Gondal poems in terms of lyric so that in this sense it forms a continuum with the non-Gondal poetry. The underlying continuity in the poetic "œuvre" is to be found in the introspection of the various speakers, Gondal and non-Gondal alike; and in the themes, especially those of loss, freedom, imprisonment and doom, which are worked out "mutatis mutandis" throughout. The "œuvre" is gender-marked if for no other reason than that it might be typical of a female poet to explicitly thematise the very problem of the voice that is to speak the poem. The emphasis throughout the study lies firmly on Emily Brontë's poetics and this is to be regarded as a corrective to the overly biographical approach so often adopted in studies of the Brontës.

Raab, Michael: *"The music hall is dying."* Die Thematisierung der Unterhaltungsindustrie im englischen Gegenwartsdrama. Tübingen, Max Niemeyer Verlag, 1989, 246 S., DM 84,–.

Die Arbeit fragt nach Gründen für den thematischen Rückgriff auf die Music Hall, die von Dramatikern wie John Osborne, Trevor Griffiths oder Terry Johnson in verschiedenem Sinne funktionalisiert wird: als Prototyp einer populären, proletarischen Unterhaltungsinstitution, die sowohl nostalgisch verklärt als auch für Aussagen über heutige Unterhaltung und ihr Publikum verwendet wird, als Symbol für den politischen und gesellschaftlichen Zustand Englands und als Paradigma für zeitgenössische Verhaltensweisen sowie als Medium der individuellen Selbstverwirklichung von historischen und fiktiven Performern. Griffiths überprüft in *Comedians* die Tradition der sinnlichen Erfahrbarkeit bestimmter Unterhaltungsformen auch praktisch auf ihre Tauglichkeit heute und schafft eine kritische Distanz gegenüber den Mechanismen des Showgeschäfts. Andere Dramatiker schreiben biographisch angelegte Stücke mit zum Teil dokumentarischem Charakter, die sich mit der Lebensgeschichte von Entertainern beschäftigen, die in der Bevölkerung noch immer einen legendenumwobenen Ruf haben. Autoren wie Osborne oder Catherine Hayes schließlich arbeiten die Music Hall-Tradition anhand von Persönlichkeitsentwürfen fiktiver Komikerfiguren auf. Zusammen mit der Analyse der Dramen wird ein Abriß über die Geschichte der Music Hall gegeben und auf die Vermittlungsprobleme eingegangen, die bei der Aufarbeitung dieser Institution in einem anderen Medium, dem Theater, entstehen.

Schneider, Klaus P.: *Small Talk.* Analysing Phatic Discourse. Marburg, Wolfram Hitzeroth Verlag, 1988, 351 S., DM 68,–.

Phatic discourse, which is often derogatorily called 'small talk', has been largely neglected by discourse analysis, despite its social significance. This book aims at a linguistically adequate description of this discourse type. After exploring pretheoretical notions of small talk the author outlines a multi-layered model of spoken discourse which attempts to integrate findings from various disciplines. This is the background for an integrative study of phatic discourse. The analyses are based on a large corpus of recorded conversations and concentrate on four areas: Politeness maxims and typical operationalisations; interactional and illocutionary patterns, particularly characteristic exchange structures; aspects of topic organization, such as lexical choice, conceptual structure, and discourse position; and a frame model of topic selection and topic development.

Anschriften der Autoren

Dr. Rolf Eichler. Universität Konstanz. Philosophische Fakultät. Fachgruppe Literaturwissenschaft – Anglistik –. Universitätsstr. 10, 7750 Konstanz.

Prof. Dr. Therese Fischer-Seidel. Justus-Liebig-Universität Gießen. Institut für Anglistik und Amerikanistik. Otto-Behaghel-Str. 10, 6300 Gießen.

Prof. Dr. Armin Geraths. Technische Universität Berlin. Institut für Englische und Amerikanische Literaturwissenschaft. Ernst-Reuter-Platz 7, 1000 Berlin 10.

Prof. Dr. Andreas Höfele. Ludwig-Maximilians-Universität München. Institut für Theaterwissenschaft. Schellingstr. 9, 8000 München 40.

Dr. Werner Huber. Universität – Gesamthochschule Paderborn. FB 3: Sprach- und Literaturwissenschaften – Anglistik –. Warburgerstr. 100, 4790 Paderborn.

Dr. Richard Humphrey. Justus-Liebig-Universität Gießen. Institut für Anglistik und Amerikanistik. Otto-Behaghel-Str. 10, 6300 Gießen

Dr. Petra Iking. FernUniversität Hagen. Feithstr. 152, 5800 Hagen 1.

Prof. Dr. Günther Klotz. Akademie der Wissenschaften der DDR. Zentralinstitut für Literaturgeschichte. Berolinastr. 9, O-1020 Berlin.

Dr. Beate Neumeier. Universität Würzburg. Institut für Englische Philologie. Am Hubland, 8700 Würzburg.

Louise Page. 38 Upper Montagu Street, Flat C, London W1H 1RP, Großbritannien.

Priv.-Doz. Dr. Bernhard Reitz. Justus-Liebig-Universität Gießen. Institut für Anglistik und Amerikanistik. Otto-Behaghel-Str. 10, 6300 Gießen.

Priv.-Doz. Dr. Hubert Zapf. Universität Gesamthochschule Paderborn. FB 3: Sprach- und Literaturwissenschaften – Anglistik –. Warburgerstr. 100, 4790 Paderborn.

Literaturwissenschaft

Hedwig Bock/Albert Wertheim (Hrsg.)
Essays on Contemporary British Drama
310 Seiten, kt. DM 29,80
ISBN 3-19-002214-3

Essays über:
John Osborne, Arnold Wesker, John Arden, Joe Orton, Peter Barnes, Tom Stoppard, Harold Pinter, Edward Bond, Simon Gray, David Storey und Trevor Griffiths.

Hedwig Bock/Albert Wertheim (Hrsg.)
Essays on Contemporary American Drama
302 Seiten, kt. DM 29,80
ISBN 3-19-002232-1

Essays über:
Sam Shepard, Tennessee Williams, Lanford Wilson, David Mamet, Ronald Ribman, Arthur Kopit, David Rabe, Arthur Miller, Edward Albee, Black Drama, Lorraine Hansberry, Ed Bullins, LeRoy Jones, Women's Drama, Chicano Drama.

Hedwig Bock/Albert Wertheim (Hrsg.)
Essays on The Contemporary American Novel
392 Seiten, kt. DM 29,80
ISBN 3-19-002255-0

Essays über:
Robert Penn Warren, Bernard Malamud, E. L. Doctorow, Norman Mailer, Non-Fiction Novel, Thomas Pynchon, John Barth, Philip Roth, Saul Bellow, Jerzy Kosinski, Toni Morrison, u. a.

Hedwig Bock/Albert Wertheim (Hrsg.)
Essays on The Contemporary British Novel
284 Seiten, kt. DM 29,80
ISBN 3-19-002254-2

Essays über:
William Golding, Anthony Burgess, Barbara Pym, Iris Murdoch, Muriel Spark, Lawrence Durell, Anthony Powell, Doris Lessing, David Storey, John Fowles, Alan Sillitoe, Kingsley Amis, Malcolm Bradbury, Margaret Drabble, Edna O'Brien.

Hedwig Bock/Albert Wertheim (Hrsg.)
Essays on Contemporary Post-Colonial Fiction
448 Seiten, kt. DM 29,80
ISBN 3-19-002346-8

Essays über:
Mulk Raj Anand, Wilson Harris, Mordecai Richler, Christina Stead, Patrick White, R. K. Naravan, Alex La Guma, Margret Laurence, Chinua Achebe, Ruth Jhabvala, u. a.

Die Essaysammlungen enthalten englischsprachige Beiträge international anerkannter Literatur-/ Theaterwissenschaftler und wenden sich an Anglistikstudenten und Englischlehrer.

sprachen der welt
hueber
Max Hueber Verlag
D-8045 Ismaning/München

WALTER SAUER

American English Pronunciation

A Drillbook

1988. 110 Seiten mit mehreren Abbildungen. Kartoniert DM 20,-
(Sprachwissenschaftliche Studienbücher. 1. Abteilung)

American English Pronunciation: A Drillbook bietet ein Intensivprogramm zur am.-engl. Aussprache („General American"/„Network English"), das als Begleittext eines Phonetikkurses konzipiert ist. „Part I" enthält einen nach Phonemen gegliederten Lautkurs zur Benutzung im Sprachlabor oder im Selbststudium. Die Übungen umfassen Einzelwörter ebenso wie „Drill Sentences" und zusammenhängende Texte. Jedem Beispielwort oder -satz ist auf der rechten Buchseite eine phonetische Umschrift beigegeben. „Part II" stellt eine nach Schwierigkeitsgrad abgestufte Sammlung von Modelltranskriptionen dar, angereichert durch mehrere phonetische Worträtsel. In der Einleitung finden sich verschiedene Tabellen und Diagramme zur Phonetik des amerikanischen Englisch. Das gesamte Übungsmaterial von „Part I" liegt auf zwei C 90 Kassetten vor, die über den Verlag erhältlich sind.

CARL WINTER · UNIVERSITÄTSVERLAG · HEIDELBERG